VOLUME EIGHT

ONI PRESS

AN ONI PRESS PUBLICATION

[adult swim]

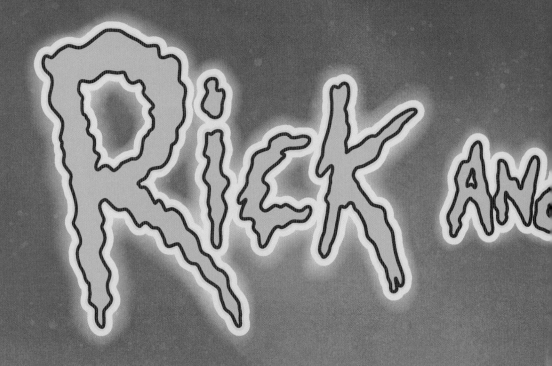

VOLUME EIGHT

RICK AND MORTY™ CREATED BY **DAN HARMON** AND **JUSTIN ROILAND**

RETAIL COVER BY
MARC ELLERBY

ONI EXCLUSIVE COVER BY
JULIETA COLÁS

EDITED BY
ARI YARWOOD WITH
SARAH GAYDOS

DESIGNED BY
HILARY THOMPSON

[adult swim]

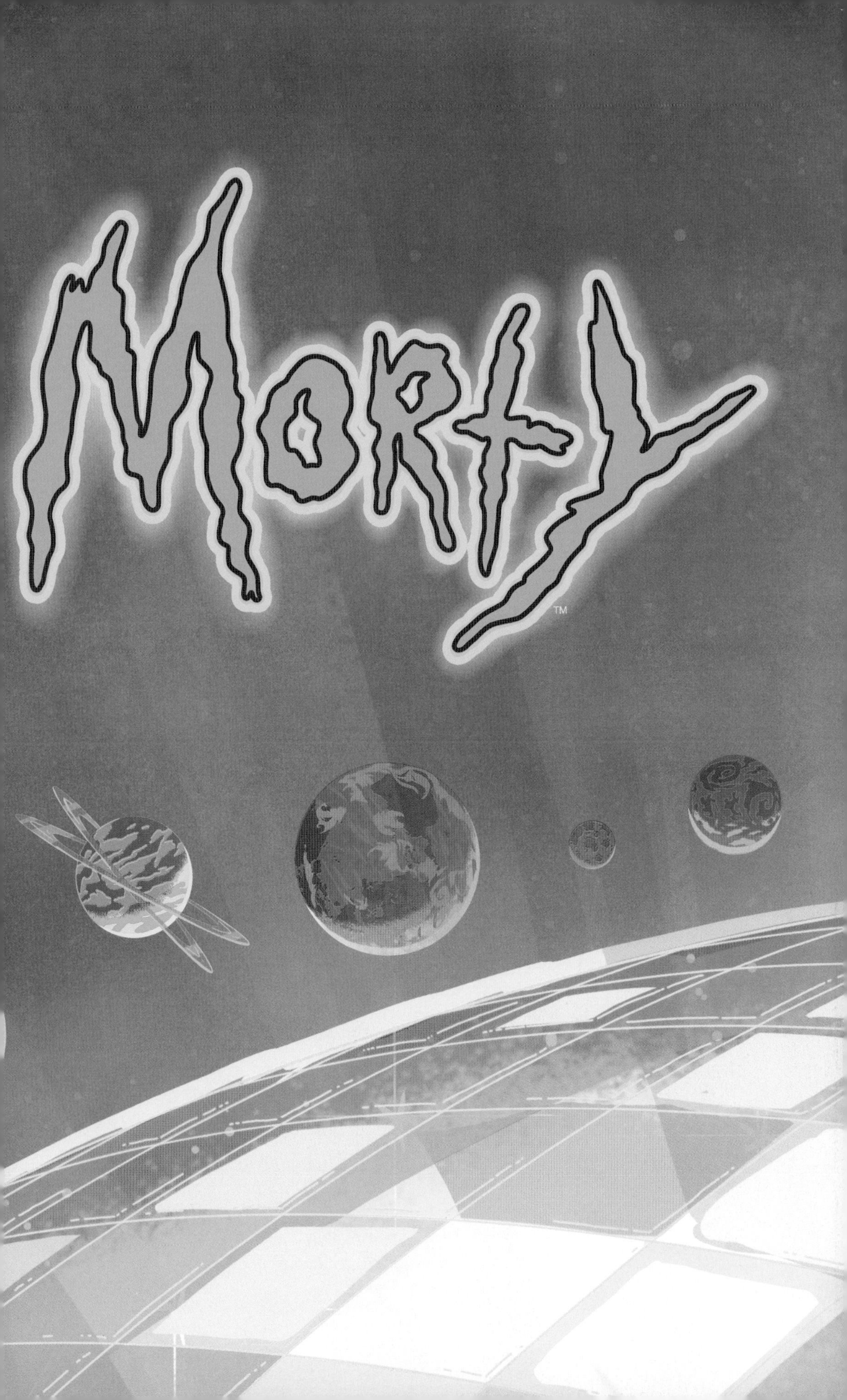
Morty™

PUBLISHED BY ONI PRESS, INC.
JOE NOZEMACK FOUNDER & CHIEF FINANCIAL OFFICER
JAMES LUCAS JONES PUBLISHER
CHARLIE CHU V.P. OF CREATIVE & BUSINESS DEVELOPMENT
BRAD ROOKS DIRECTOR OF OPERATIONS
MELISSA MESZAROS DIRECTOR OF PUBLICITY
MARGOT WOOD DIRECTOR OF SALES
SANDY TANAKA MARKETING DESIGN MANAGER
AMBER O'NEILL SPECIAL PROJECTS MANAGER
TROY LOOK DIRECTOR OF DESIGN & PRODUCTION
KATE Z. STONE SENIOR GRAPHIC DESIGNER
SONJA SYNAK GRAPHIC DESIGNER
ANGIE KNOWLES DIGITAL PREPRESS LEAD
ARI YARWOOD EXECUTIVE EDITOR
SARAH GAYDOS EDITORIAL DIRECTOR OF LICENSED PUBLISHING
ROBIN HERRERA SENIOR EDITOR
DESIREE WILSON ASSOCIATE EDITOR
MICHELLE NGUYEN EXECUTIVE ASSISTANT
JUNG LEE LOGISTICS COORDINATOR
SCOTT SHARKEY WAREHOUSE ASSISTANT

ONI PRESS

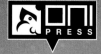

[adult swim]

ONIPRESS.COM
FACEBOOK.COM/ONIPRESS
TWITTER.COM/ONIPRESS
INSTAGRAM.COM/ONIPRESS
ADULTSWIM.COM
TWITTER.COM/RICKANDMORTY
FACEBOOK.COM/RICKANDMORTY

THIS VOLUME COLLECTS ISSUES #36-40
OF THE ONI PRESS SERIES *RICK AND MORTY*™.

FIRST EDITION: DECEMBER 2018

ISBN 978-1-62010-549-8
EISBN 978-1-62010-550-4
ONI EXCLUSIVE ISBN 978-1-62010-558-0

PRINTED IN USA.

LIBRARY OF CONGRESS CONTROL NUMBER: 2018947001

1 2 3 4 5 6 7 8 9 10

SPECIAL THANKS TO JUSTIN ROILAND, DAN HARMON, MARISA MARIONAKIS, ELYSE SALAZAR, MIKE MENDEL, JANET NO, AND MEAGAN BIRNEY.

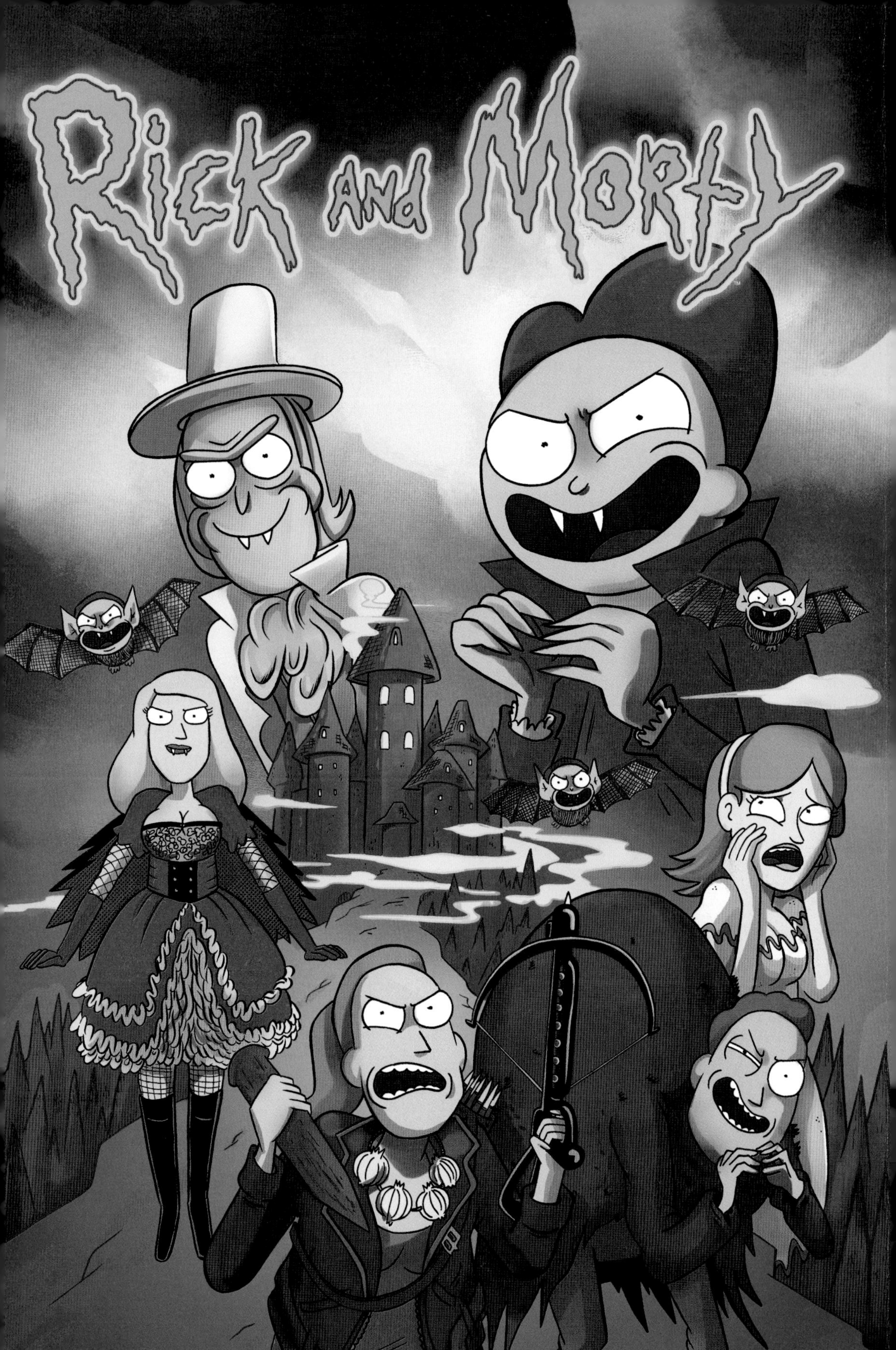
Rick and Morty

"LET THE RICK ONE IN, PART ONE"

WRITTEN BY **KYLE STARKS** & **TINI HOWARD** ILLUSTRATED BY **MARC ELLERBY** COLORED BY **SARAH STERN** LETTERED BY **CRANK!**

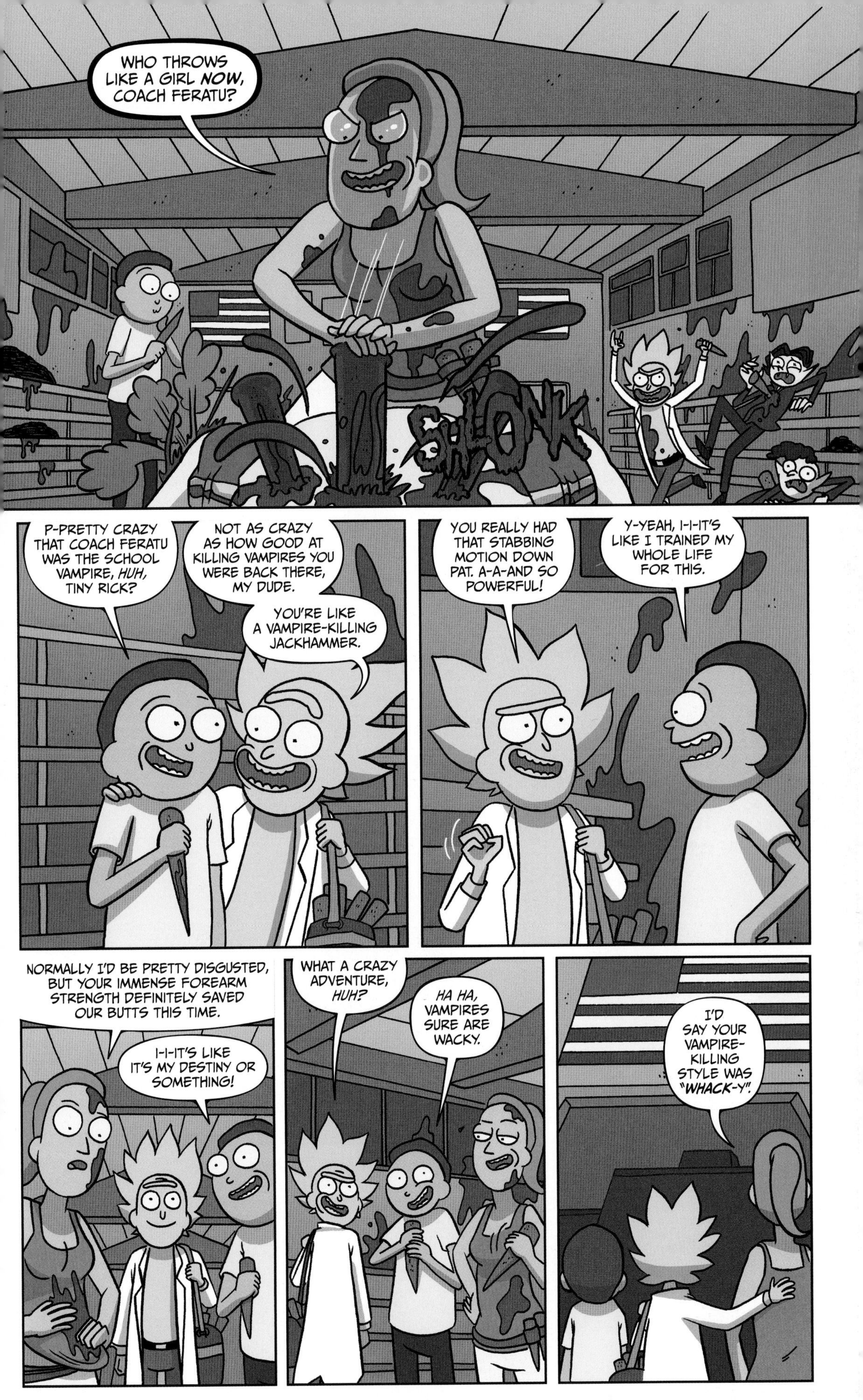
WHO THROWS LIKE A GIRL *NOW*, COACH FERATU?
SHLONK
P-PRETTY CRAZY THAT COACH FERATU WAS THE SCHOOL VAMPIRE, *HUH*, TINY RICK?
NOT AS CRAZY AS HOW GOOD AT KILLING VAMPIRES YOU WERE BACK THERE, MY DUDE.
YOU'RE LIKE A VAMPIRE-KILLING JACKHAMMER.
YOU REALLY HAD THAT STABBING MOTION DOWN PAT. A-A-AND SO POWERFUL!
Y-YEAH, I-I-IT'S LIKE I TRAINED MY WHOLE LIFE FOR THIS.
NORMALLY I'D BE PRETTY DISGUSTED, BUT YOUR IMMENSE FOREARM STRENGTH DEFINITELY SAVED OUR BUTTS THIS TIME.
I-I-IT'S LIKE IT'S MY DESTINY OR SOMETHING!
WHAT A CRAZY ADVENTURE, *HUH?*
HA HA, VAMPIRES SURE ARE WACKY.
I'D SAY YOUR VAMPIRE-KILLING STYLE WAS "*WHACK*-Y".

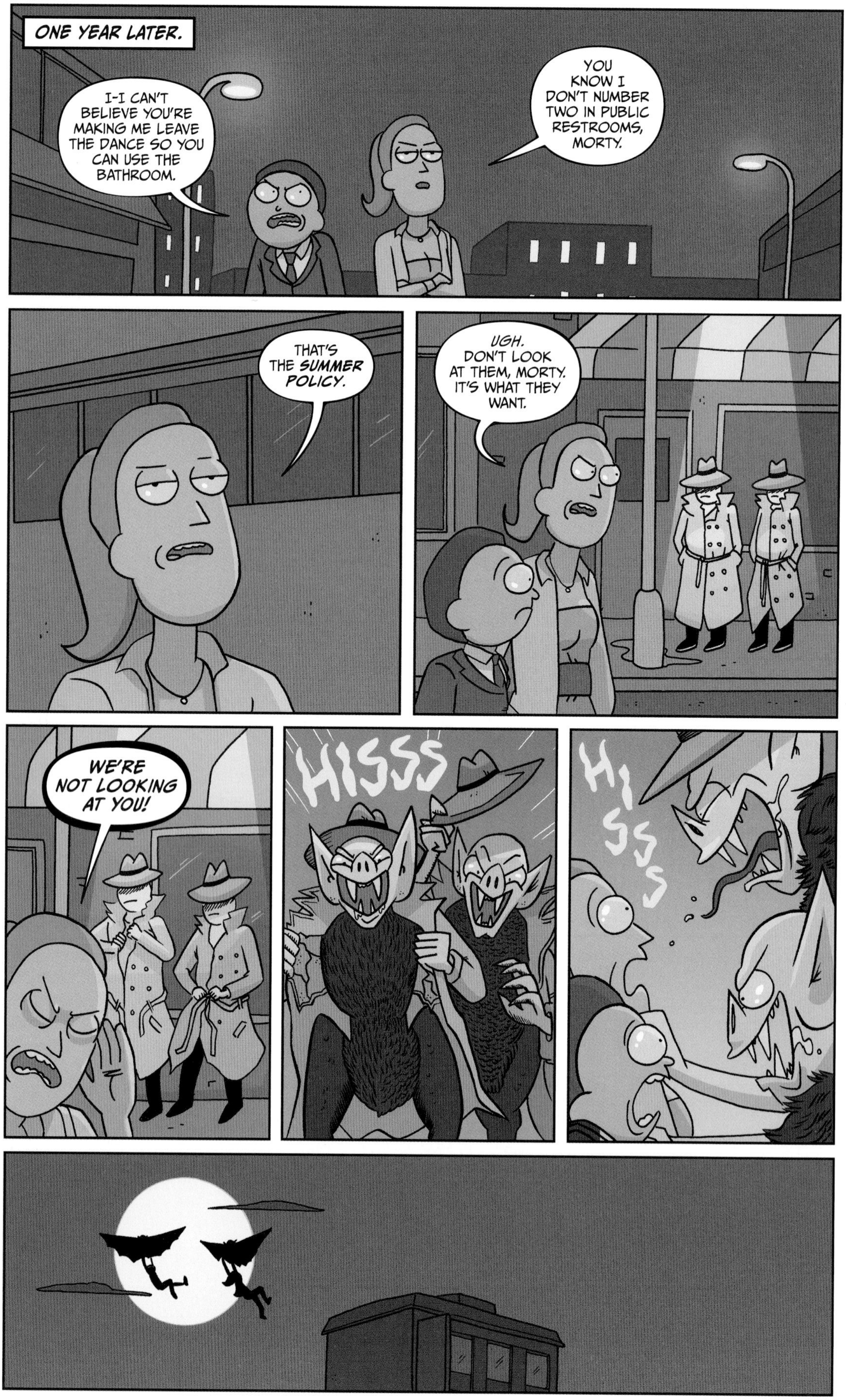
ONE YEAR LATER.
I-I CAN'T BELIEVE YOU'RE MAKING ME LEAVE THE DANCE SO YOU CAN USE THE BATHROOM.
YOU KNOW I DON'T NUMBER TWO IN PUBLIC RESTROOMS, MORTY.
THAT'S THE SUMMER POLICY.
UGH. DON'T LOOK AT THEM, MORTY. IT'S WHAT THEY WANT.
WE'RE NOT LOOKING AT YOU!
HISSS
HISSS

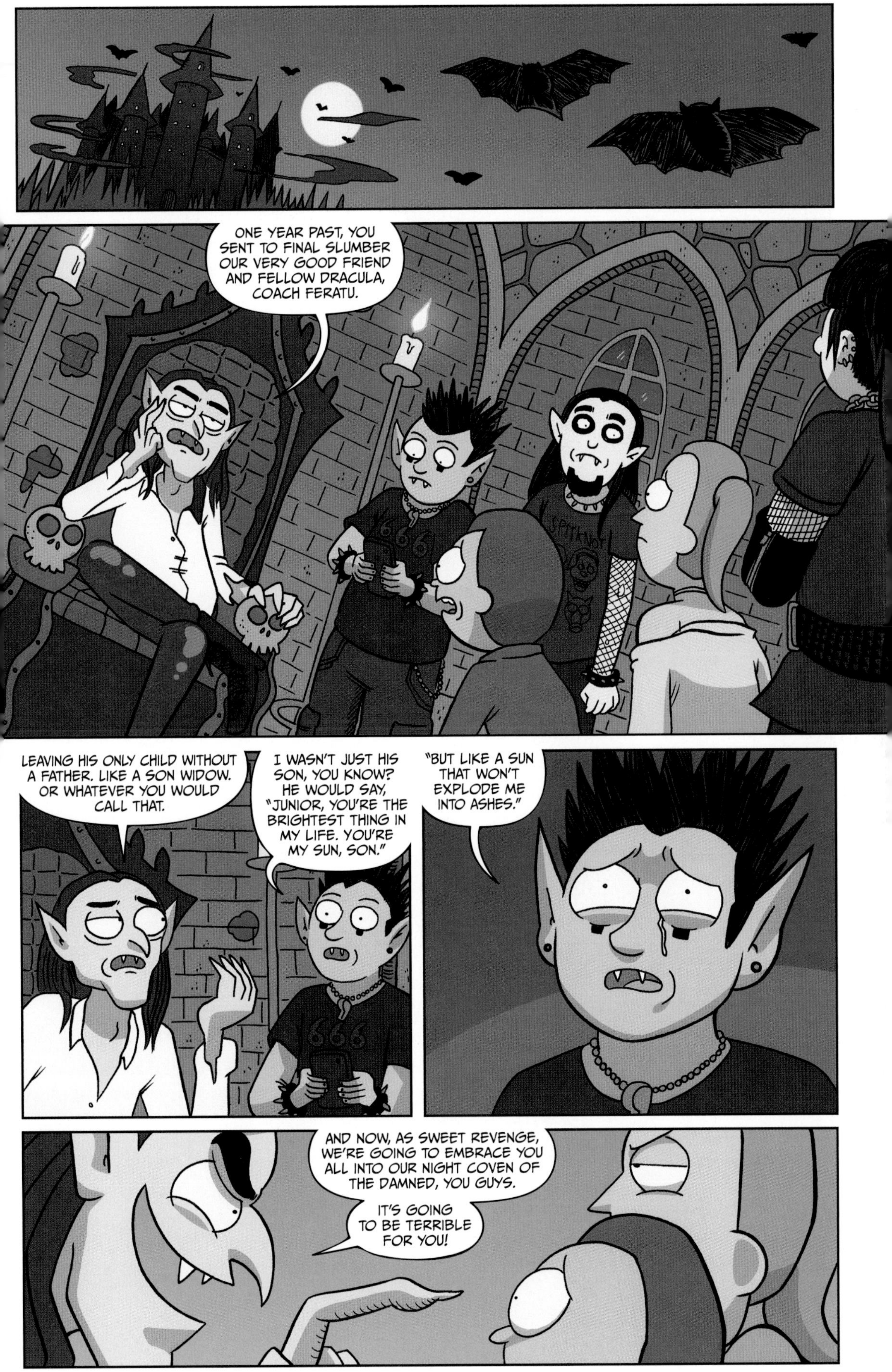
ONE YEAR PAST, YOU SENT TO FINAL SLUMBER OUR VERY GOOD FRIEND AND FELLOW DRACULA, COACH FERATU.
SPITKNOT
LEAVING HIS ONLY CHILD WITHOUT A FATHER. LIKE A SON WIDOW. OR WHATEVER YOU WOULD CALL THAT.
I WASN'T JUST HIS SON, YOU KNOW? HE WOULD SAY, "JUNIOR, YOU'RE THE BRIGHTEST THING IN MY LIFE. YOU'RE MY SUN, SON."
"BUT LIKE A SUN THAT WON'T EXPLODE ME INTO ASHES."
AND NOW, AS SWEET REVENGE, WE'RE GOING TO EMBRACE YOU ALL INTO OUR NIGHT COVEN OF THE DAMNED, YOU GUYS.
IT'S GOING TO BE TERRIBLE FOR YOU!

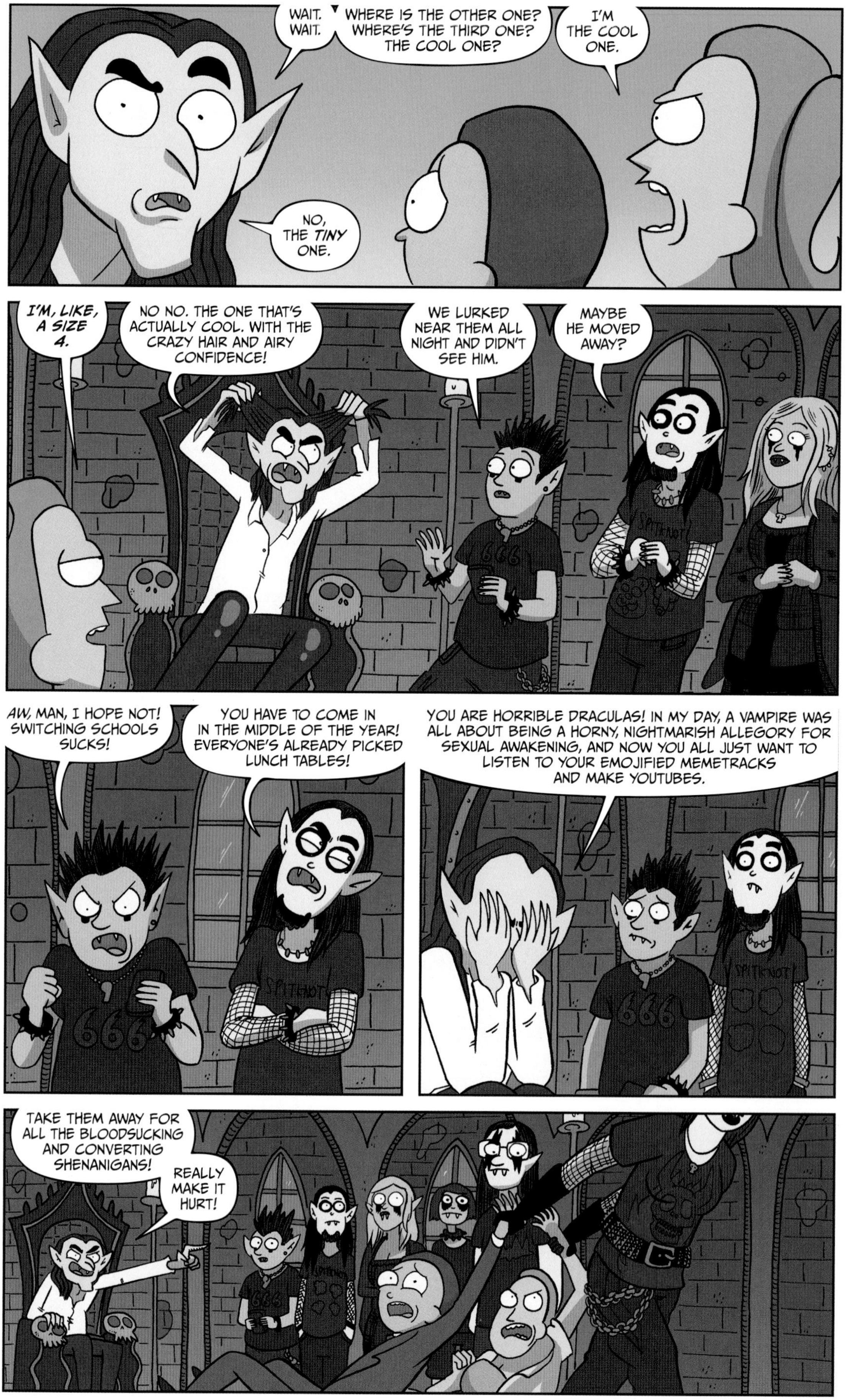
WAIT. WAIT.
WHERE IS THE OTHER ONE? WHERE'S THE THIRD ONE? THE COOL ONE?
I'M THE COOL ONE.
NO, THE *TINY* ONE.
I'M, LIKE, A SIZE 4.
NO NO. THE ONE THAT'S ACTUALLY COOL. WITH THE CRAZY HAIR AND AIRY CONFIDENCE!
WE LURKED NEAR THEM ALL NIGHT AND DIDN'T SEE HIM.
MAYBE HE MOVED AWAY?
AW, MAN, I HOPE NOT! SWITCHING SCHOOLS SUCKS!
YOU HAVE TO COME IN IN THE MIDDLE OF THE YEAR! EVERYONE'S ALREADY PICKED LUNCH TABLES!
YOU ARE HORRIBLE DRACULAS! IN MY DAY, A VAMPIRE WAS ALL ABOUT BEING A HORNY, NIGHTMARISH ALLEGORY FOR SEXUAL AWAKENING, AND NOW YOU ALL JUST WANT TO LISTEN TO YOUR EMOJIFIED MEMETRACKS AND MAKE YOUTUBES.
TAKE THEM AWAY FOR ALL THE BLOODSUCKING AND CONVERTING SHENANIGANS!
REALLY MAKE IT HURT!

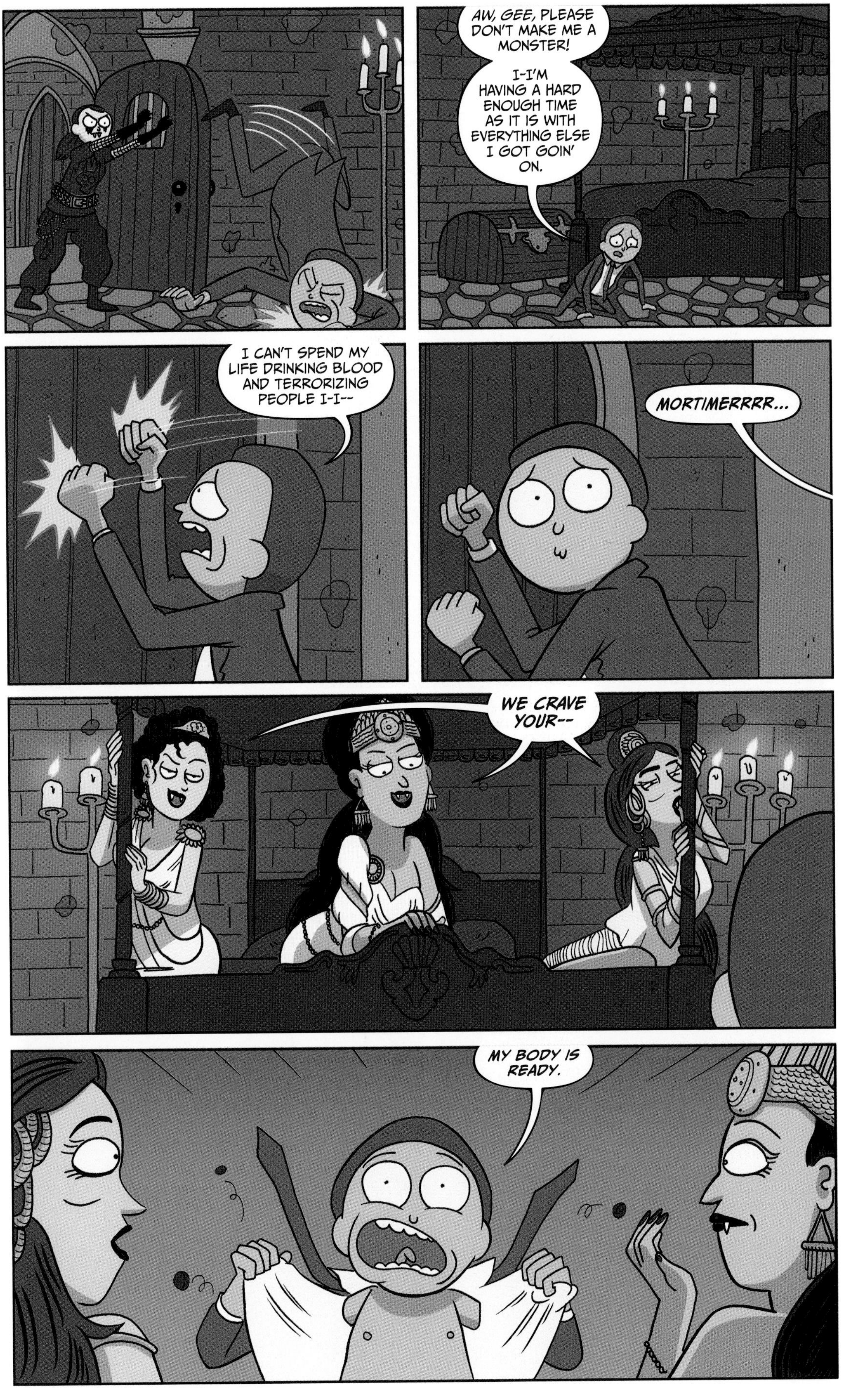
AW, GEE, PLEASE DON'T MAKE ME A MONSTER!
I-I'M HAVING A HARD ENOUGH TIME AS IT IS WITH EVERYTHING ELSE I GOT GOIN' ON.
I CAN'T SPEND MY LIFE DRINKING BLOOD AND TERRORIZING PEOPLE I-I--
MORTIMERRRR...
WE CRAVE YOUR--
MY BODY IS READY.

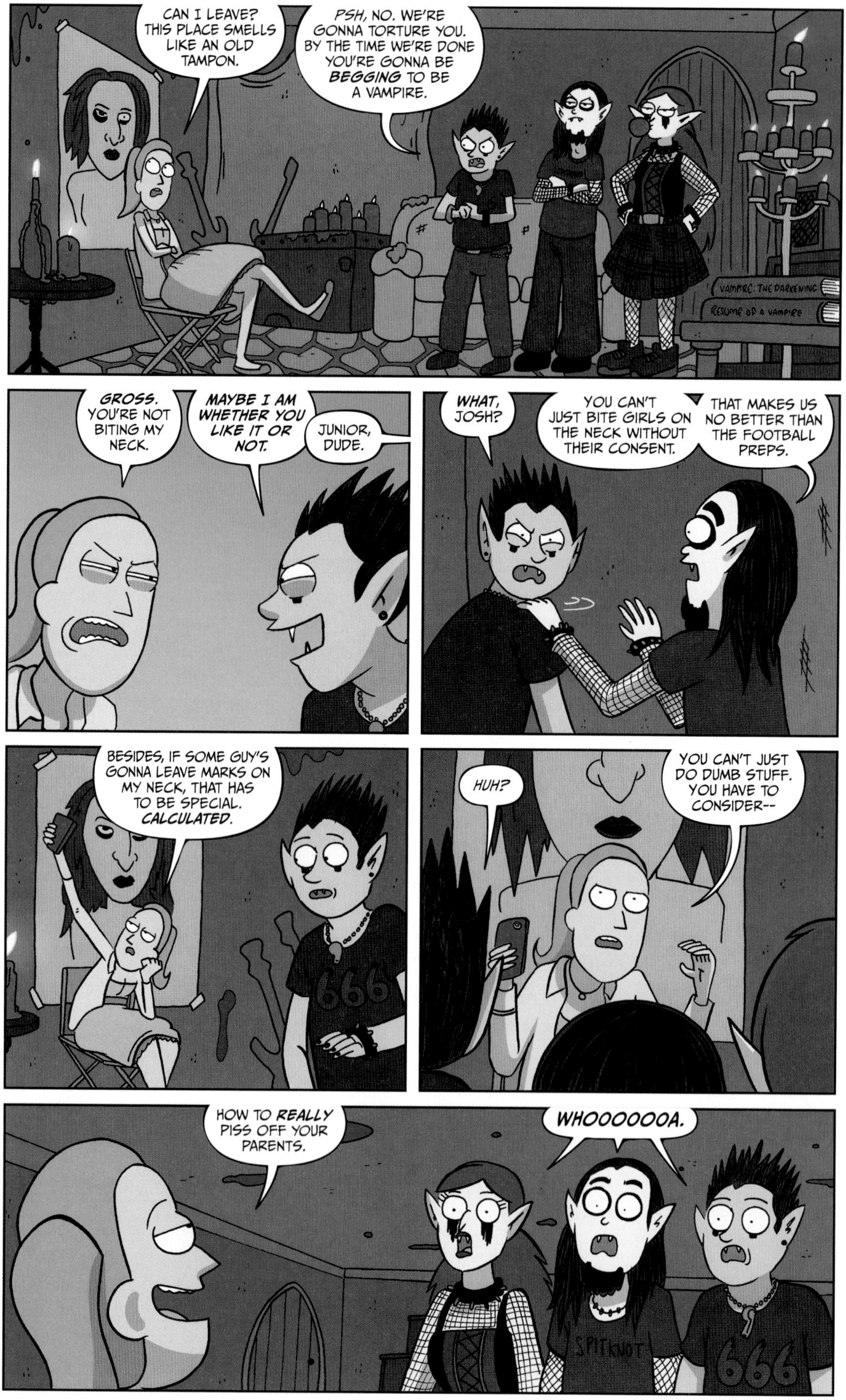
CAN I LEAVE? THIS PLACE SMELLS LIKE AN OLD TAMPON.
PSH, NO. WE'RE GONNA TORTURE YOU. BY THE TIME WE'RE DONE YOU'RE GONNA BE ***BEGGING*** TO BE A VAMPIRE.
VAMPIRE: THE DARKENING
RESUME OF A VAMPIRE
GROSS. YOU'RE NOT BITING MY NECK.
MAYBE I AM WHETHER YOU LIKE IT OR NOT.
JUNIOR, DUDE.
WHAT, JOSH?
YOU CAN'T JUST BITE GIRLS ON THE NECK WITHOUT THEIR CONSENT.
THAT MAKES US NO BETTER THAN THE FOOTBALL PREPS.
BESIDES, IF SOME GUY'S GONNA LEAVE MARKS ON MY NECK, THAT HAS TO BE SPECIAL. ***CALCULATED.***
666
HUH?
YOU CAN'T JUST DO DUMB STUFF. YOU HAVE TO CONSIDER--
HOW TO ***REALLY*** PISS OFF YOUR PARENTS.
WHOOOOOOA.
SPITKNOT
666

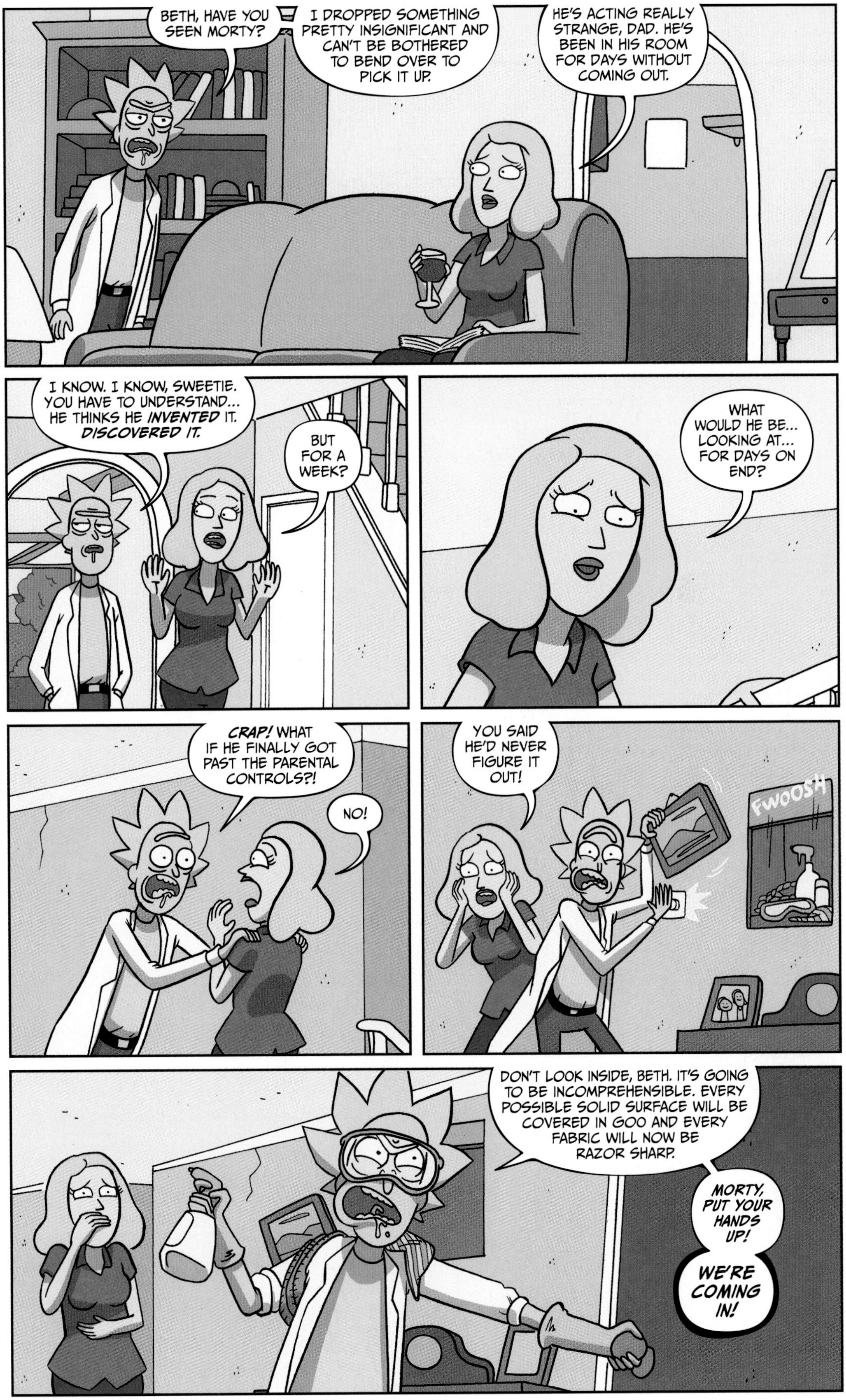
BETH, HAVE YOU SEEN MORTY?
I DROPPED SOMETHING PRETTY INSIGNIFICANT AND CAN'T BE BOTHERED TO BEND OVER TO PICK IT UP.
HE'S ACTING REALLY STRANGE, DAD. HE'S BEEN IN HIS ROOM FOR DAYS WITHOUT COMING OUT.
I KNOW. I KNOW, SWEETIE. YOU HAVE TO UNDERSTAND... HE THINKS HE *INVENTED* IT. ***DISCOVERED IT.***
BUT FOR A WEEK?
WHAT WOULD HE BE... LOOKING AT... FOR DAYS ON END?
CRAP! WHAT IF HE FINALLY GOT PAST THE PARENTAL CONTROLS?!
NO!
YOU SAID HE'D NEVER FIGURE IT OUT!
FWOOSH
DON'T LOOK INSIDE, BETH. IT'S GOING TO BE INCOMPREHENSIBLE. EVERY POSSIBLE SOLID SURFACE WILL BE COVERED IN GOO AND EVERY FABRIC WILL NOW BE RAZOR SHARP.
MORTY, PUT YOUR HANDS UP!
WE'RE COMING IN!

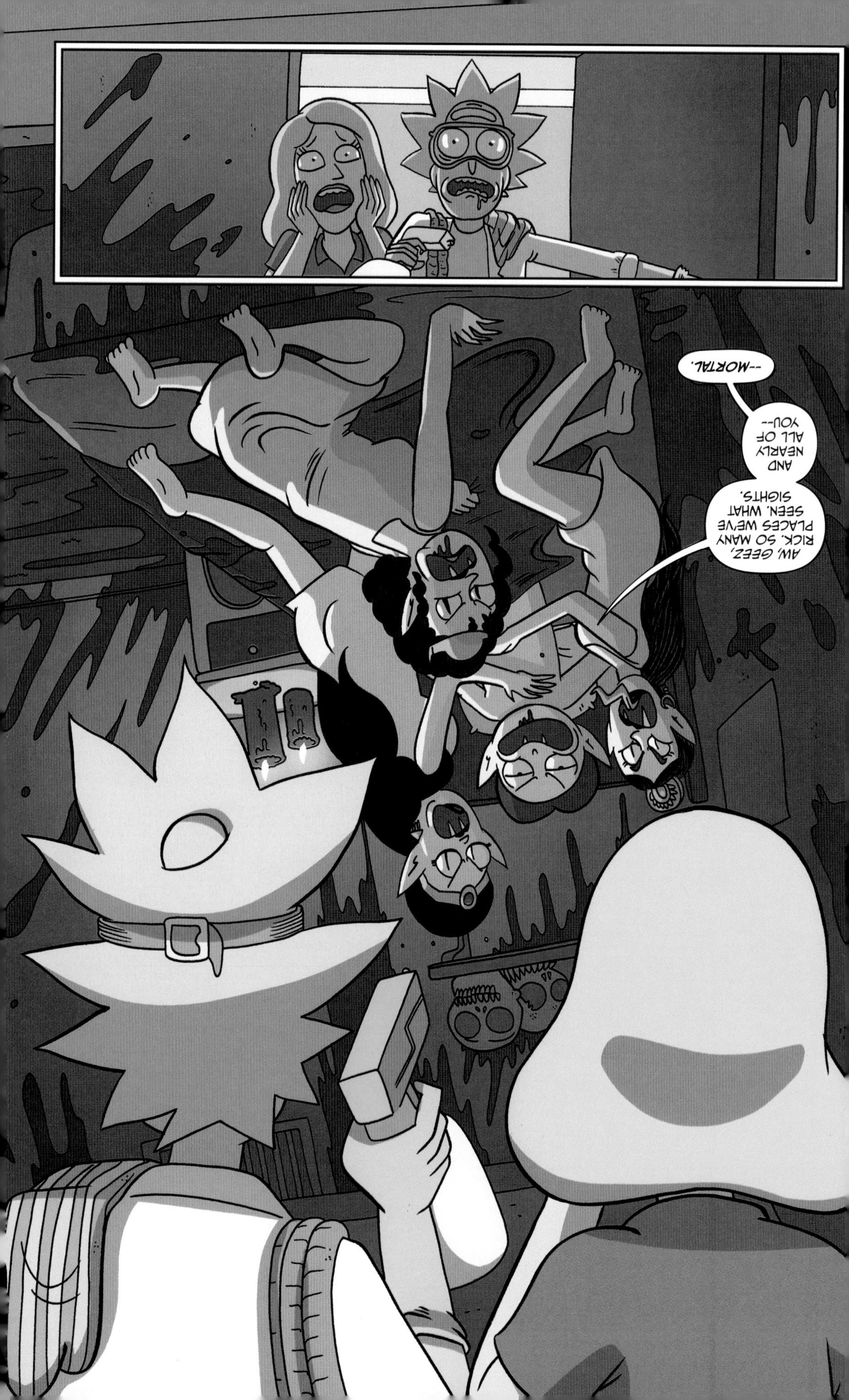
AW, GEEZ, RICK. SO MANY PLACES WE'VE SEEN. WHAT SIGHTS.
AND NEARLY ALL OF YOU--
--MORTAL.

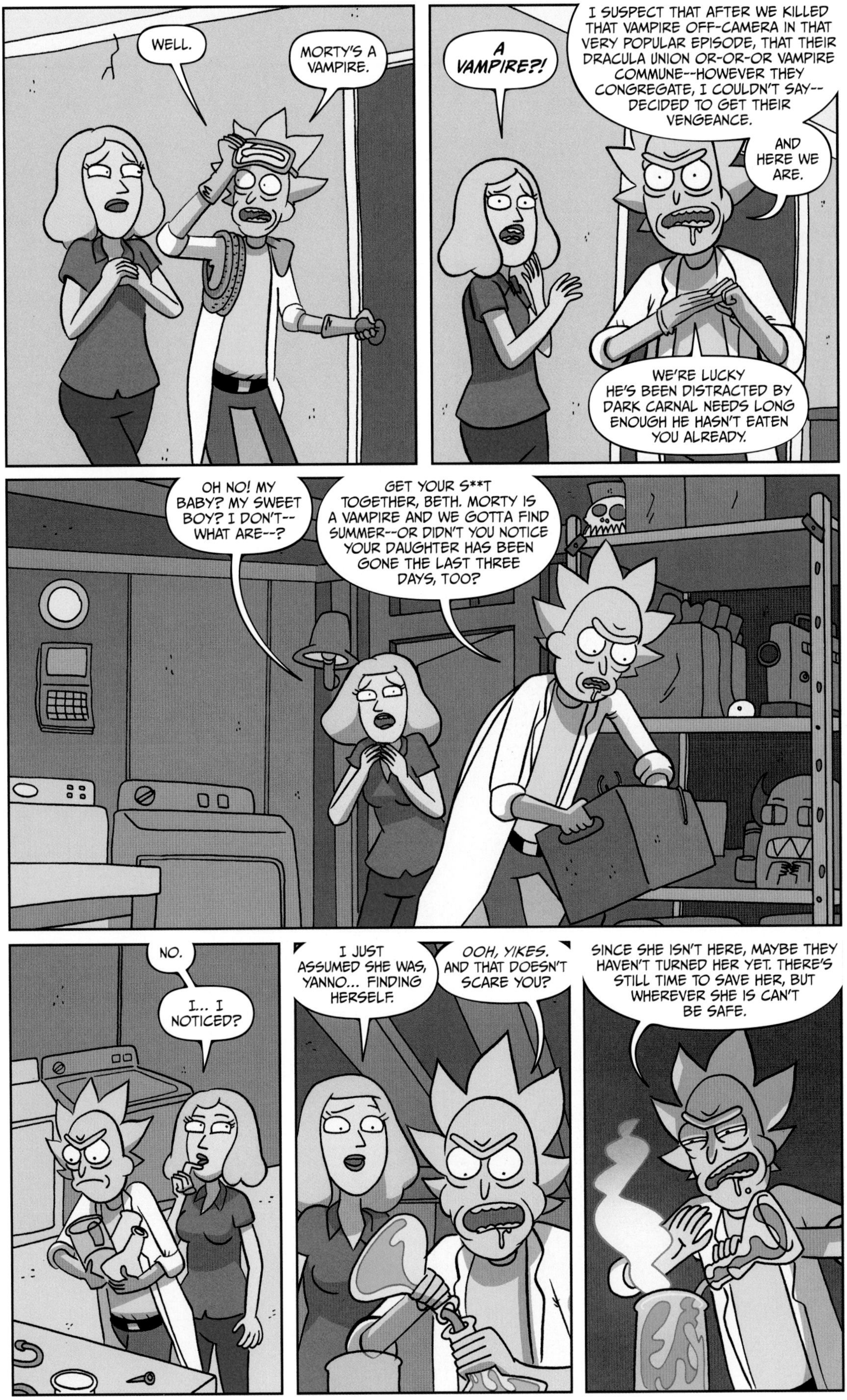

WELL.
MORTY'S A VAMPIRE.
A VAMPIRE?!
I SUSPECT THAT AFTER WE KILLED THAT VAMPIRE OFF-CAMERA IN THAT VERY POPULAR EPISODE, THAT THEIR DRACULA UNION OR-OR-OR VAMPIRE COMMUNE--HOWEVER THEY CONGREGATE, I COULDN'T SAY--DECIDED TO GET THEIR VENGEANCE.
AND HERE WE ARE.
WE'RE LUCKY HE'S BEEN DISTRACTED BY DARK CARNAL NEEDS LONG ENOUGH HE HASN'T EATEN YOU ALREADY.
OH NO! MY BABY? MY SWEET BOY? I DON'T-- WHAT ARE--?
GET YOUR S**T TOGETHER, BETH. MORTY IS A VAMPIRE AND WE GOTTA FIND SUMMER--OR DIDN'T YOU NOTICE YOUR DAUGHTER HAS BEEN GONE THE LAST THREE DAYS, TOO?
NO.
I... I NOTICED?
I JUST ASSUMED SHE WAS, YANNO... FINDING HERSELF.
OOH, YIKES. AND THAT DOESN'T SCARE YOU?
SINCE SHE ISN'T HERE, MAYBE THEY HAVEN'T TURNED HER YET. THERE'S STILL TIME TO SAVE HER, BUT WHEREVER SHE IS CAN'T BE SAFE.

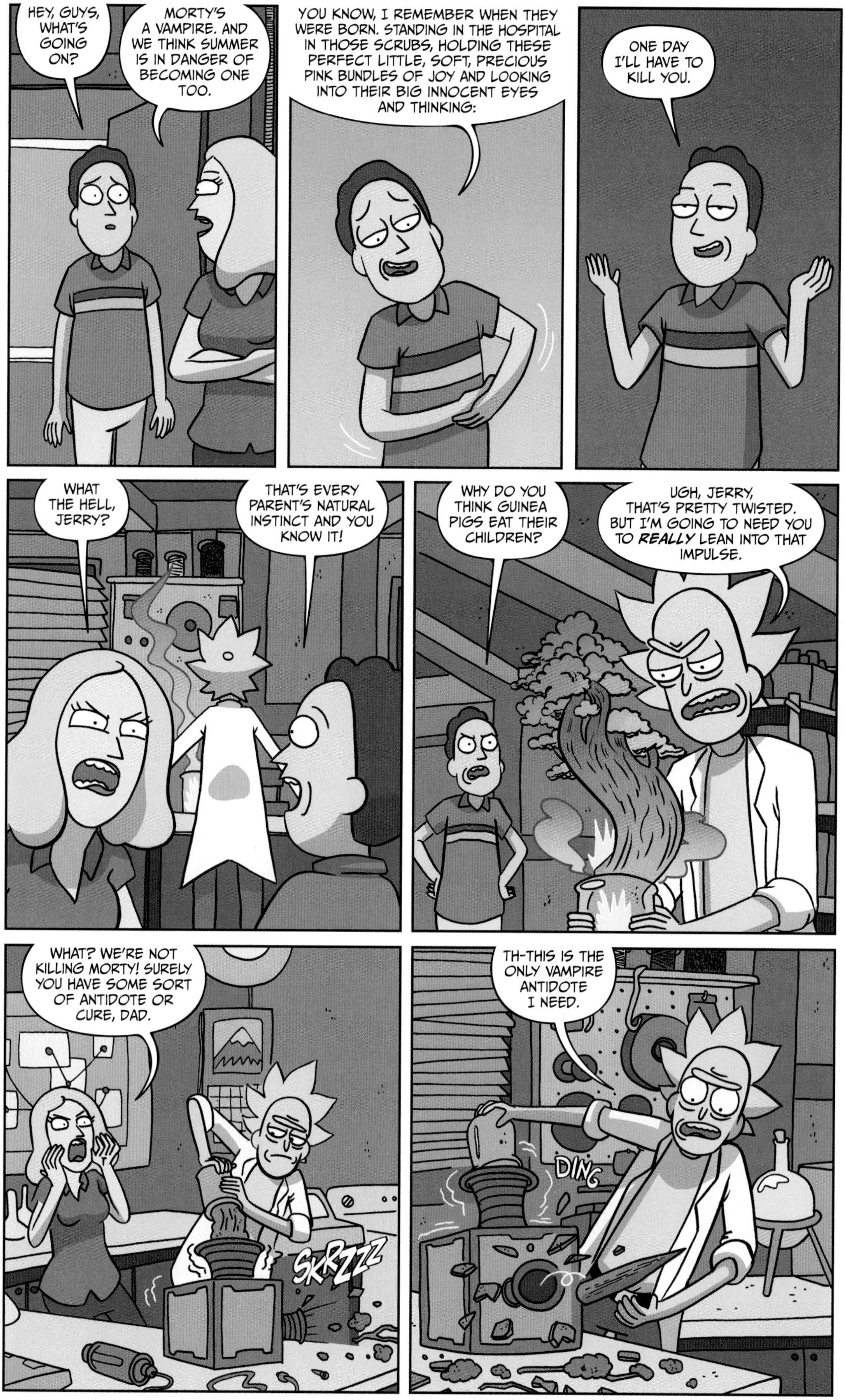
HEY, GUYS, WHAT'S GOING ON?
MORTY'S A VAMPIRE. AND WE THINK SUMMER IS IN DANGER OF BECOMING ONE TOO.
YOU KNOW, I REMEMBER WHEN THEY WERE BORN. STANDING IN THE HOSPITAL IN THOSE SCRUBS, HOLDING THESE PERFECT LITTLE, SOFT, PRECIOUS PINK BUNDLES OF JOY AND LOOKING INTO THEIR BIG INNOCENT EYES AND THINKING:
ONE DAY I'LL HAVE TO KILL YOU.
WHAT THE HELL, JERRY?
THAT'S EVERY PARENT'S NATURAL INSTINCT AND YOU KNOW IT!
WHY DO YOU THINK GUINEA PIGS EAT THEIR CHILDREN?
UGH, JERRY, THAT'S PRETTY TWISTED. BUT I'M GOING TO NEED YOU TO *REALLY* LEAN INTO THAT IMPULSE.
WHAT? WE'RE NOT KILLING MORTY! SURELY YOU HAVE SOME SORT OF ANTIDOTE OR CURE, DAD.
SKRZZZ
TH-THIS IS THE ONLY VAMPIRE ANTIDOTE I NEED.
DING

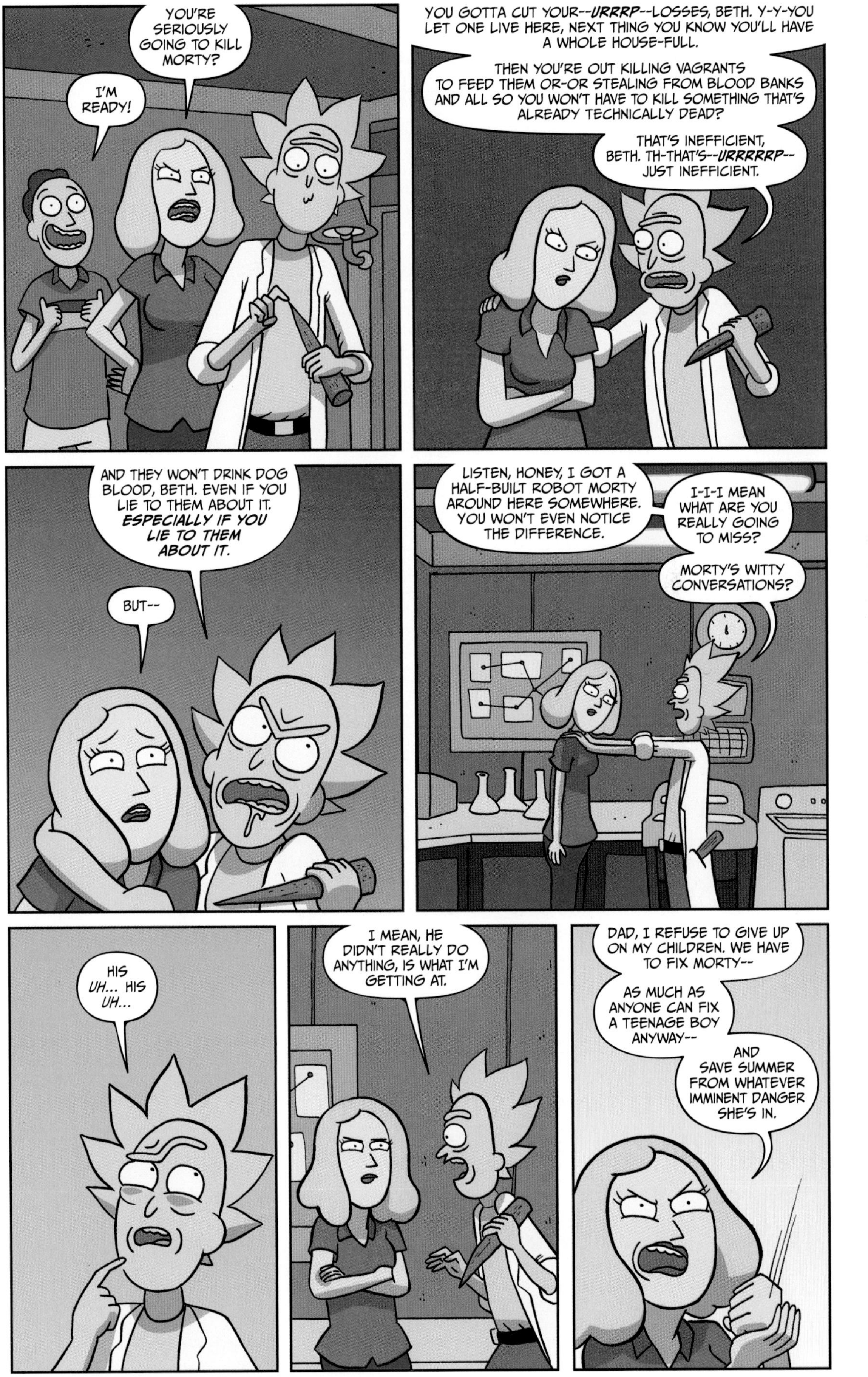
YOU'RE SERIOUSLY GOING TO KILL MORTY?
I'M READY!
YOU GOTTA CUT YOUR--URRRP--LOSSES, BETH. Y-Y-YOU LET ONE LIVE HERE, NEXT THING YOU KNOW YOU'LL HAVE A WHOLE HOUSE-FULL.
THEN YOU'RE OUT KILLING VAGRANTS TO FEED THEM OR-OR STEALING FROM BLOOD BANKS AND ALL SO YOU WON'T HAVE TO KILL SOMETHING THAT'S ALREADY TECHNICALLY DEAD?
THAT'S INEFFICIENT, BETH. TH-THAT'S--URRRRRP--JUST INEFFICIENT.
AND THEY WON'T DRINK DOG BLOOD, BETH. EVEN IF YOU LIE TO THEM ABOUT IT. ESPECIALLY IF YOU LIE TO THEM ABOUT IT.
BUT--
LISTEN, HONEY, I GOT A HALF-BUILT ROBOT MORTY AROUND HERE SOMEWHERE. YOU WON'T EVEN NOTICE THE DIFFERENCE.
I-I-I MEAN WHAT ARE YOU REALLY GOING TO MISS?
MORTY'S WITTY CONVERSATIONS?
HIS UH... HIS UH...
I MEAN, HE DIDN'T REALLY DO ANYTHING, IS WHAT I'M GETTING AT.
DAD, I REFUSE TO GIVE UP ON MY CHILDREN. WE HAVE TO FIX MORTY--
AS MUCH AS ANYONE CAN FIX A TEENAGE BOY ANYWAY--
AND SAVE SUMMER FROM WHATEVER IMMINENT DANGER SHE'S IN.

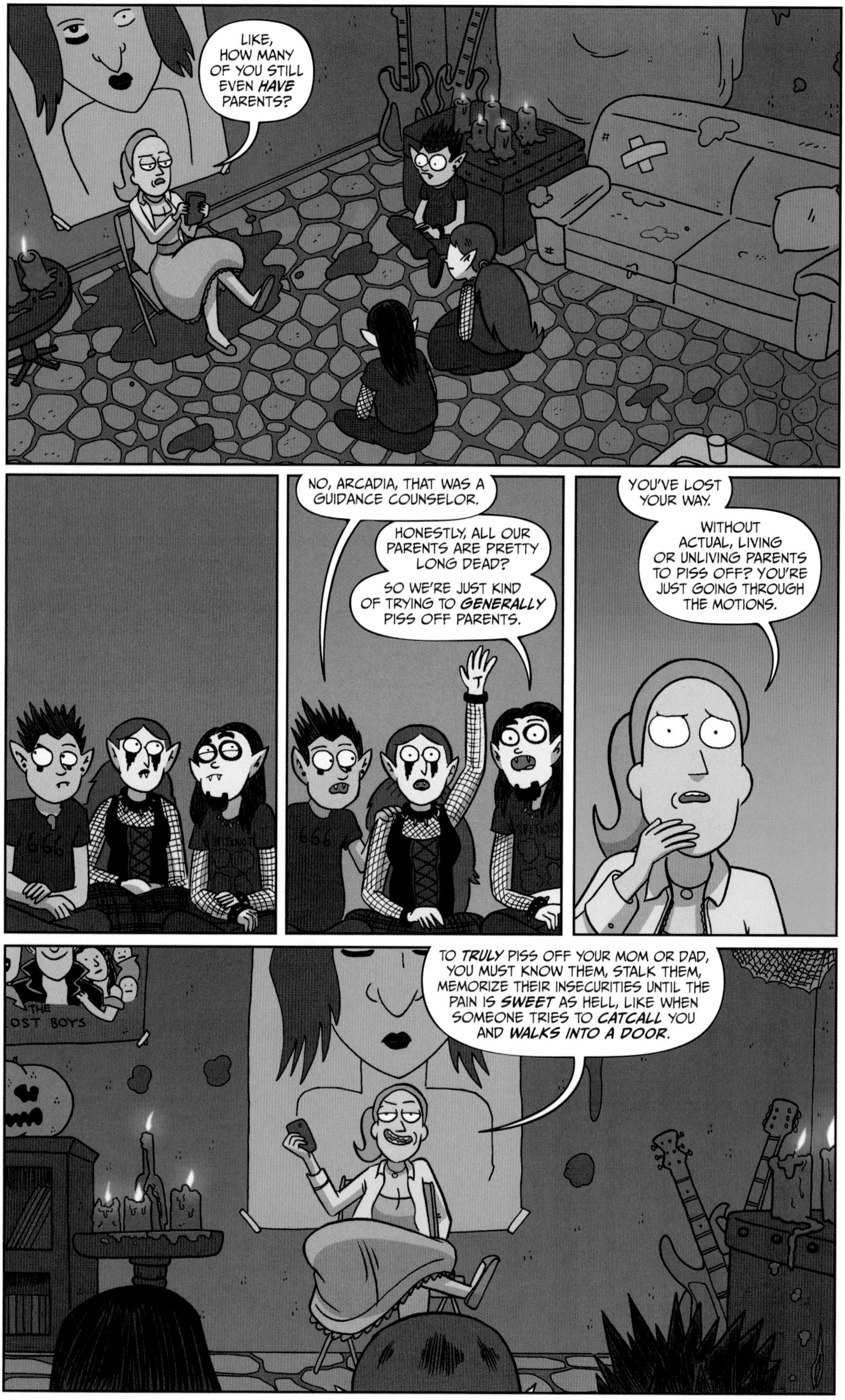
LIKE, HOW MANY OF YOU STILL EVEN *HAVE* PARENTS?
NO, ARCADIA, THAT WAS A GUIDANCE COUNSELOR.
HONESTLY, ALL OUR PARENTS ARE PRETTY LONG DEAD?
SO WE'RE JUST KIND OF TRYING TO *GENERALLY* PISS OFF PARENTS.
YOU'VE LOST YOUR WAY.
WITHOUT ACTUAL, LIVING OR UNLIVING PARENTS TO PISS OFF? YOU'RE JUST GOING THROUGH THE MOTIONS.
THE
OST BOYS
TO *TRULY* PISS OFF YOUR MOM OR DAD, YOU MUST KNOW THEM, STALK THEM, MEMORIZE THEIR INSECURITIES UNTIL THE PAIN IS *SWEET* AS HELL, LIKE WHEN SOMEONE TRIES TO *CATCALL* YOU AND *WALKS INTO A DOOR*.

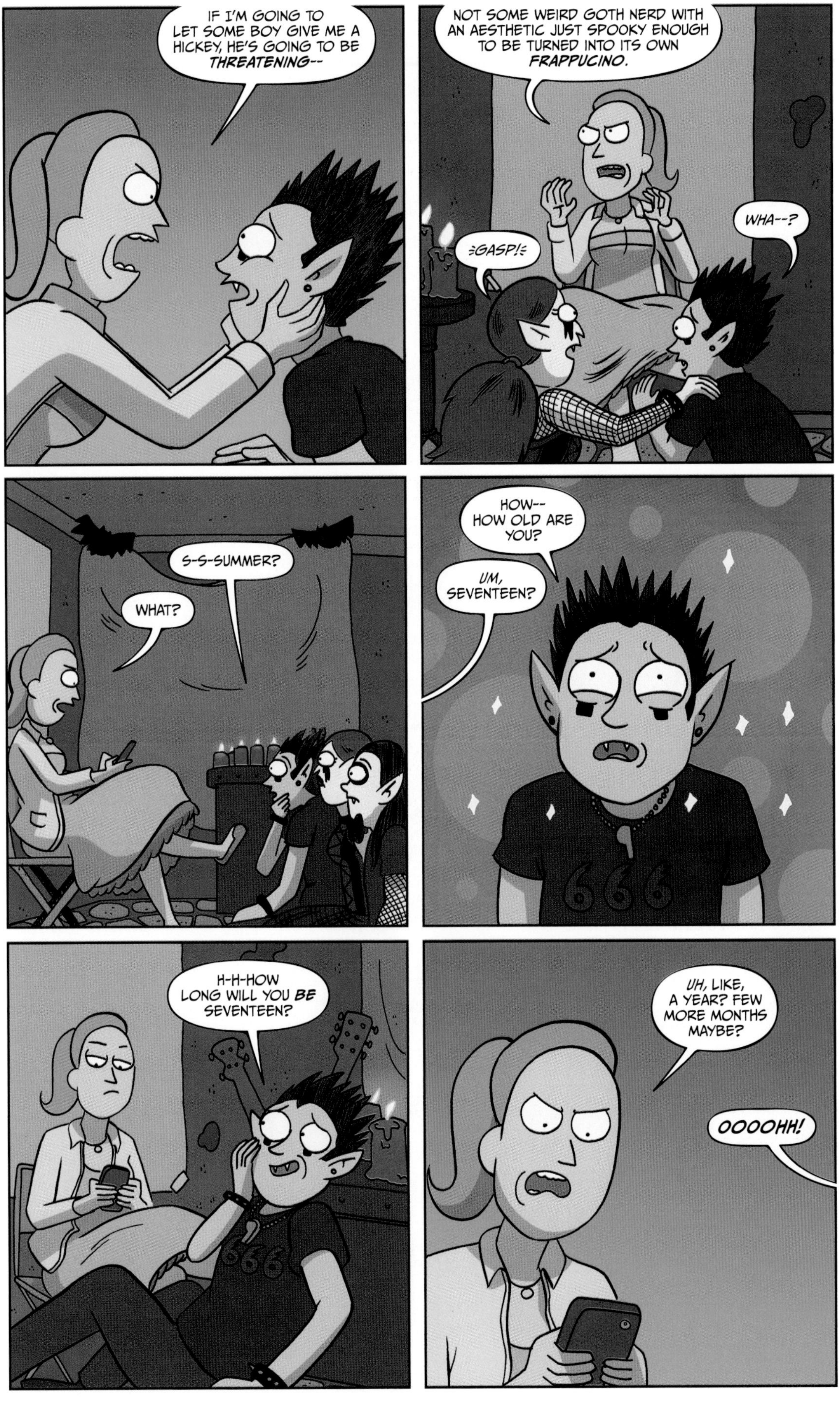
IF I'M GOING TO LET SOME BOY GIVE ME A HICKEY, HE'S GOING TO BE *THREATENING--*
NOT SOME WEIRD GOTH NERD WITH AN AESTHETIC JUST SPOOKY ENOUGH TO BE TURNED INTO ITS OWN *FRAPPUCINO.*
GASP!
WHA--?
S-S-SUMMER?
WHAT?
HOW-- HOW OLD ARE YOU?
UM, SEVENTEEN?
H-H-HOW LONG WILL YOU *BE* SEVENTEEN?
UH, LIKE, A YEAR? FEW MORE MONTHS MAYBE?
OOOOHH!

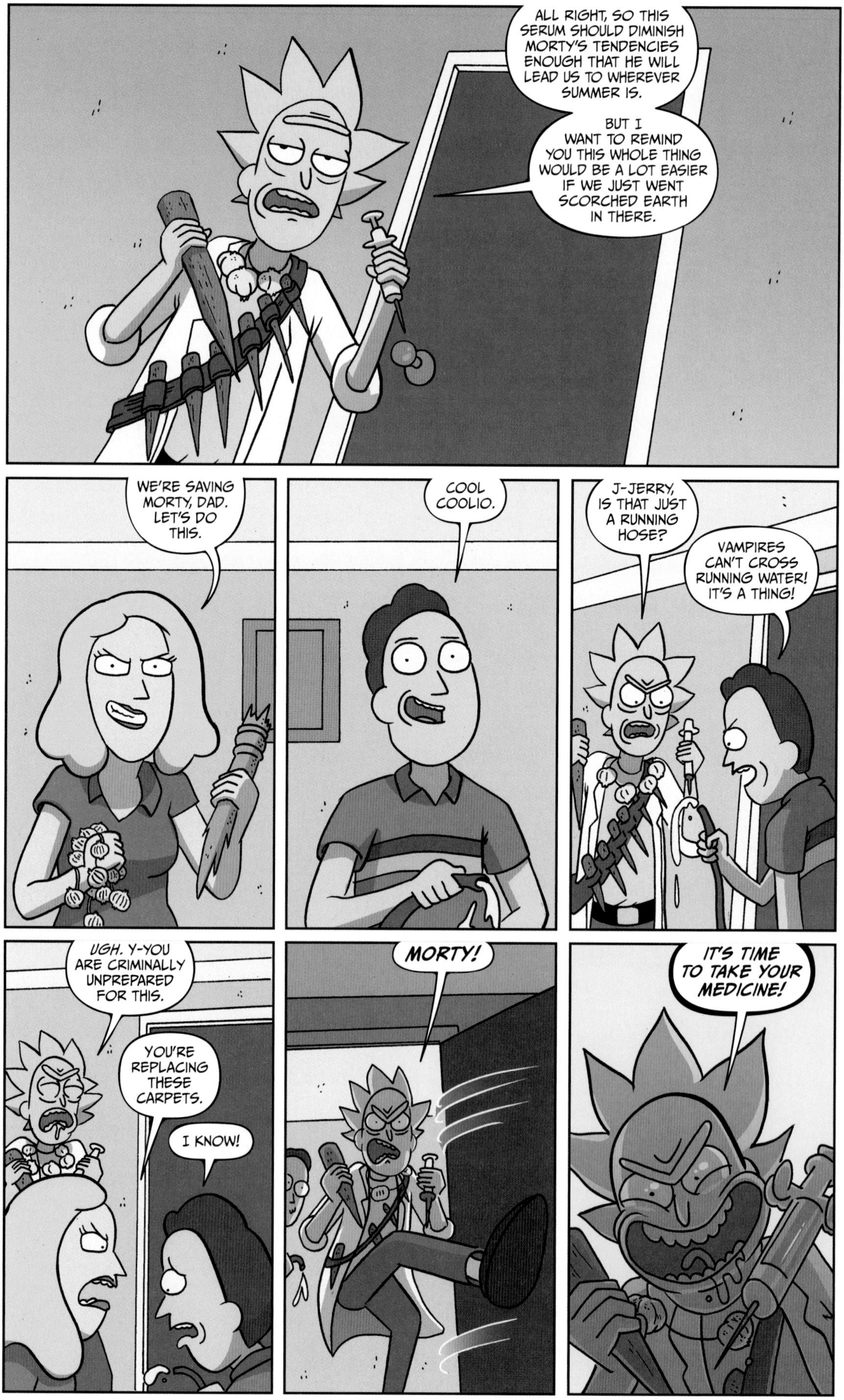
ALL RIGHT, SO THIS SERUM SHOULD DIMINISH MORTY'S TENDENCIES ENOUGH THAT HE WILL LEAD US TO WHEREVER SUMMER IS.
BUT I WANT TO REMIND YOU THIS WHOLE THING WOULD BE A LOT EASIER IF WE JUST WENT SCORCHED EARTH IN THERE.
WE'RE SAVING MORTY, DAD. LET'S DO THIS.
COOL COOLIO.
J-JERRY, IS THAT JUST A RUNNING HOSE?
VAMPIRES CAN'T CROSS RUNNING WATER! IT'S A THING!
UGH. Y-YOU ARE CRIMINALLY UNPREPARED FOR THIS.
YOU'RE REPLACING THESE CARPETS.
I KNOW!
MORTY!
IT'S TIME TO TAKE YOUR MEDICINE!

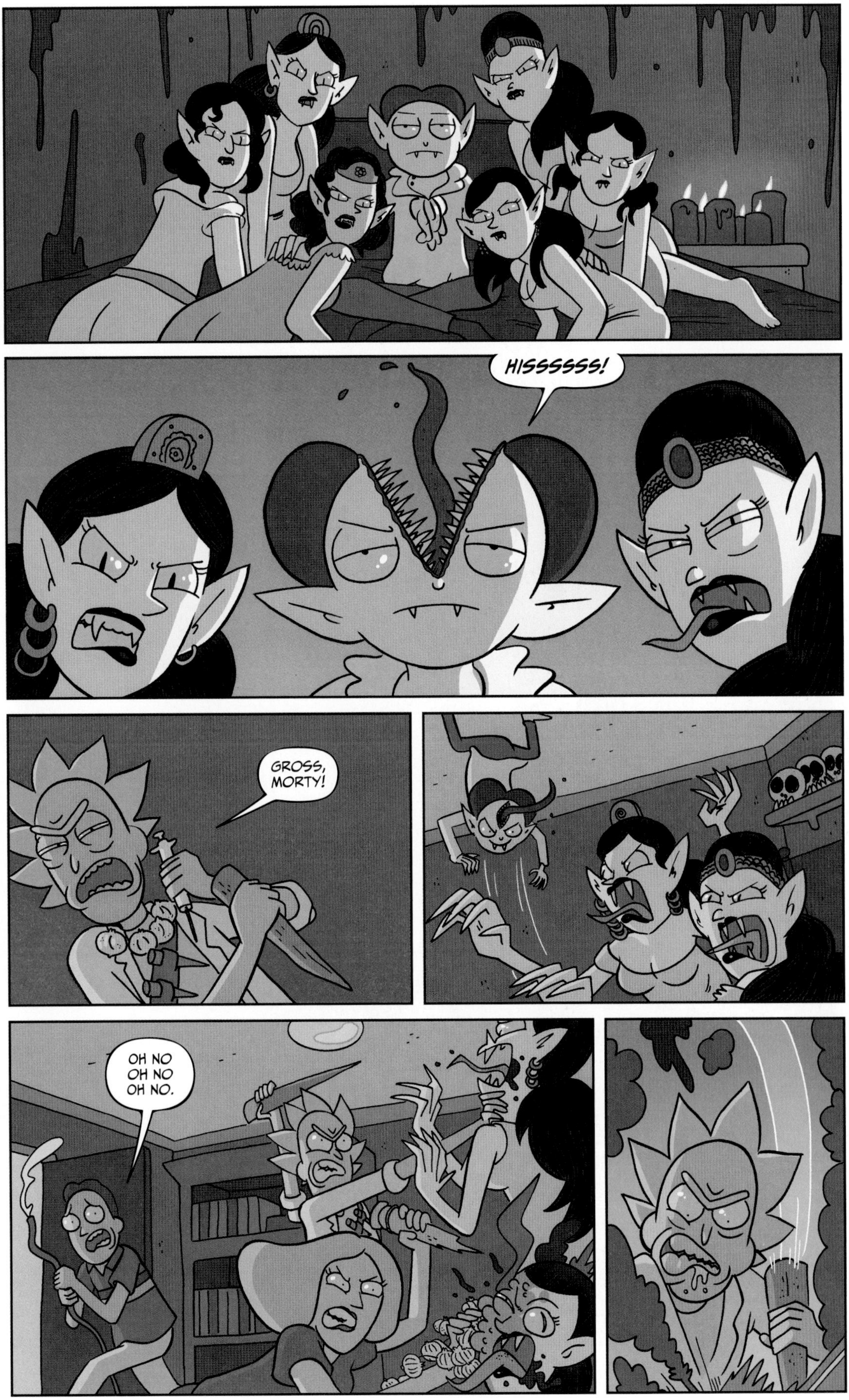
HISSSSSS!
GROSS, MORTY!
OH NO OH NO OH NO.

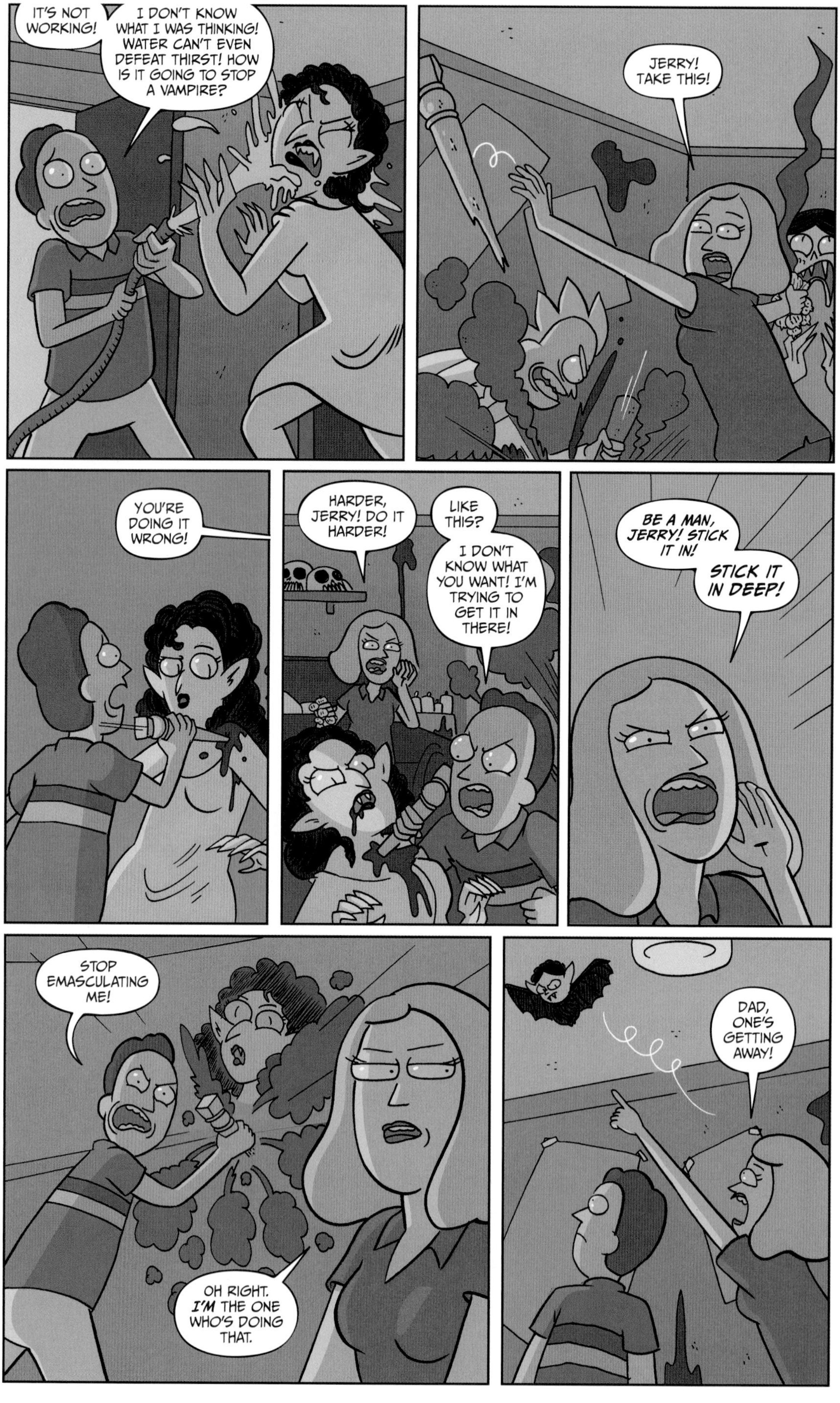
IT'S NOT WORKING!
I DON'T KNOW WHAT I WAS THINKING! WATER CAN'T EVEN DEFEAT THIRST! HOW IS IT GOING TO STOP A VAMPIRE?
JERRY! TAKE THIS!
YOU'RE DOING IT WRONG!
HARDER, JERRY! DO IT HARDER!
LIKE THIS?
I DON'T KNOW WHAT YOU WANT! I'M TRYING TO GET IT IN THERE!
BE A MAN, JERRY! STICK IT IN!
STICK IT IN DEEP!
STOP EMASCULATING ME!
OH RIGHT. *I'M* THE ONE WHO'S DOING THAT.
DAD, ONE'S GETTING AWAY!

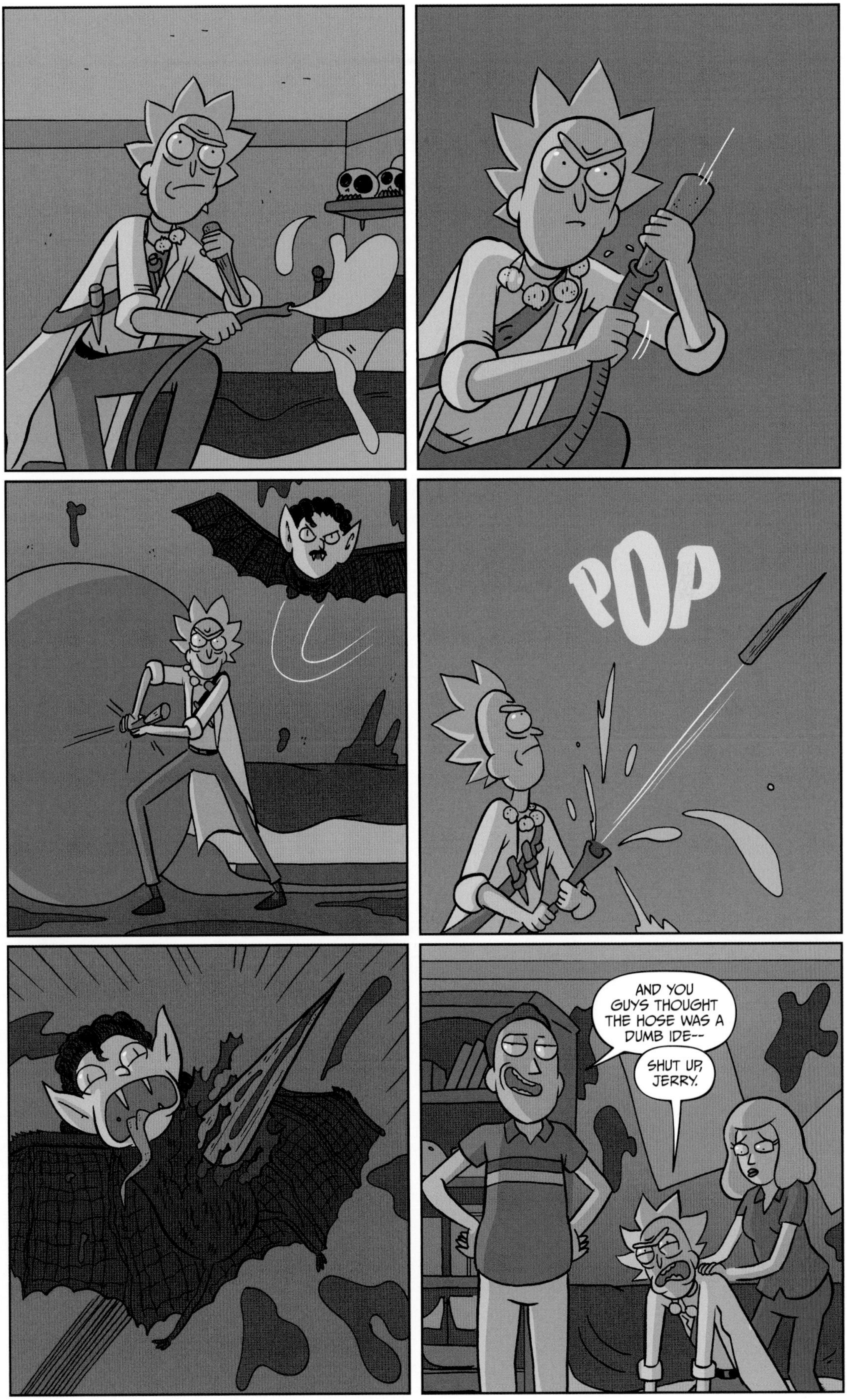
POP
AND YOU GUYS THOUGHT THE HOSE WAS A DUMB IDE--
SHUT UP, JERRY.

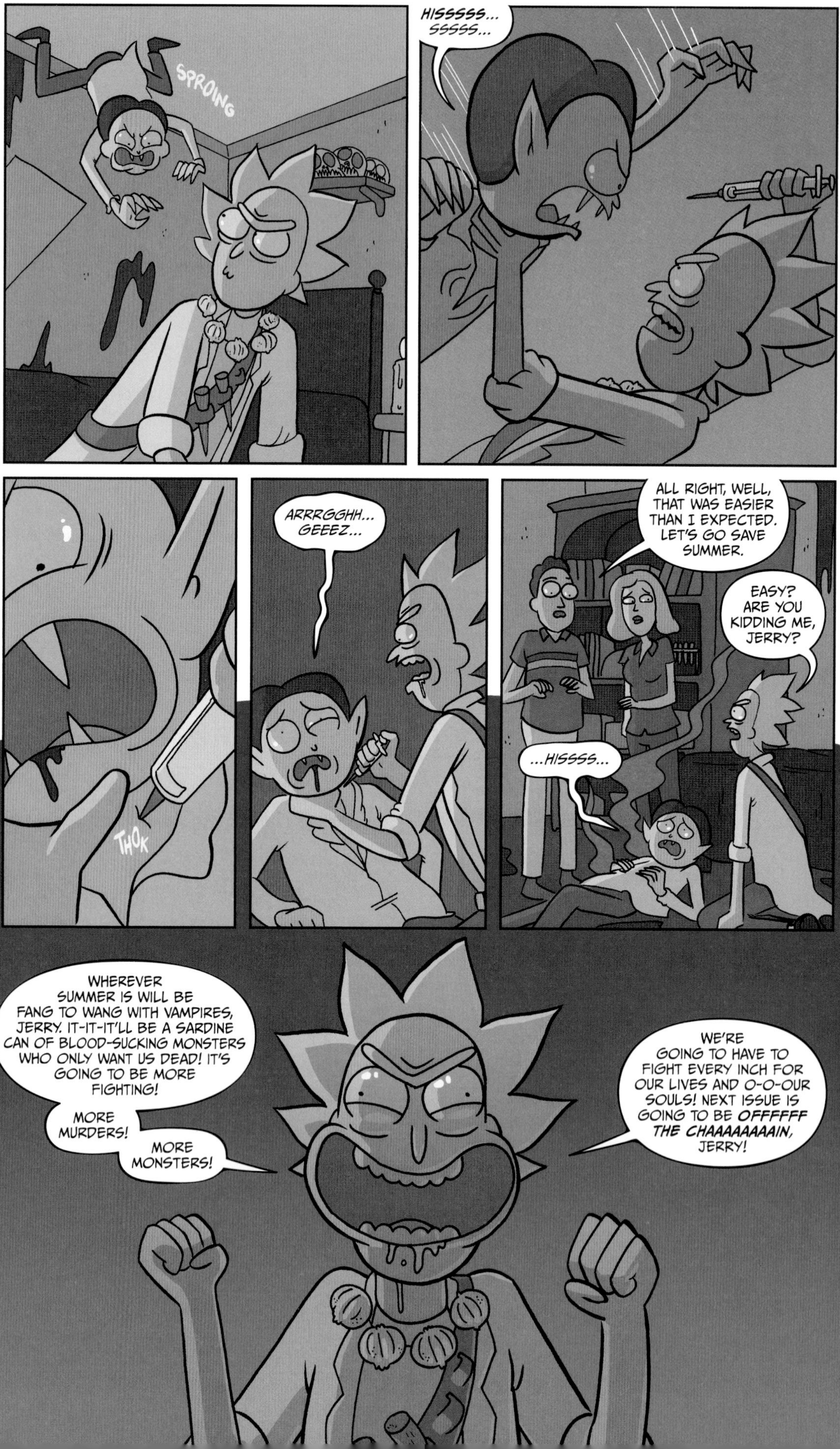
SPROING
HISSSSS... SSSSS...
THOK
ARRRGGHH... GEEEZ...
ALL RIGHT, WELL, THAT WAS EASIER THAN I EXPECTED. LET'S GO SAVE SUMMER.
EASY? ARE YOU KIDDING ME, JERRY?
...HISSSS...
WHEREVER SUMMER IS WILL BE FANG TO WANG WITH VAMPIRES, JERRY. IT-IT-IT'LL BE A SARDINE CAN OF BLOOD-SUCKING MONSTERS WHO ONLY WANT US DEAD! IT'S GOING TO BE MORE FIGHTING!
MORE MURDERS!
MORE MONSTERS!
WE'RE GOING TO HAVE TO FIGHT EVERY INCH FOR OUR LIVES AND O-O-OUR SOULS! NEXT ISSUE IS GOING TO BE OFFFFFF THE CHAAAAAAAAIN, JERRY!

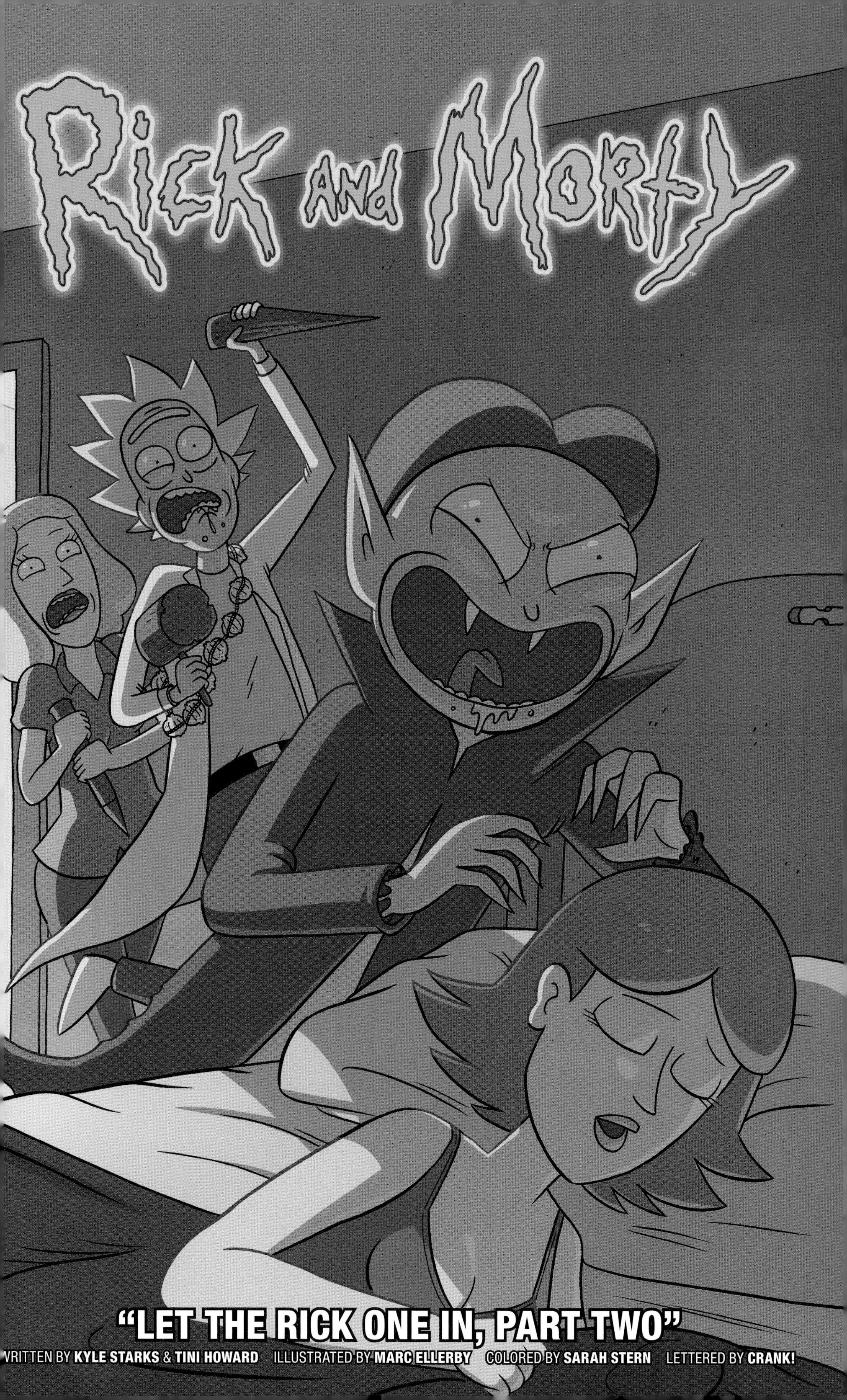
Rick and Morty

"LET THE RICK ONE IN, PART TWO"

WRITTEN BY **KYLE STARKS** & **TINI HOWARD** ILLUSTRATED BY **MARC ELLERBY** COLORED BY **SARAH STERN** LETTERED BY **CRANK!**

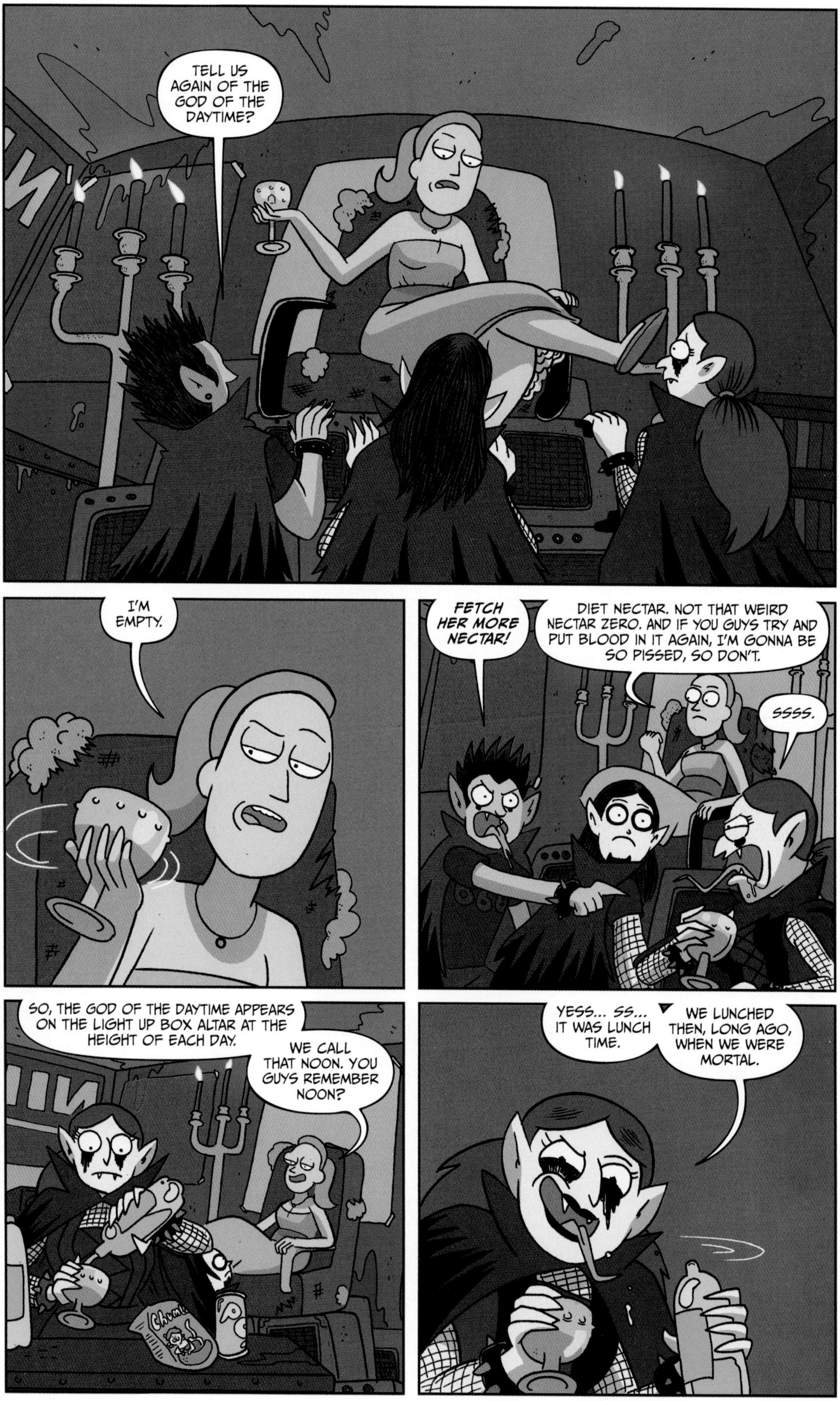
TELL US AGAIN OF THE GOD OF THE DAYTIME?
I'M EMPTY.
FETCH HER MORE NECTAR!
DIET NECTAR. NOT THAT WEIRD NECTAR ZERO. AND IF YOU GUYS TRY AND PUT BLOOD IN IT AGAIN, I'M GONNA BE SO PISSED, SO DON'T.
SSSS.
SO, THE GOD OF THE DAYTIME APPEARS ON THE LIGHT UP BOX ALTAR AT THE HEIGHT OF EACH DAY.
WE CALL THAT NOON. YOU GUYS REMEMBER NOON?
YESS... SS... IT WAS LUNCH TIME.
WE LUNCHED THEN, LONG AGO, WHEN WE WERE MORTAL.

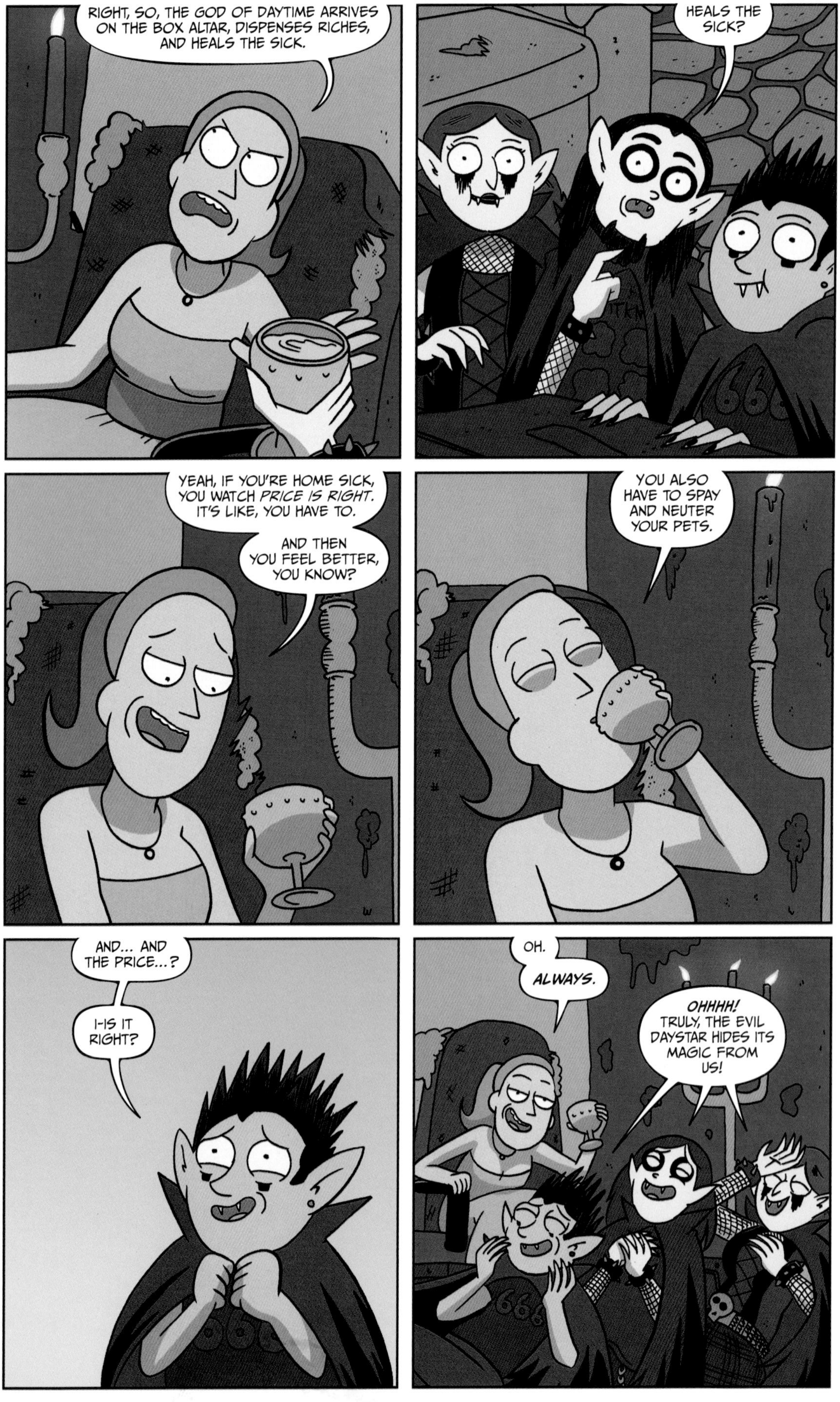
RIGHT, SO, THE GOD OF DAYTIME ARRIVES ON THE BOX ALTAR, DISPENSES RICHES, AND HEALS THE SICK.
HEALS THE SICK?
YEAH, IF YOU'RE HOME SICK, YOU WATCH *PRICE IS RIGHT*. IT'S LIKE, YOU HAVE TO.
AND THEN YOU FEEL BETTER, YOU KNOW?
YOU ALSO HAVE TO SPAY AND NEUTER YOUR PETS.
AND... AND THE PRICE...?
I-IS IT RIGHT?
OH.
ALWAYS.
OHHHH! TRULY, THE EVIL DAYSTAR HIDES ITS MAGIC FROM US!

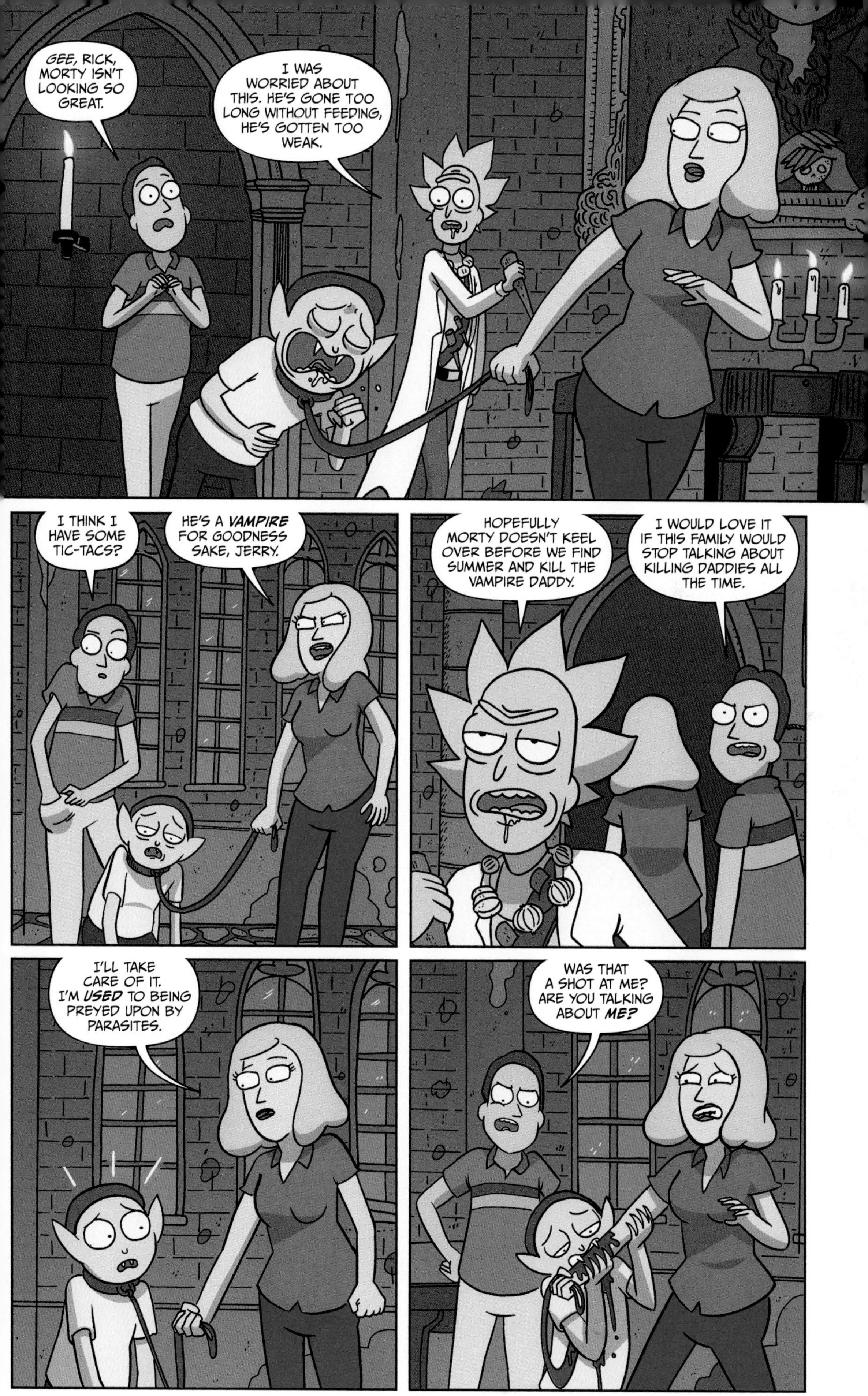
GEE, RICK, MORTY ISN'T LOOKING SO GREAT.
I WAS WORRIED ABOUT THIS. HE'S GONE TOO LONG WITHOUT FEEDING, HE'S GOTTEN TOO WEAK.
I THINK I HAVE SOME TIC-TACS?
HE'S A VAMPIRE FOR GOODNESS SAKE, JERRY.
HOPEFULLY MORTY DOESN'T KEEL OVER BEFORE WE FIND SUMMER AND KILL THE VAMPIRE DADDY.
I WOULD LOVE IT IF THIS FAMILY WOULD STOP TALKING ABOUT KILLING DADDIES ALL THE TIME.
I'LL TAKE CARE OF IT. I'M USED TO BEING PREYED UPON BY PARASITES.
WAS THAT A SHOT AT ME? ARE YOU TALKING ABOUT ME?

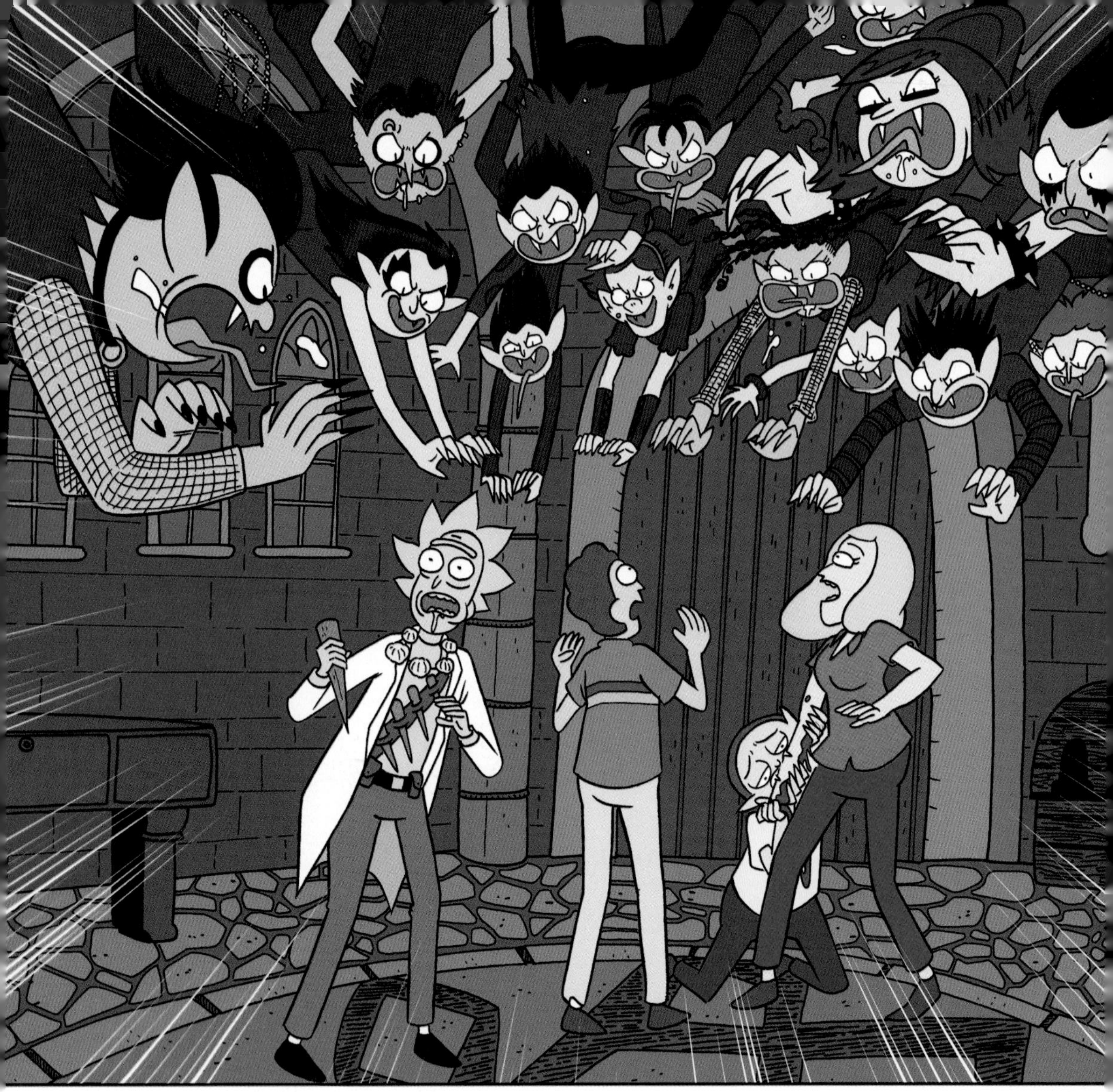

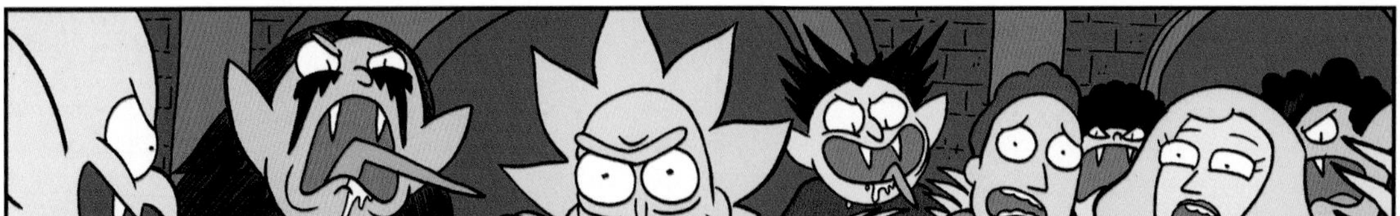

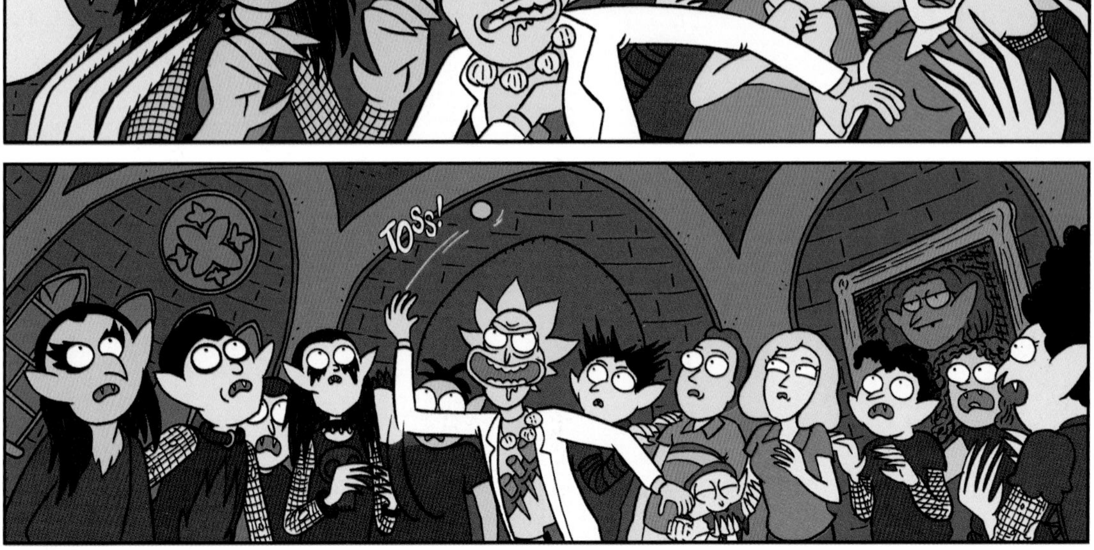
TOSS!

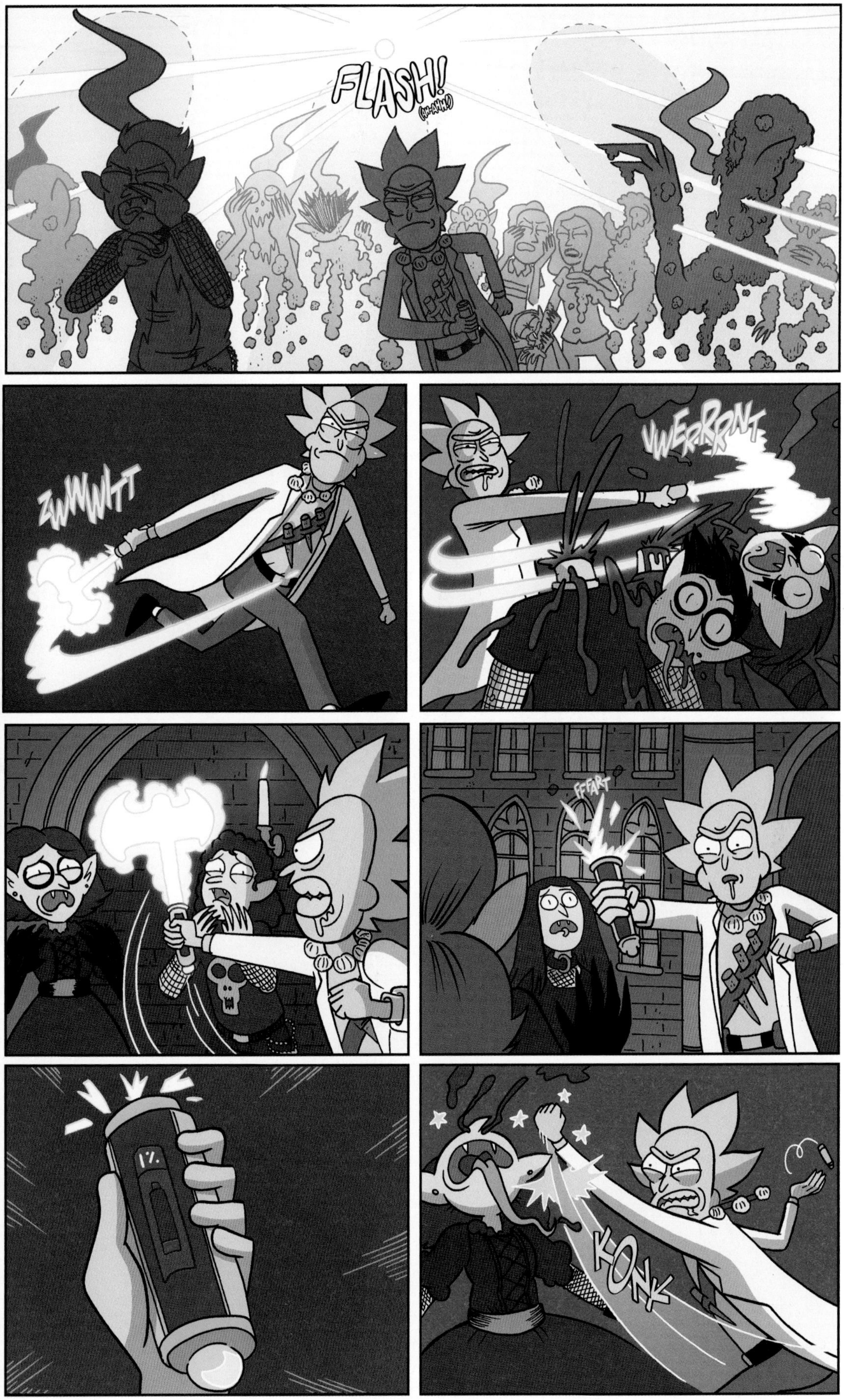
FLASH!
(AH-AHH!)
ZWWWITT
VWERRRNT
FFFART
1%
KONK

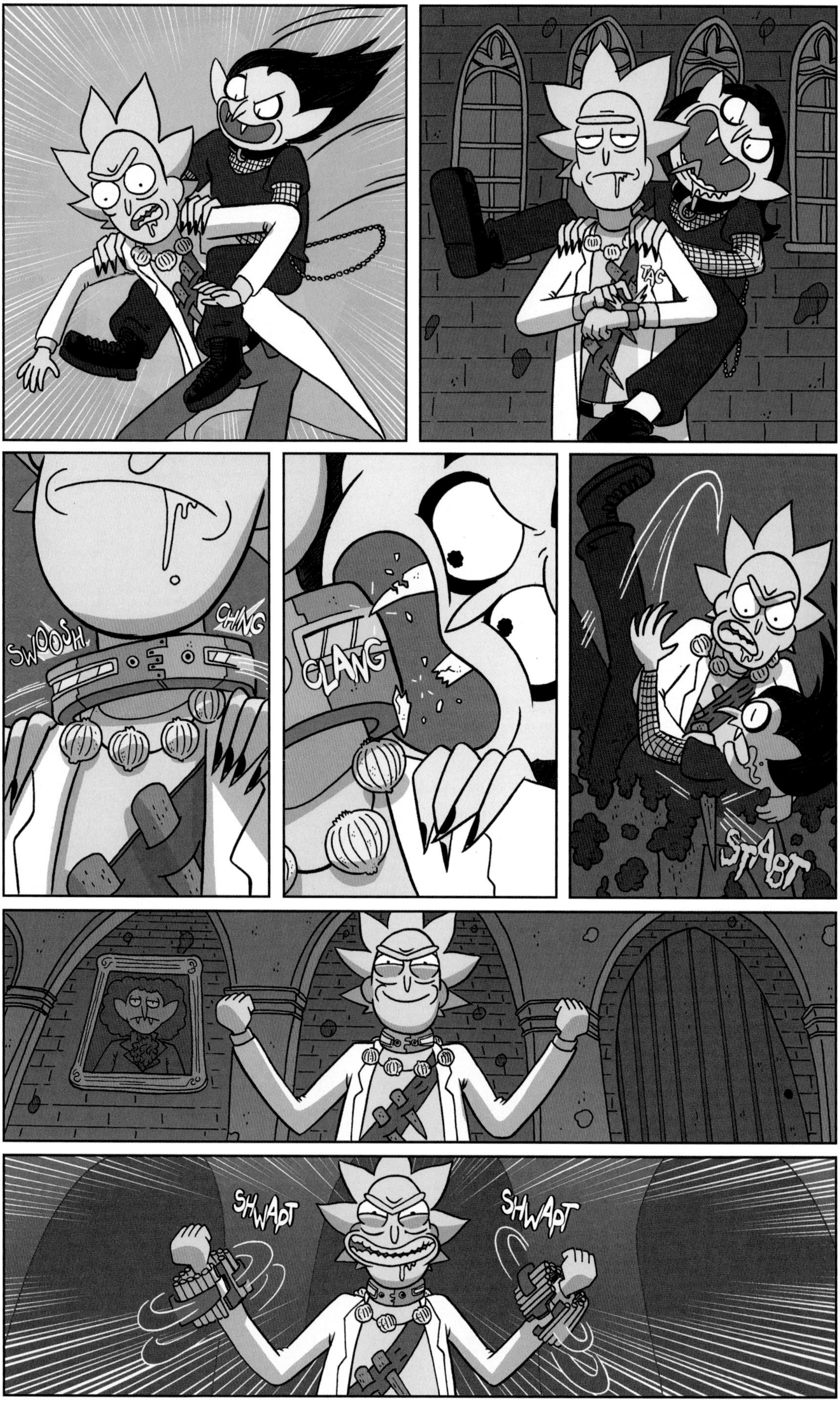
TAC
SWOOSH
CHING
CLANG
STABT
SHWAPT
SHWAPT

TWIP TWIP TWIP TWIR TWIP

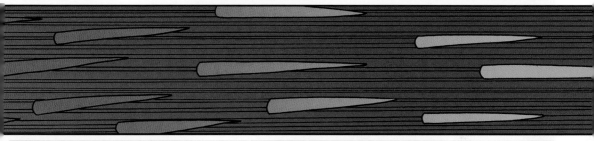

SHUNK SHUNK SHUNK SHUNK STREE VAMPS

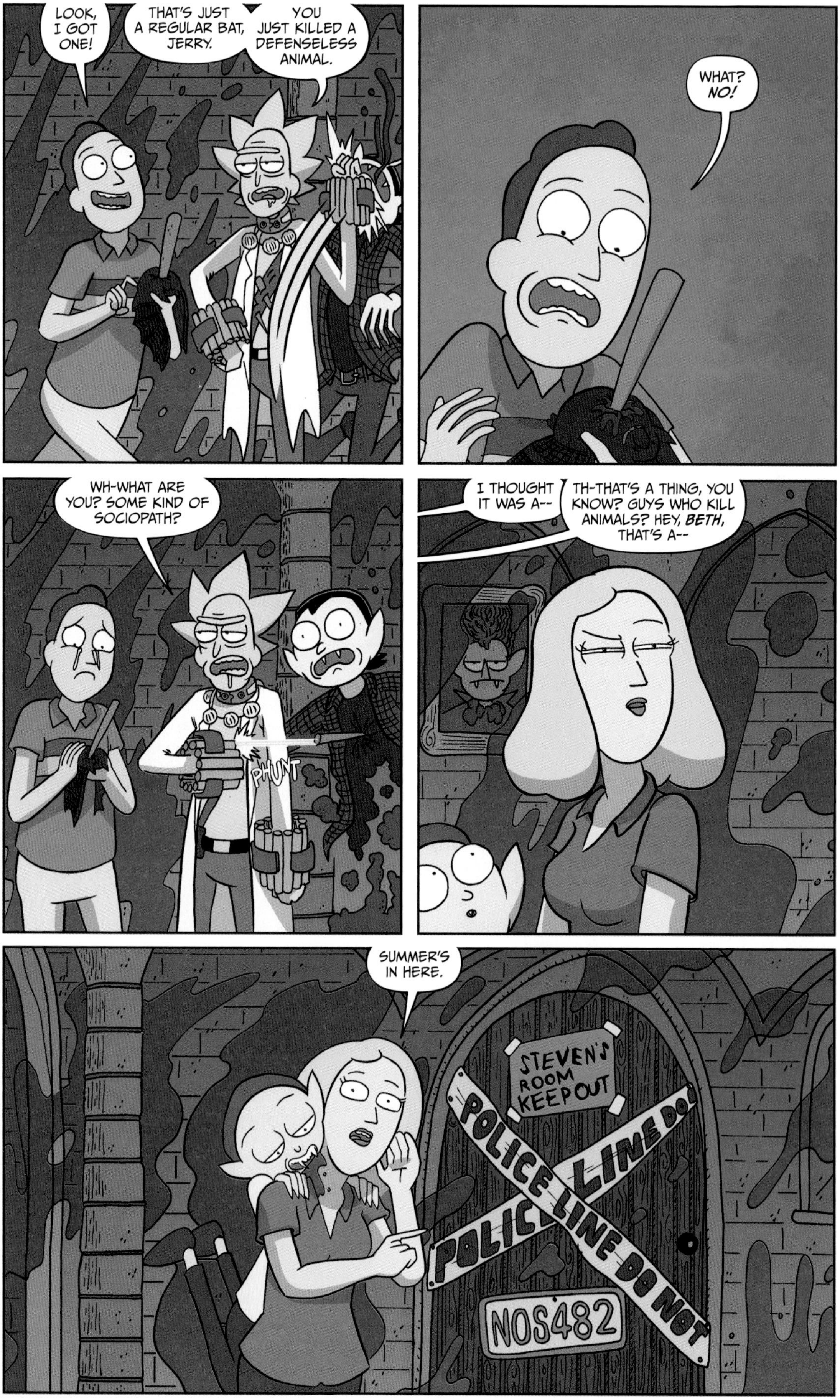
LOOK, I GOT ONE!
THAT'S JUST A REGULAR BAT, JERRY.
YOU JUST KILLED A DEFENSELESS ANIMAL.
WHAT? NO!
WH-WHAT ARE YOU? SOME KIND OF SOCIOPATH?
PHUNT
I THOUGHT IT WAS A--
TH-THAT'S A THING, YOU KNOW? GUYS WHO KILL ANIMALS? HEY, BETH, THAT'S A--
SUMMER'S IN HERE.
STEVEN'S ROOM KEEP OUT
POLICE LINE DO
POLICE LINE DO NOT
NOS482

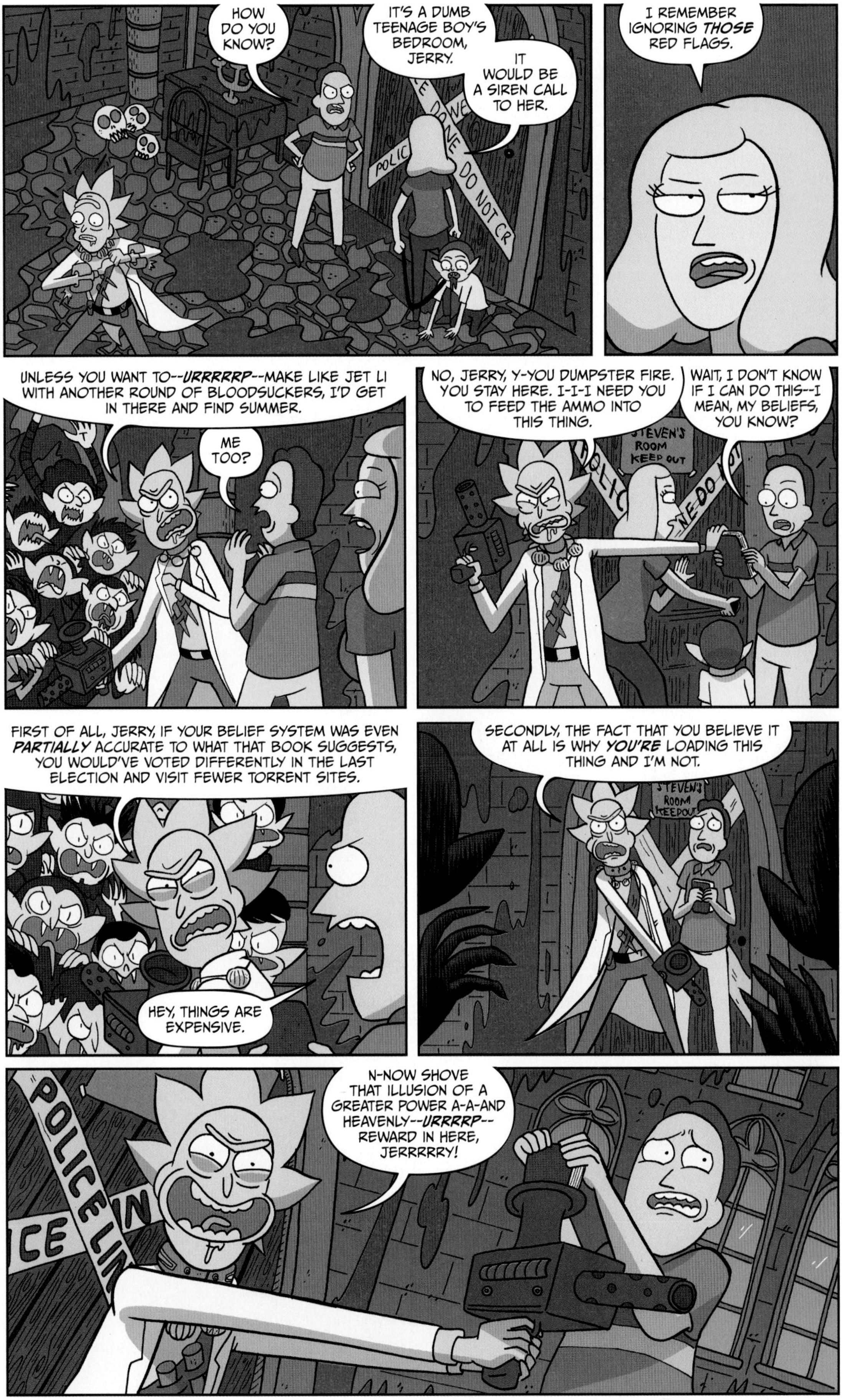
HOW DO YOU KNOW?
IT'S A DUMB TEENAGE BOY'S BEDROOM, JERRY.
IT WOULD BE A SIREN CALL TO HER.
I REMEMBER IGNORING ***THOSE*** RED FLAGS.
UNLESS YOU WANT TO--***URRRRRP***--MAKE LIKE JET LI WITH ANOTHER ROUND OF BLOODSUCKERS, I'D GET IN THERE AND FIND SUMMER.
ME TOO?
NO, JERRY, Y-YOU DUMPSTER FIRE. YOU STAY HERE. I-I-I NEED YOU TO FEED THE AMMO INTO THIS THING.
STEVEN'S ROOM KEEP OUT
WAIT, I DON'T KNOW IF I CAN DO THIS--I MEAN, MY BELIEFS, YOU KNOW?
FIRST OF ALL, JERRY, IF YOUR BELIEF SYSTEM WAS EVEN ***PARTIALLY*** ACCURATE TO WHAT THAT BOOK SUGGESTS, YOU WOULD'VE VOTED DIFFERENTLY IN THE LAST ELECTION AND VISIT FEWER TORRENT SITES.
HEY, THINGS ARE EXPENSIVE.
SECONDLY, THE FACT THAT YOU BELIEVE IT AT ALL IS WHY ***YOU'RE*** LOADING THIS THING AND I'M NOT.
N-NOW SHOVE THAT ILLUSION OF A GREATER POWER A-A-AND HEAVENLY--***URRRRP***--REWARD IN HERE, JERRRRRY!

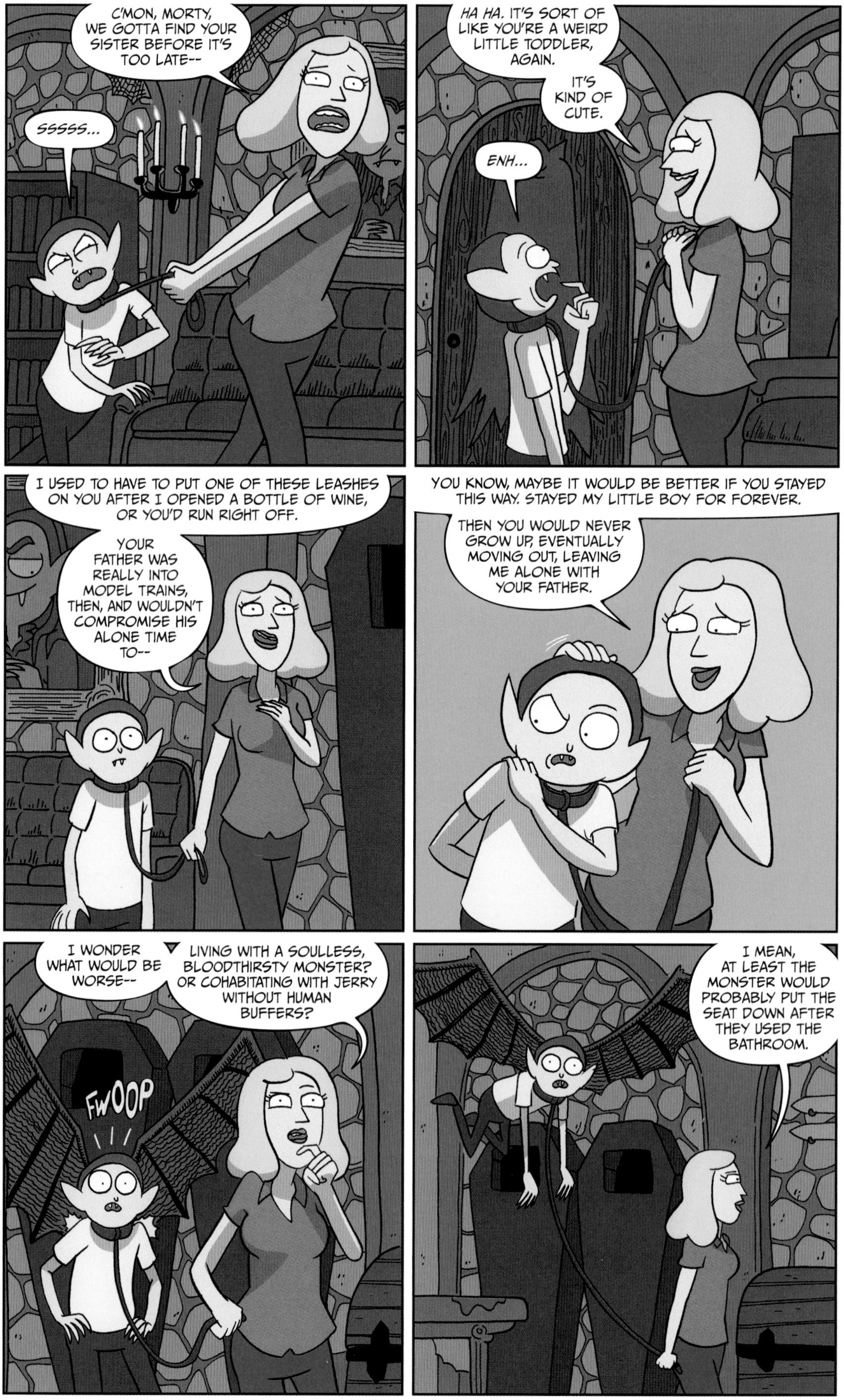
C'MON, MORTY, WE GOTTA FIND YOUR SISTER BEFORE IT'S TOO LATE--
SSSSS...
HA HA. IT'S SORT OF LIKE YOU'RE A WEIRD LITTLE TODDLER, AGAIN.
IT'S KIND OF CUTE.
ENH...
I USED TO HAVE TO PUT ONE OF THESE LEASHES ON YOU AFTER I OPENED A BOTTLE OF WINE, OR YOU'D RUN RIGHT OFF.
YOUR FATHER WAS REALLY INTO MODEL TRAINS, THEN, AND WOULDN'T COMPROMISE HIS ALONE TIME TO--
YOU KNOW, MAYBE IT WOULD BE BETTER IF YOU STAYED THIS WAY. STAYED MY LITTLE BOY FOR FOREVER.
THEN YOU WOULD NEVER GROW UP, EVENTUALLY MOVING OUT, LEAVING ME ALONE WITH YOUR FATHER.
I WONDER WHAT WOULD BE WORSE--
LIVING WITH A SOULLESS, BLOODTHIRSTY MONSTER? OR COHABITATING WITH JERRY WITHOUT HUMAN BUFFERS?
FWOOP
I MEAN, AT LEAST THE MONSTER WOULD PROBABLY PUT THE SEAT DOWN AFTER THEY USED THE BATHROOM.

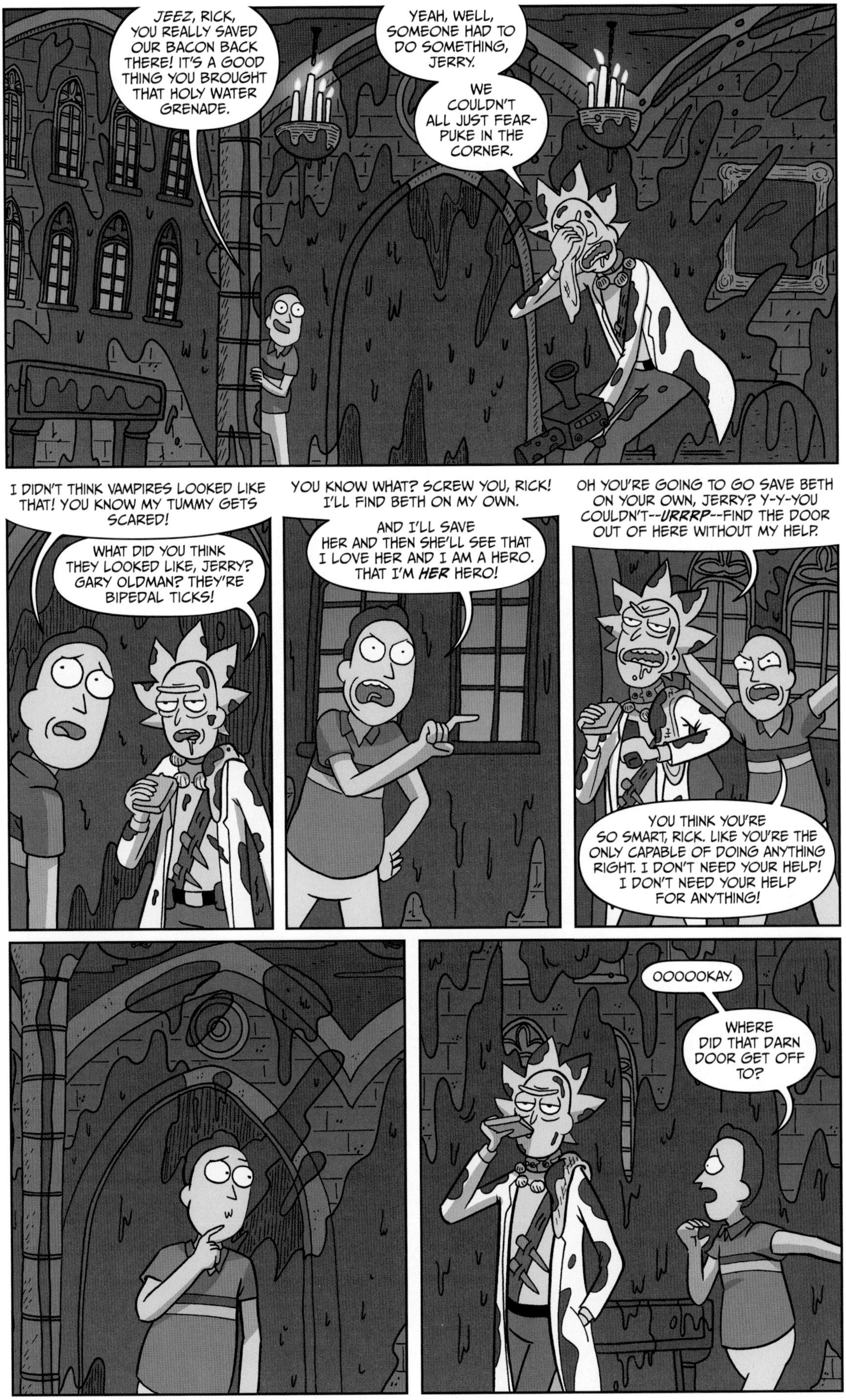
JEEZ, RICK, YOU REALLY SAVED OUR BACON BACK THERE! IT'S A GOOD THING YOU BROUGHT THAT HOLY WATER GRENADE.
YEAH, WELL, SOMEONE HAD TO DO SOMETHING, JERRY.
WE COULDN'T ALL JUST FEAR-PUKE IN THE CORNER.
I DIDN'T THINK VAMPIRES LOOKED LIKE THAT! YOU KNOW MY TUMMY GETS SCARED!
WHAT DID YOU THINK THEY LOOKED LIKE, JERRY? GARY OLDMAN? THEY'RE BIPEDAL TICKS!
YOU KNOW WHAT? SCREW YOU, RICK! I'LL FIND BETH ON MY OWN.
AND I'LL SAVE HER AND THEN SHE'LL SEE THAT I LOVE HER AND I AM A HERO. THAT I'M *HER* HERO!
OH YOU'RE GOING TO GO SAVE BETH ON YOUR OWN, JERRY? Y-Y-YOU COULDN'T--*URRRP*--FIND THE DOOR OUT OF HERE WITHOUT MY HELP.
YOU THINK YOU'RE SO SMART, RICK. LIKE YOU'RE THE ONLY CAPABLE OF DOING ANYTHING RIGHT. I DON'T NEED YOUR HELP! I DON'T NEED YOUR HELP FOR ANYTHING!
OOOOOKAY.
WHERE DID THAT DARN DOOR GET OFF TO?

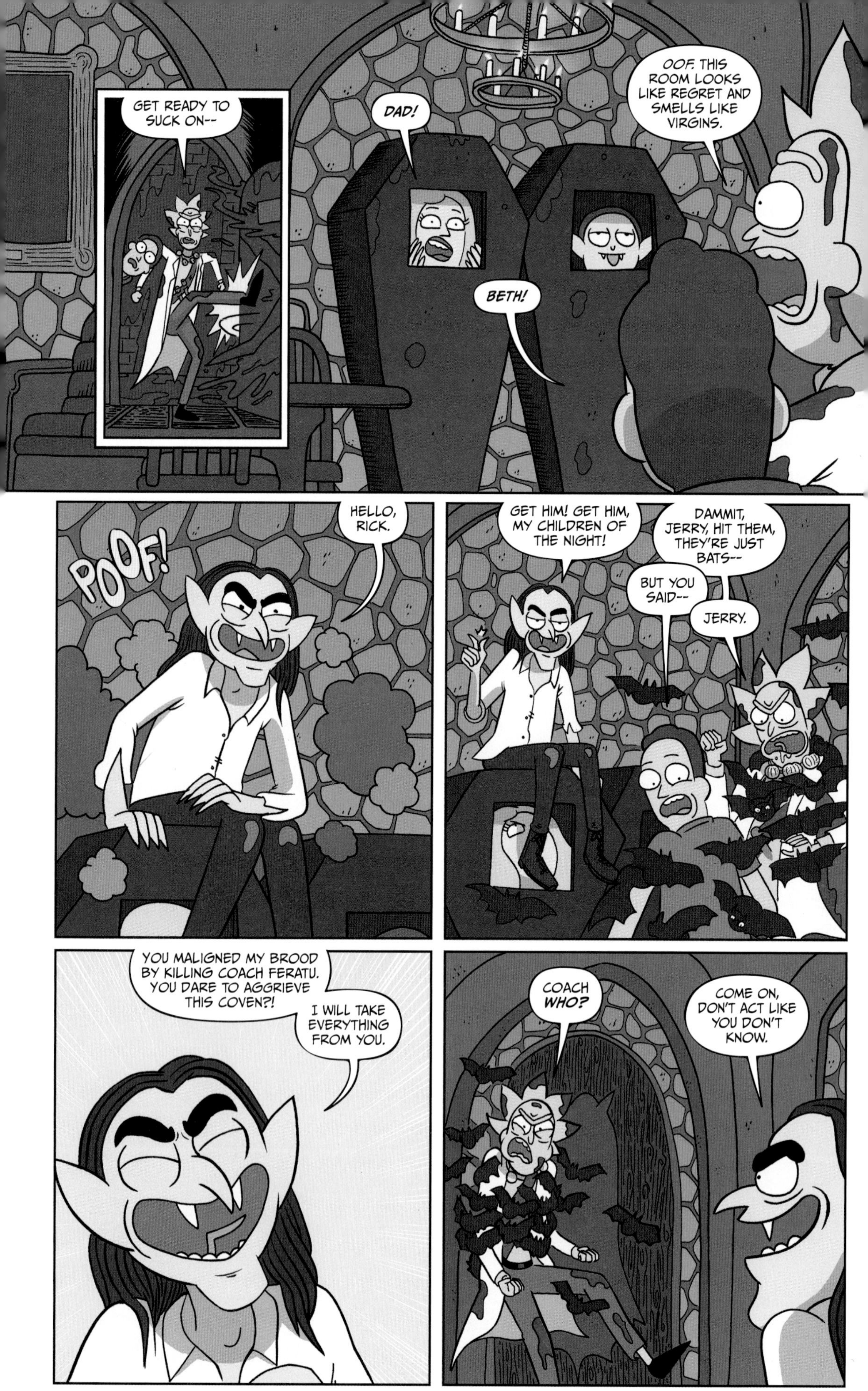
GET READY TO SUCK ON--
DAD!
OOF. THIS ROOM LOOKS LIKE REGRET AND SMELLS LIKE VIRGINS.
BETH!
POOF!
HELLO, RICK.
GET HIM! GET HIM, MY CHILDREN OF THE NIGHT!
DAMMIT, JERRY, HIT THEM, THEY'RE JUST BATS--
BUT YOU SAID--
JERRY.
YOU MALIGNED MY BROOD BY KILLING COACH FERATU. YOU DARE TO AGGRIEVE THIS COVEN?!
I WILL TAKE EVERYTHING FROM YOU.
COACH WHO?
COME ON, DON'T ACT LIKE YOU DON'T KNOW.

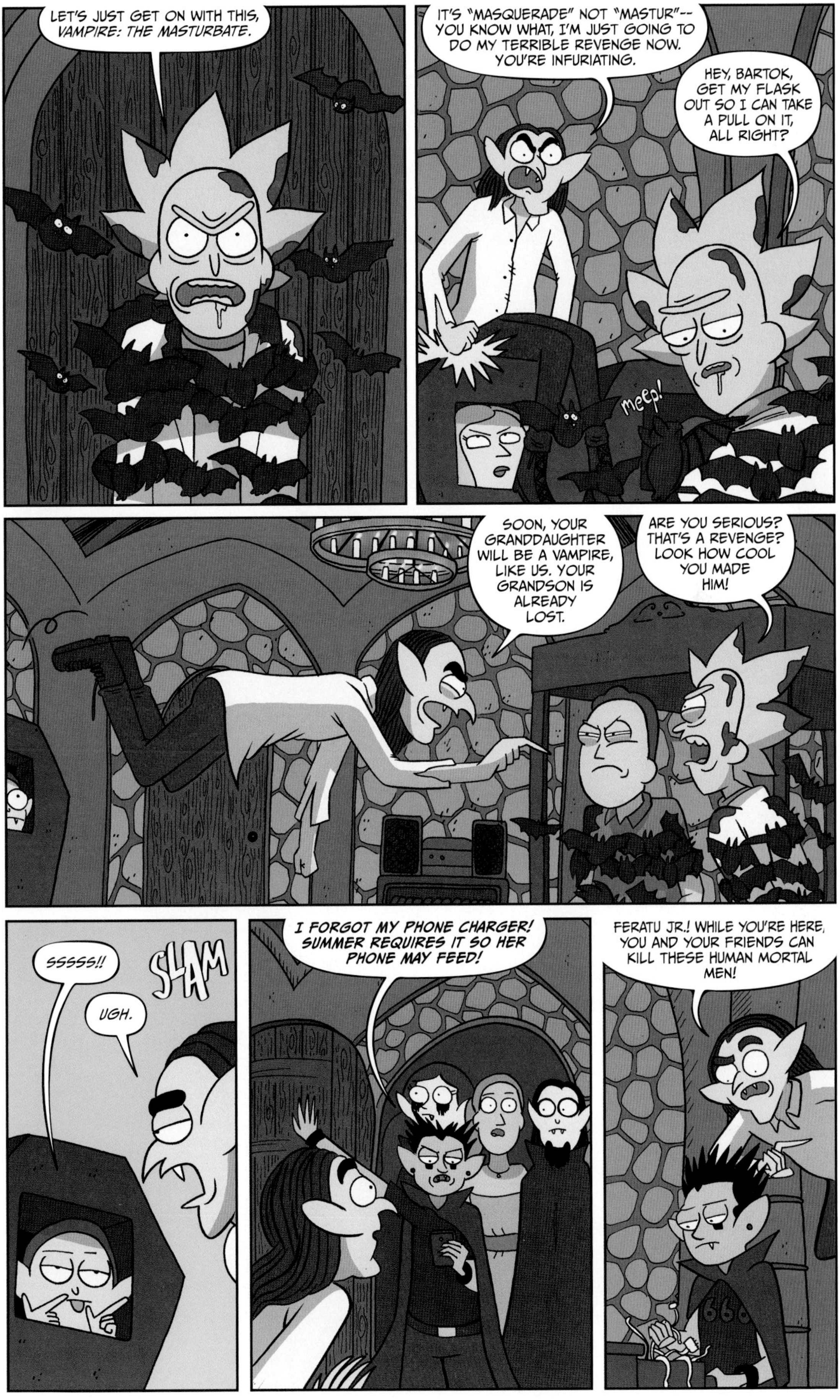
LET'S JUST GET ON WITH THIS, *VAMPIRE: THE MASTURBATE.*
IT'S "MASQUERADE" NOT "MASTUR"-- YOU KNOW WHAT, I'M JUST GOING TO DO MY TERRIBLE REVENGE NOW. YOU'RE INFURIATING.
HEY, BARTOK, GET MY FLASK OUT SO I CAN TAKE A PULL ON IT, ALL RIGHT?
meep!
SOON, YOUR GRANDDAUGHTER WILL BE A VAMPIRE, LIKE US. YOUR GRANDSON IS ALREADY LOST.
ARE YOU SERIOUS? THAT'S A REVENGE? LOOK HOW COOL YOU MADE HIM!
SSSSS!!
SLAM
UGH.
I FORGOT MY PHONE CHARGER! SUMMER REQUIRES IT SO HER PHONE MAY FEED!
FERATU JR.! WHILE YOU'RE HERE, YOU AND YOUR FRIENDS CAN KILL THESE HUMAN MORTAL MEN!

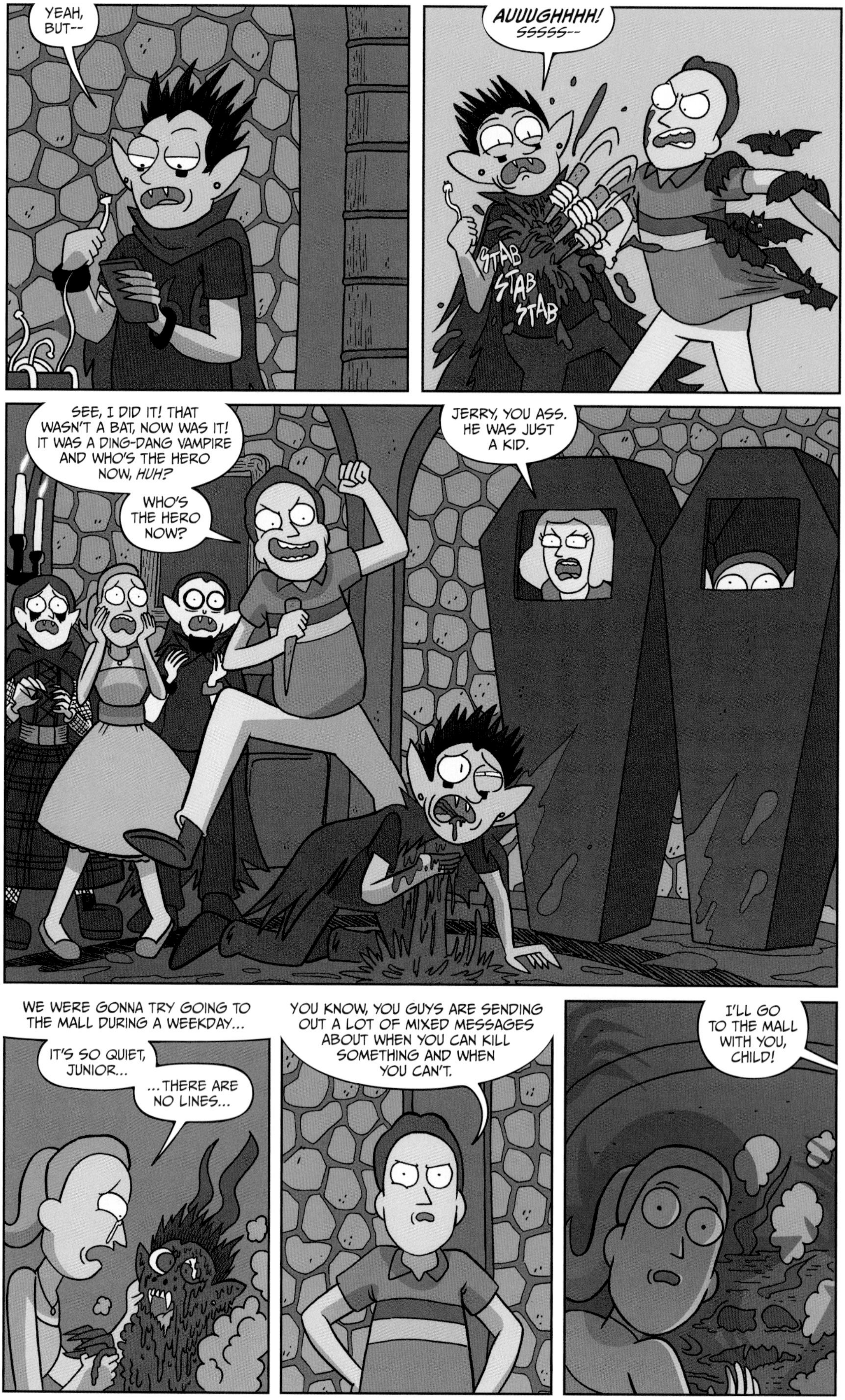
YEAH, BUT--
AUUUGHHHH! SSSSS--
STAB STAB STAB
SEE, I DID IT! THAT WASN'T A BAT, NOW WAS IT! IT WAS A DING-DANG VAMPIRE AND WHO'S THE HERO NOW, *HUH?*
WHO'S THE HERO NOW?
JERRY, YOU ASS. HE WAS JUST A KID.
WE WERE GONNA TRY GOING TO THE MALL DURING A WEEKDAY...
IT'S SO QUIET, JUNIOR...
...THERE ARE NO LINES...
YOU KNOW, YOU GUYS ARE SENDING OUT A LOT OF MIXED MESSAGES ABOUT WHEN YOU CAN KILL SOMETHING AND WHEN YOU CAN'T.
I'LL GO TO THE MALL WITH YOU, CHILD!

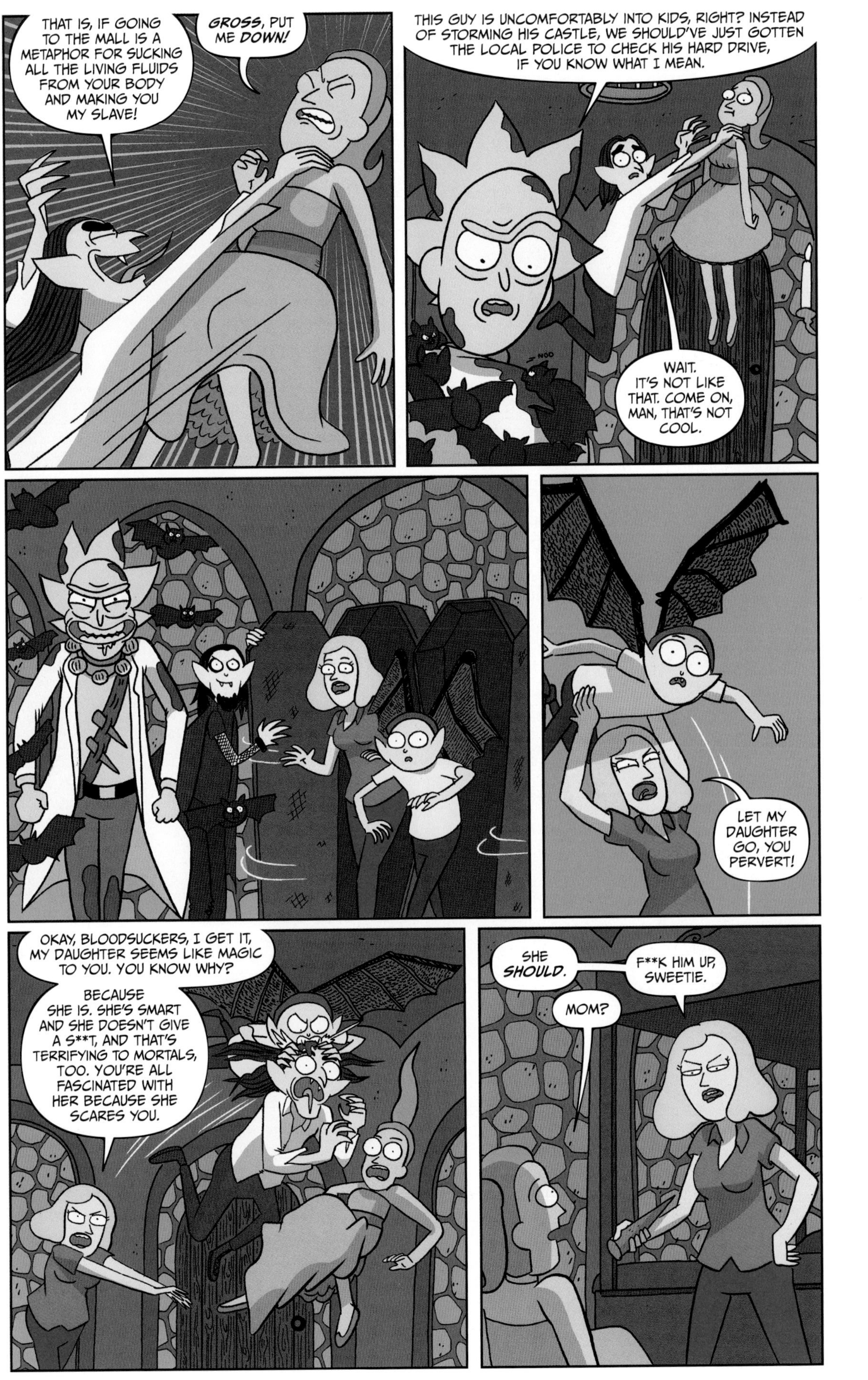
THAT IS, IF GOING TO THE MALL IS A METAPHOR FOR SUCKING ALL THE LIVING FLUIDS FROM YOUR BODY AND MAKING YOU MY SLAVE!
GROSS, PUT ME DOWN!
THIS GUY IS UNCOMFORTABLY INTO KIDS, RIGHT? INSTEAD OF STORMING HIS CASTLE, WE SHOULD'VE JUST GOTTEN THE LOCAL POLICE TO CHECK HIS HARD DRIVE, IF YOU KNOW WHAT I MEAN.
WAIT. IT'S NOT LIKE THAT. COME ON, MAN, THAT'S NOT COOL.
LET MY DAUGHTER GO, YOU PERVERT!
OKAY, BLOODSUCKERS, I GET IT, MY DAUGHTER SEEMS LIKE MAGIC TO YOU. YOU KNOW WHY?
BECAUSE SHE IS. SHE'S SMART AND SHE DOESN'T GIVE A S**T, AND THAT'S TERRIFYING TO MORTALS, TOO. YOU'RE ALL FASCINATED WITH HER BECAUSE SHE SCARES YOU.
SHE SHOULD.
F**K HIM UP, SWEETIE.
MOM?

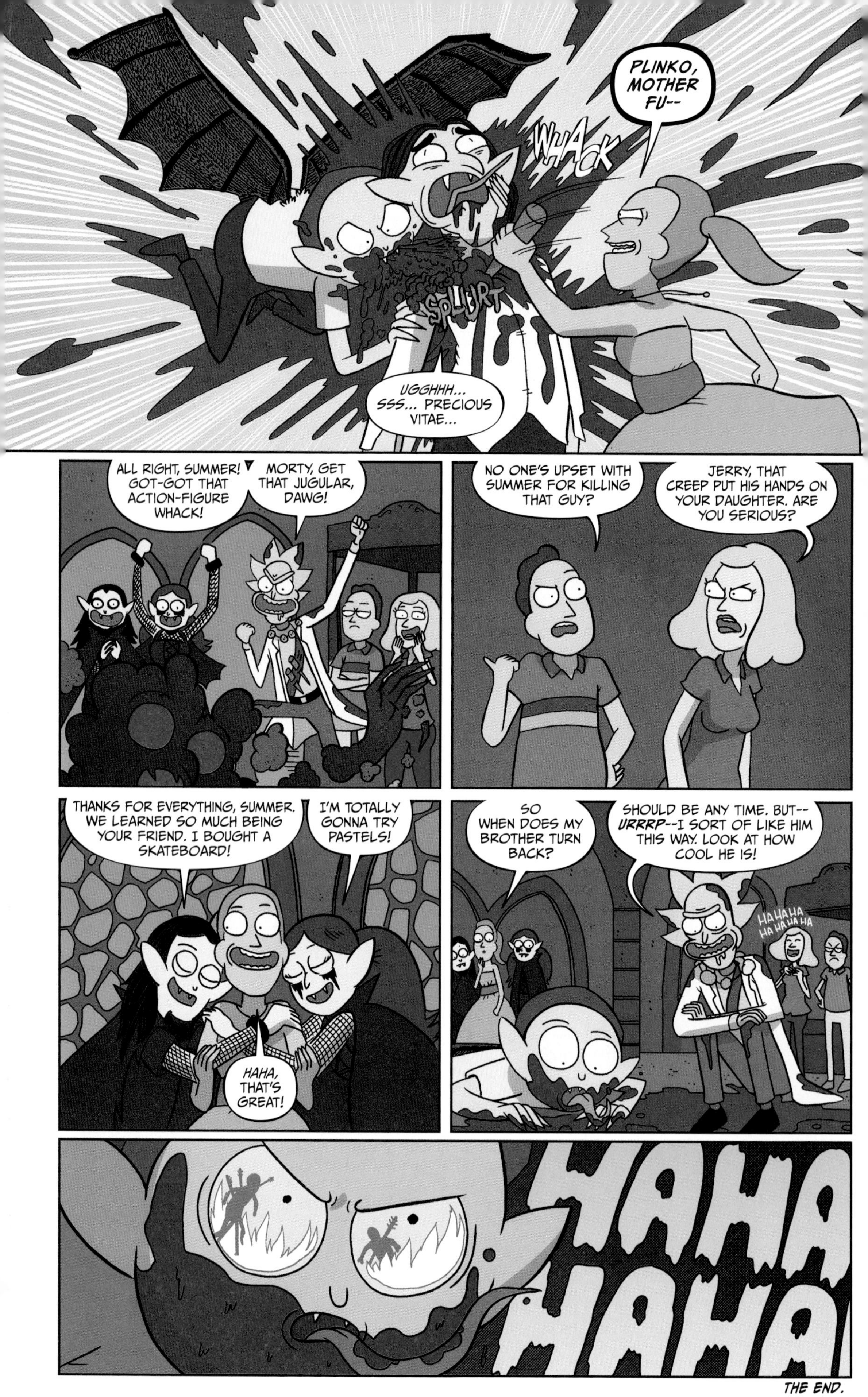
PLINKO, MOTHER FU--
WHACK
SPLURT
UGGHHH... SSS... PRECIOUS VITAE...
ALL RIGHT, SUMMER! GOT-GOT THAT ACTION-FIGURE WHACK!
MORTY, GET THAT JUGULAR, DAWG!
NO ONE'S UPSET WITH SUMMER FOR KILLING THAT GUY?
JERRY, THAT CREEP PUT HIS HANDS ON YOUR DAUGHTER. ARE YOU SERIOUS?
THANKS FOR EVERYTHING, SUMMER. WE LEARNED SO MUCH BEING YOUR FRIEND. I BOUGHT A SKATEBOARD!
I'M TOTALLY GONNA TRY PASTELS!
HAHA, THAT'S GREAT!
SO WHEN DOES MY BROTHER TURN BACK?
SHOULD BE ANY TIME. BUT--URRRP--I SORT OF LIKE HIM THIS WAY. LOOK AT HOW COOL HE IS!
HA HA HA HA HA HA HA
HAHA HAHA

THE END.

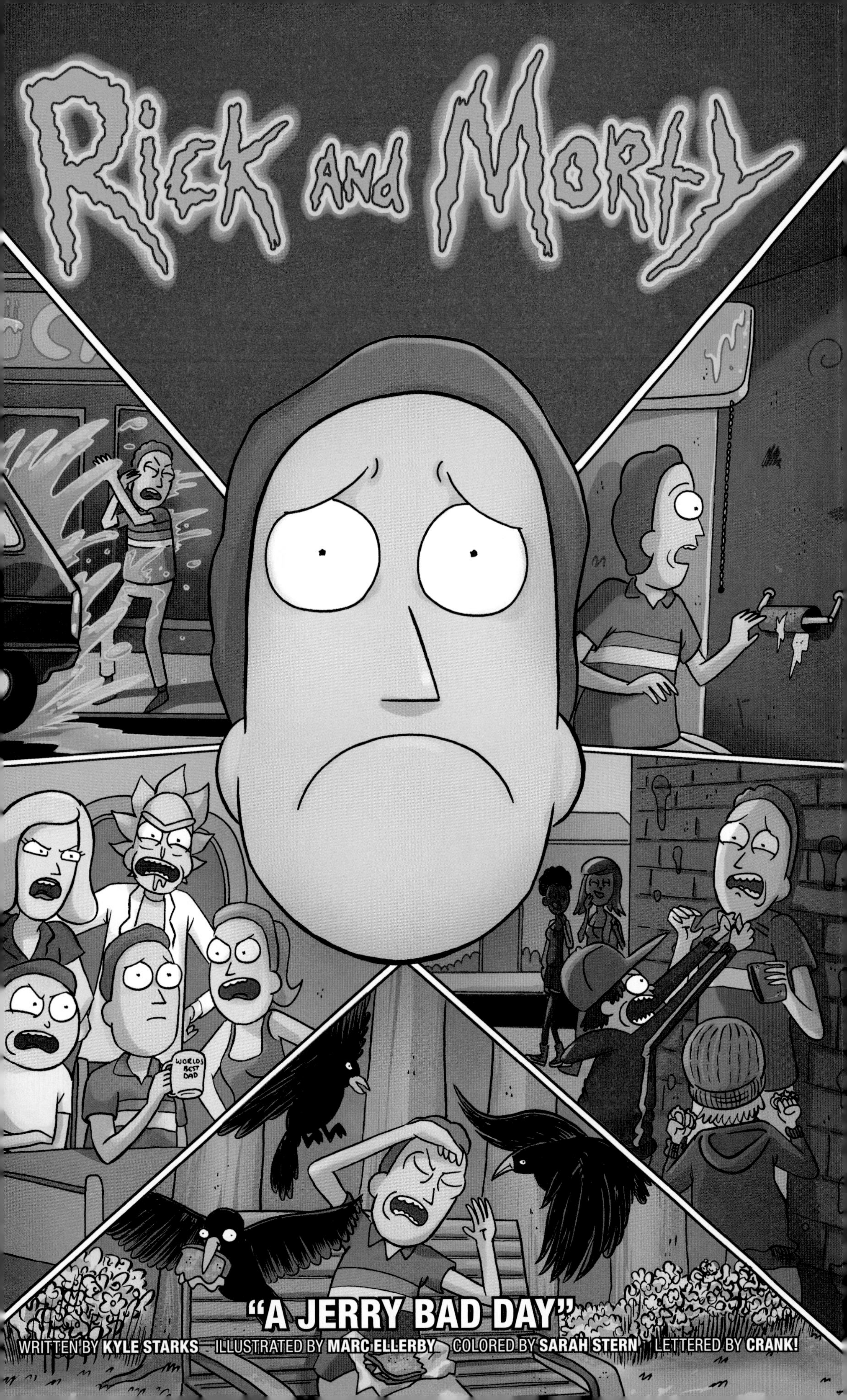
Rick and Morty
WORLD'S BEST DAD
"A JERRY BAD DAY"
WRITTEN BY KYLE STARKS ILLUSTRATED BY MARC ELLERBY COLORED BY SARAH STERN LETTERED BY CRANK!

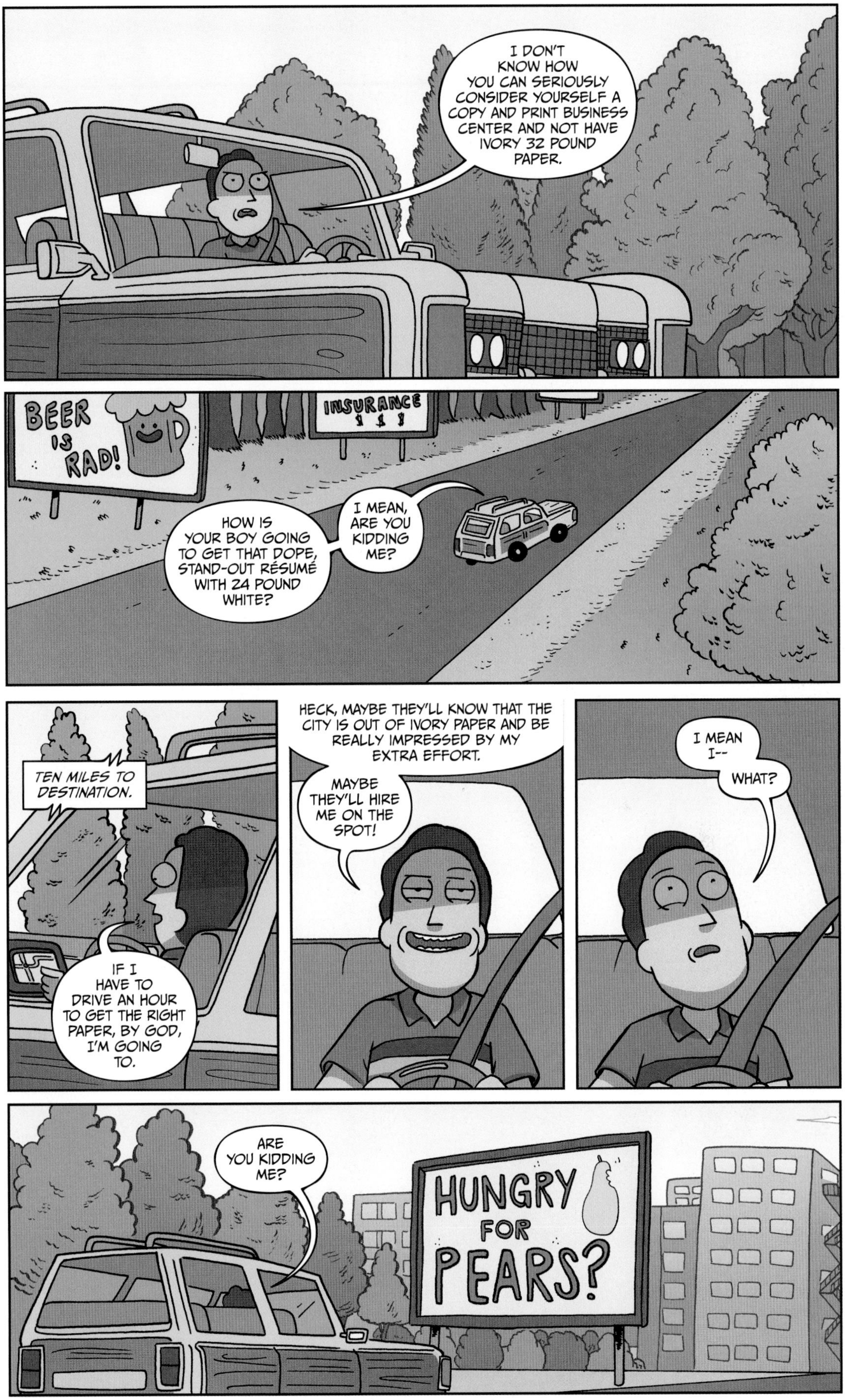
I DON'T KNOW HOW YOU CAN SERIOUSLY CONSIDER YOURSELF A COPY AND PRINT BUSINESS CENTER AND NOT HAVE IVORY 32 POUND PAPER.
BEER IS RAD!
INSURANCE
HOW IS YOUR BOY GOING TO GET THAT DOPE, STAND-OUT RÉSUMÉ WITH 24 POUND WHITE?
I MEAN, ARE YOU KIDDING ME?
TEN MILES TO DESTINATION.
IF I HAVE TO DRIVE AN HOUR TO GET THE RIGHT PAPER, BY GOD, I'M GOING TO.
HECK, MAYBE THEY'LL KNOW THAT THE CITY IS OUT OF IVORY PAPER AND BE REALLY IMPRESSED BY MY EXTRA EFFORT.
MAYBE THEY'LL HIRE ME ON THE SPOT!
I MEAN I--
WHAT?
ARE YOU KIDDING ME?
HUNGRY FOR PEARS?

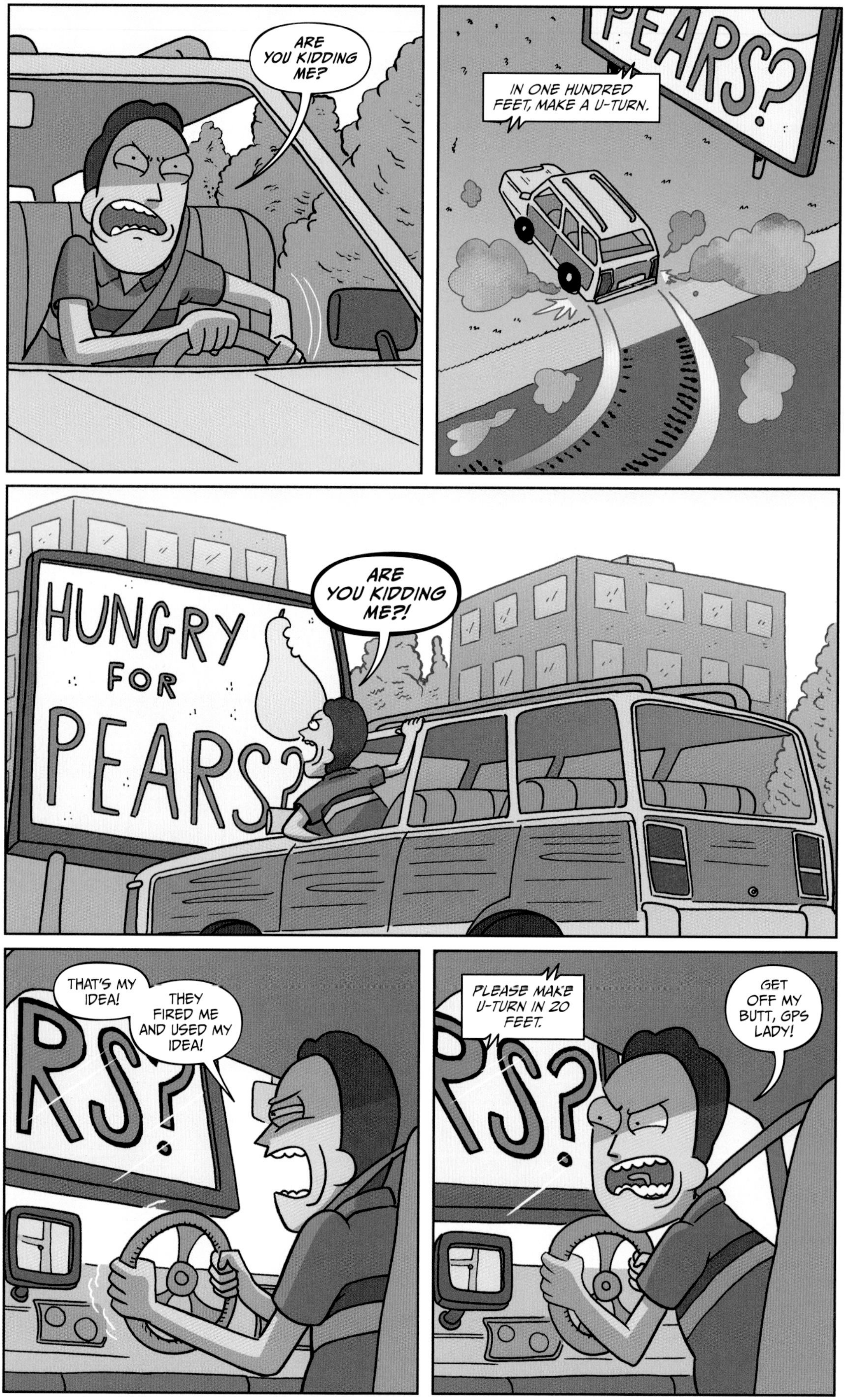
ARE YOU KIDDING ME?
PEARS?
IN ONE HUNDRED FEET, MAKE A U-TURN.
HUNGRY FOR PEARS?
ARE YOU KIDDING ME?!
RS?
THAT'S MY IDEA!
THEY FIRED ME AND USED MY IDEA!
PLEASE MAKE U-TURN IN 20 FEET.
RS?
GET OFF MY BUTT, GPS LADY!

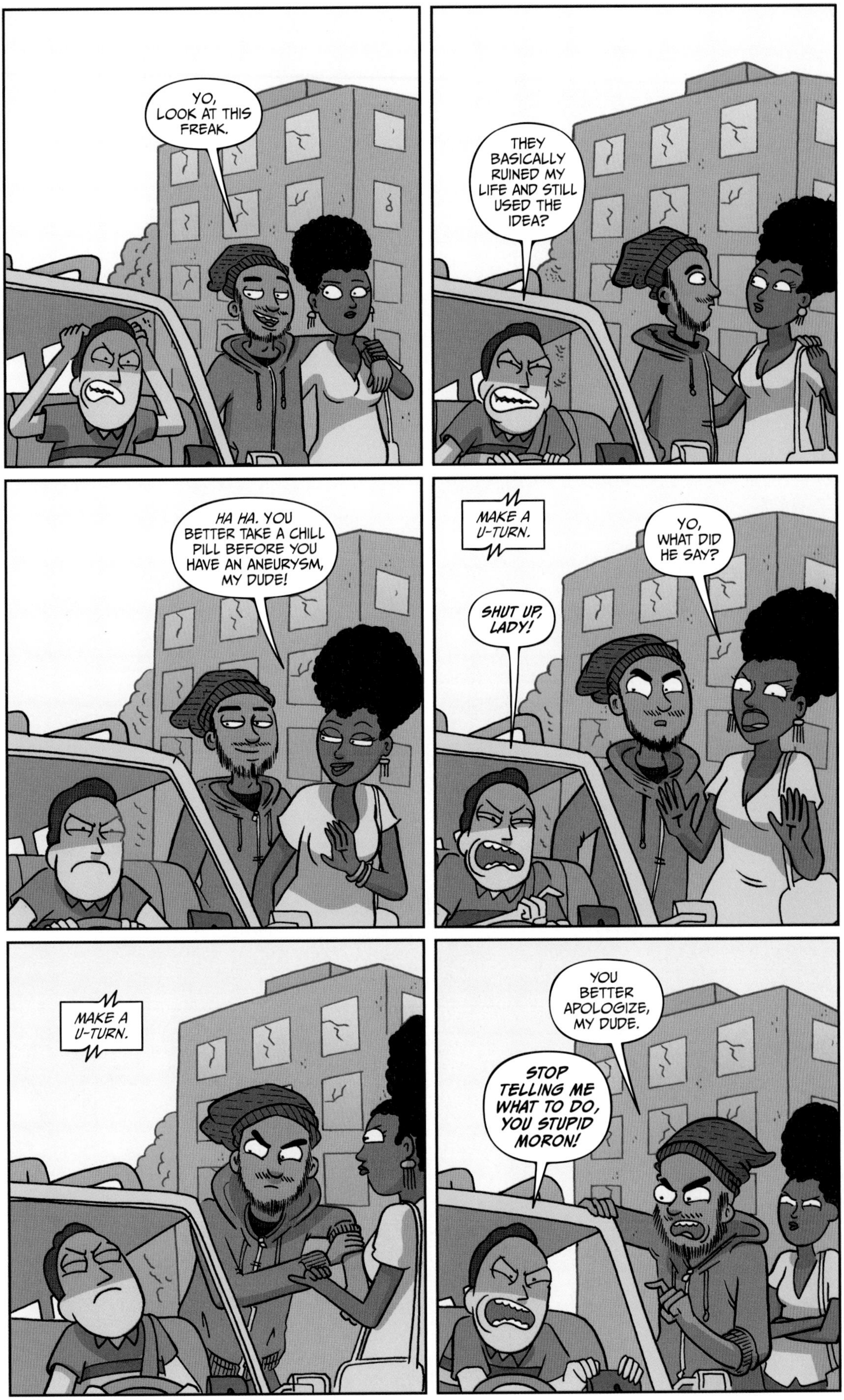
YO, LOOK AT THIS FREAK.
THEY BASICALLY RUINED MY LIFE AND STILL USED THE IDEA?
HA HA. YOU BETTER TAKE A CHILL PILL BEFORE YOU HAVE AN ANEURYSM, MY DUDE!
MAKE A U-TURN.
YO, WHAT DID HE SAY?
SHUT UP, LADY!
MAKE A U-TURN.
YOU BETTER APOLOGIZE, MY DUDE.
STOP TELLING ME WHAT TO DO, YOU STUPID MORON!

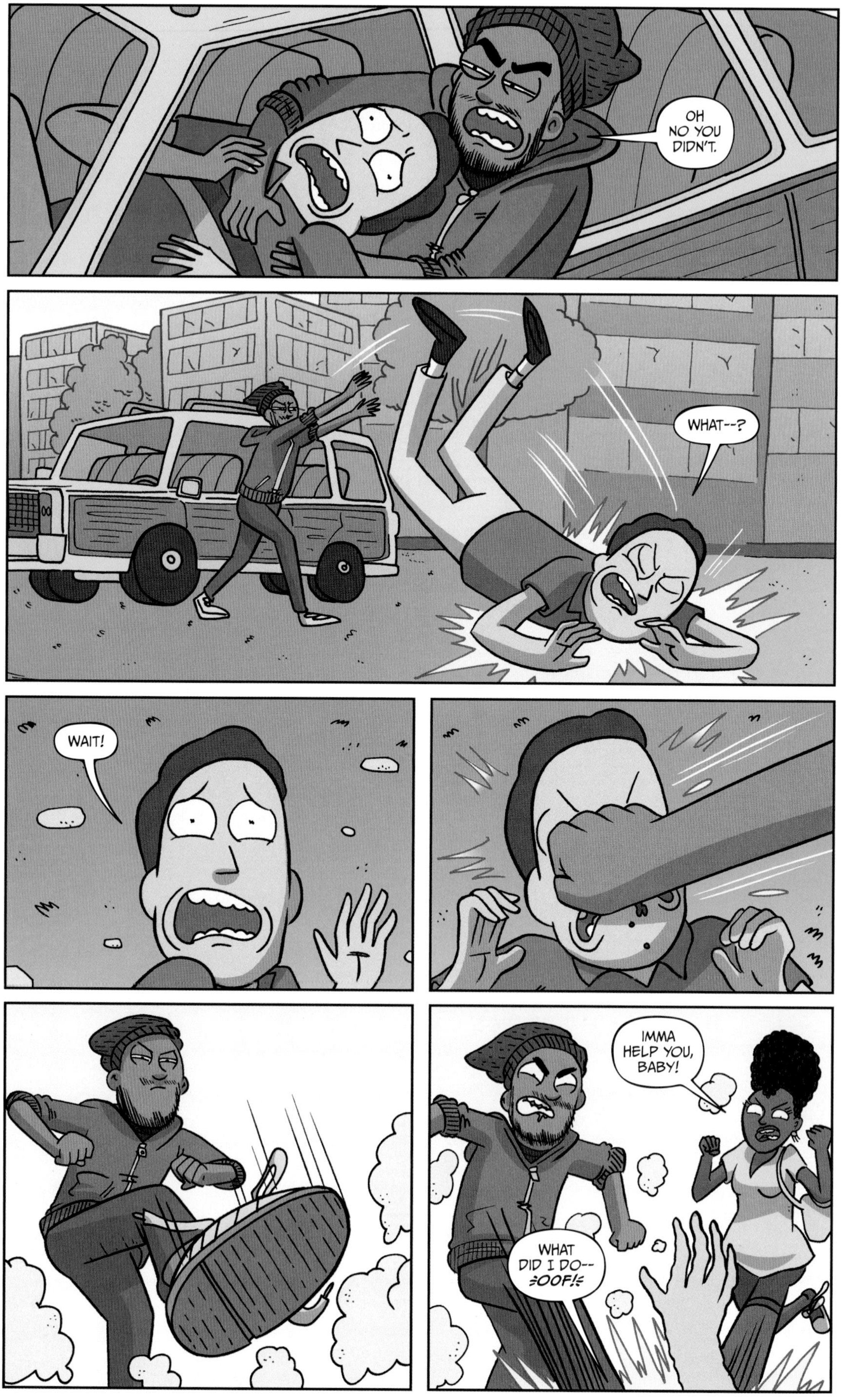
OH NO YOU DIDN'T.
WHAT--?
WAIT!
IMMA HELP YOU, BABY!
WHAT DID I DO-- OOF!

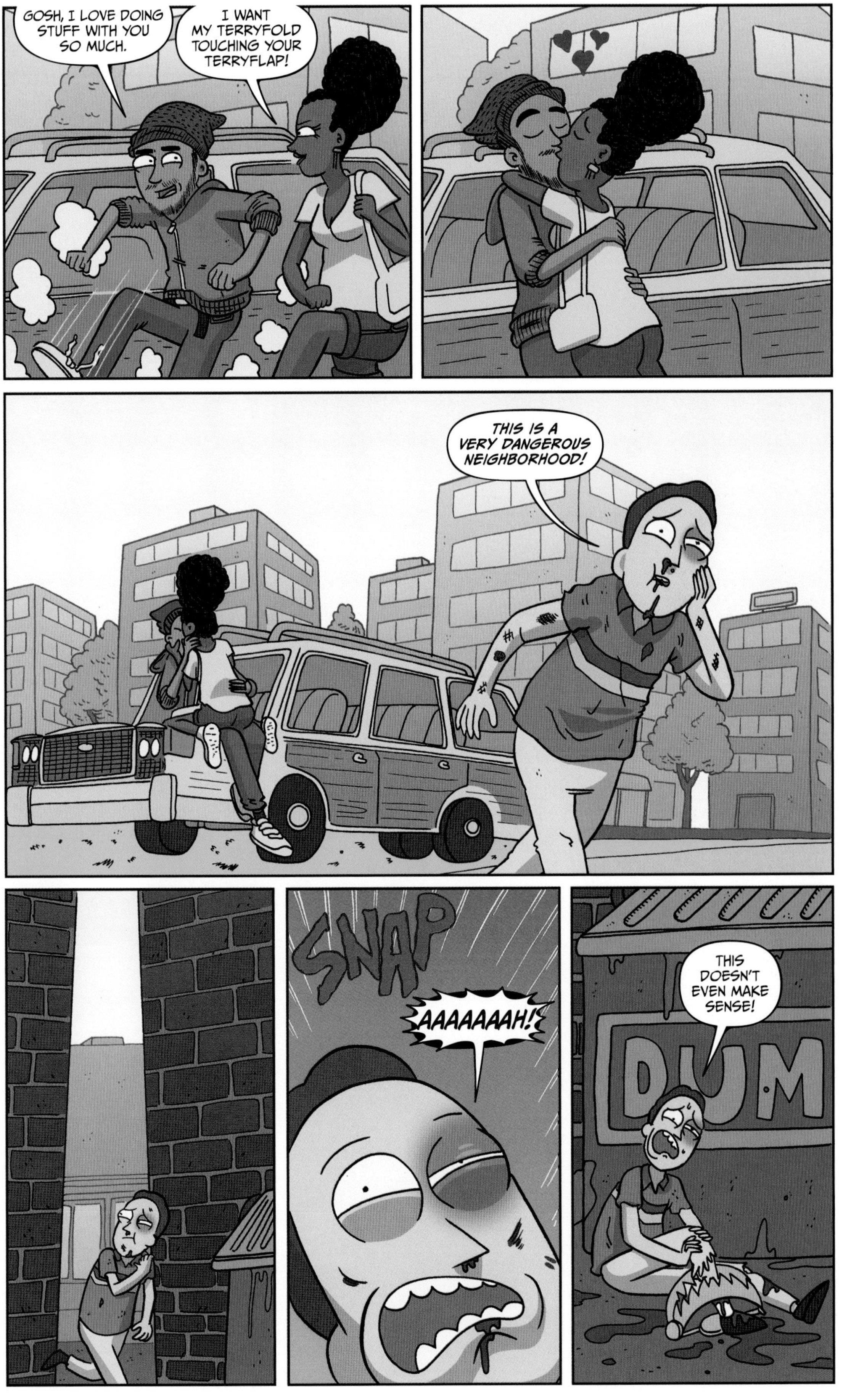
GOSH, I LOVE DOING STUFF WITH YOU SO MUCH.
I WANT MY TERRYFOLD TOUCHING YOUR TERRYFLAP!
THIS IS A VERY DANGEROUS NEIGHBORHOOD!
SNAP
AAAAAAAH!
THIS DOESN'T EVEN MAKE SENSE!
DUM

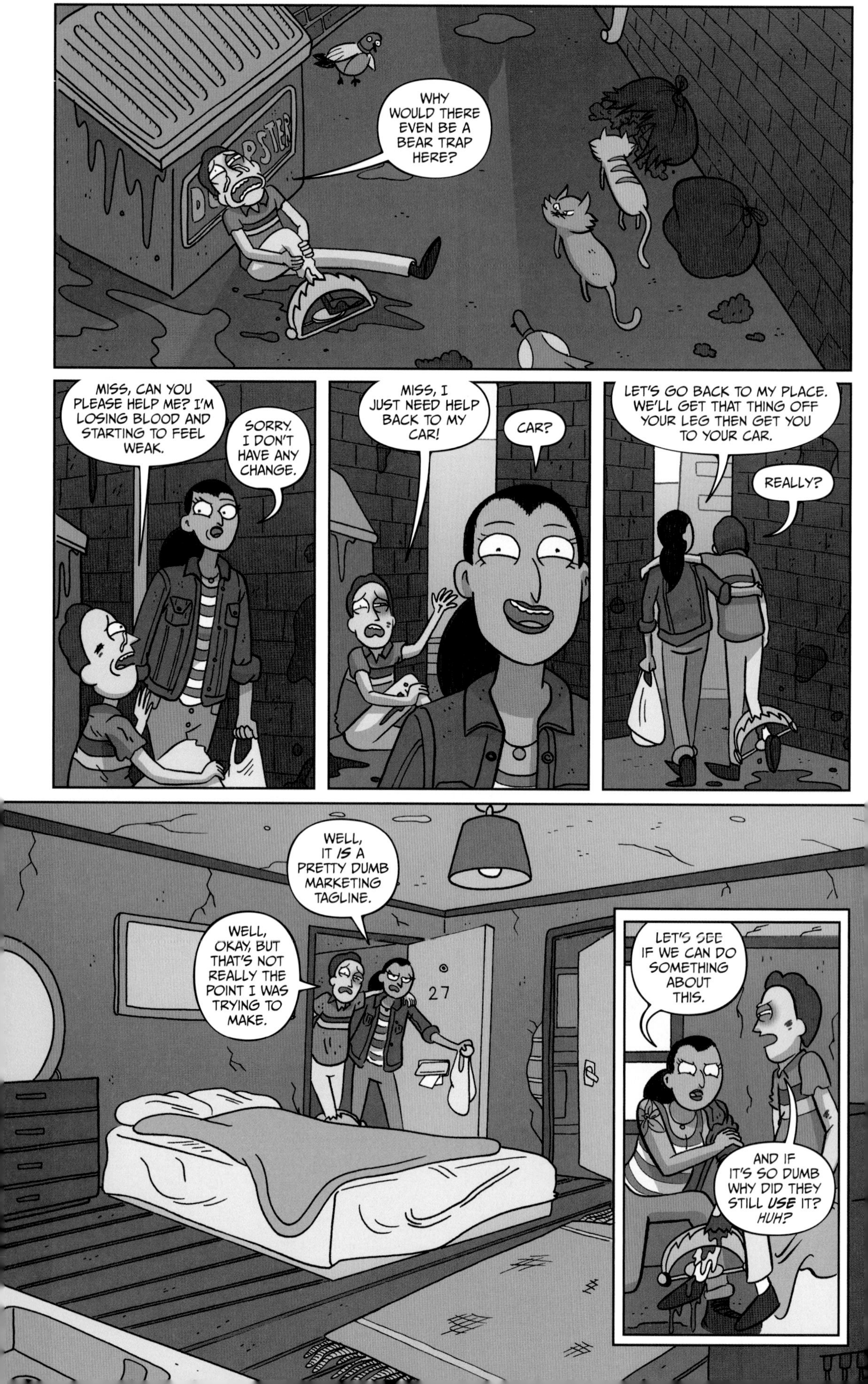
WHY WOULD THERE EVEN BE A BEAR TRAP HERE?
MISS, CAN YOU PLEASE HELP ME? I'M LOSING BLOOD AND STARTING TO FEEL WEAK.
SORRY. I DON'T HAVE ANY CHANGE.
MISS, I JUST NEED HELP BACK TO MY CAR!
CAR?
LET'S GO BACK TO MY PLACE. WE'LL GET THAT THING OFF YOUR LEG THEN GET YOU TO YOUR CAR.
REALLY?
WELL, OKAY, BUT THAT'S NOT REALLY THE POINT I WAS TRYING TO MAKE.
WELL, IT *IS* A PRETTY DUMB MARKETING TAGLINE.
27
LET'S SEE IF WE CAN DO SOMETHING ABOUT THIS.
AND IF IT'S SO DUMB WHY DID THEY STILL *USE* IT? *HUH?*

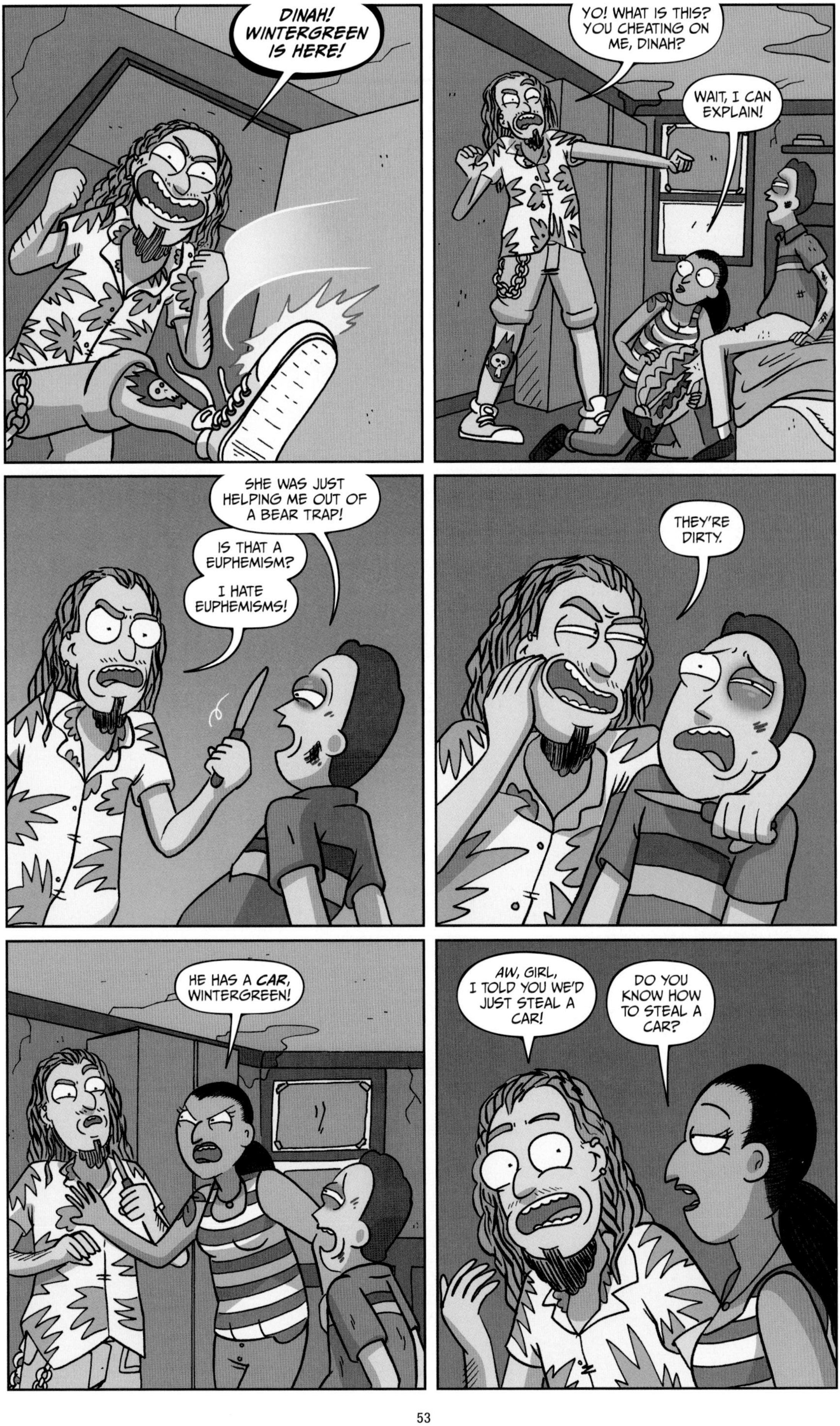
DINAH! WINTERGREEN IS HERE!
YO! WHAT IS THIS? YOU CHEATING ON ME, DINAH?
WAIT, I CAN EXPLAIN!
SHE WAS JUST HELPING ME OUT OF A BEAR TRAP!
IS THAT A EUPHEMISM?
I HATE EUPHEMISMS!
THEY'RE DIRTY.
HE HAS A CAR, WINTERGREEN!
AW, GIRL, I TOLD YOU WE'D JUST STEAL A CAR!
DO YOU KNOW HOW TO STEAL A CAR?

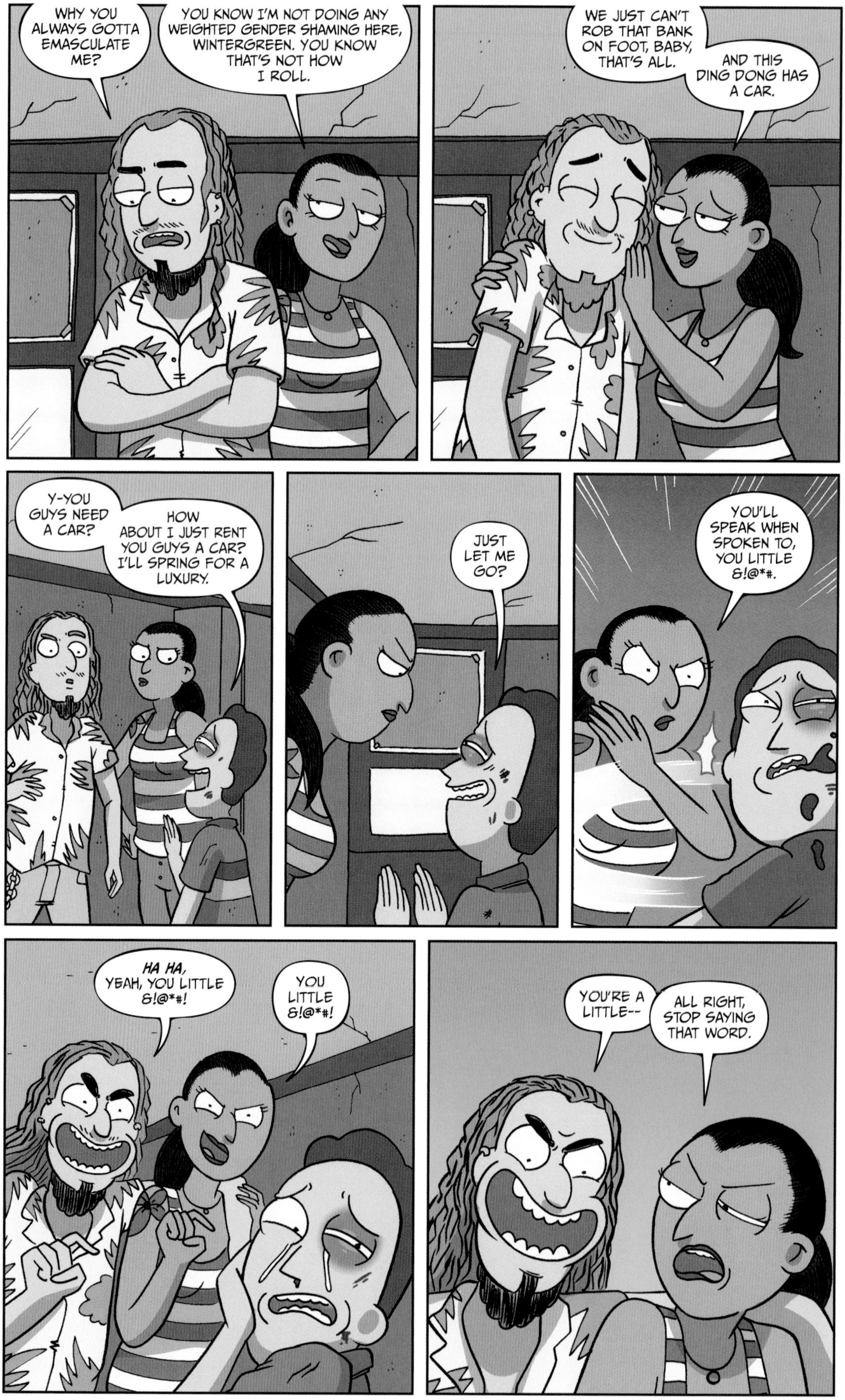
WHY YOU ALWAYS GOTTA EMASCULATE ME?
YOU KNOW I'M NOT DOING ANY WEIGHTED GENDER SHAMING HERE, WINTERGREEN. YOU KNOW THAT'S NOT HOW I ROLL.
WE JUST CAN'T ROB THAT BANK ON FOOT, BABY, THAT'S ALL.
AND THIS DING DONG HAS A CAR.
Y-YOU GUYS NEED A CAR?
HOW ABOUT I JUST RENT YOU GUYS A CAR? I'LL SPRING FOR A LUXURY.
JUST LET ME GO?
YOU'LL SPEAK WHEN SPOKEN TO, YOU LITTLE &!@*#.
HA HA, YEAH, YOU LITTLE &!@*#!
YOU LITTLE &!@*#!
YOU'RE A LITTLE--
ALL RIGHT, STOP SAYING THAT WORD.

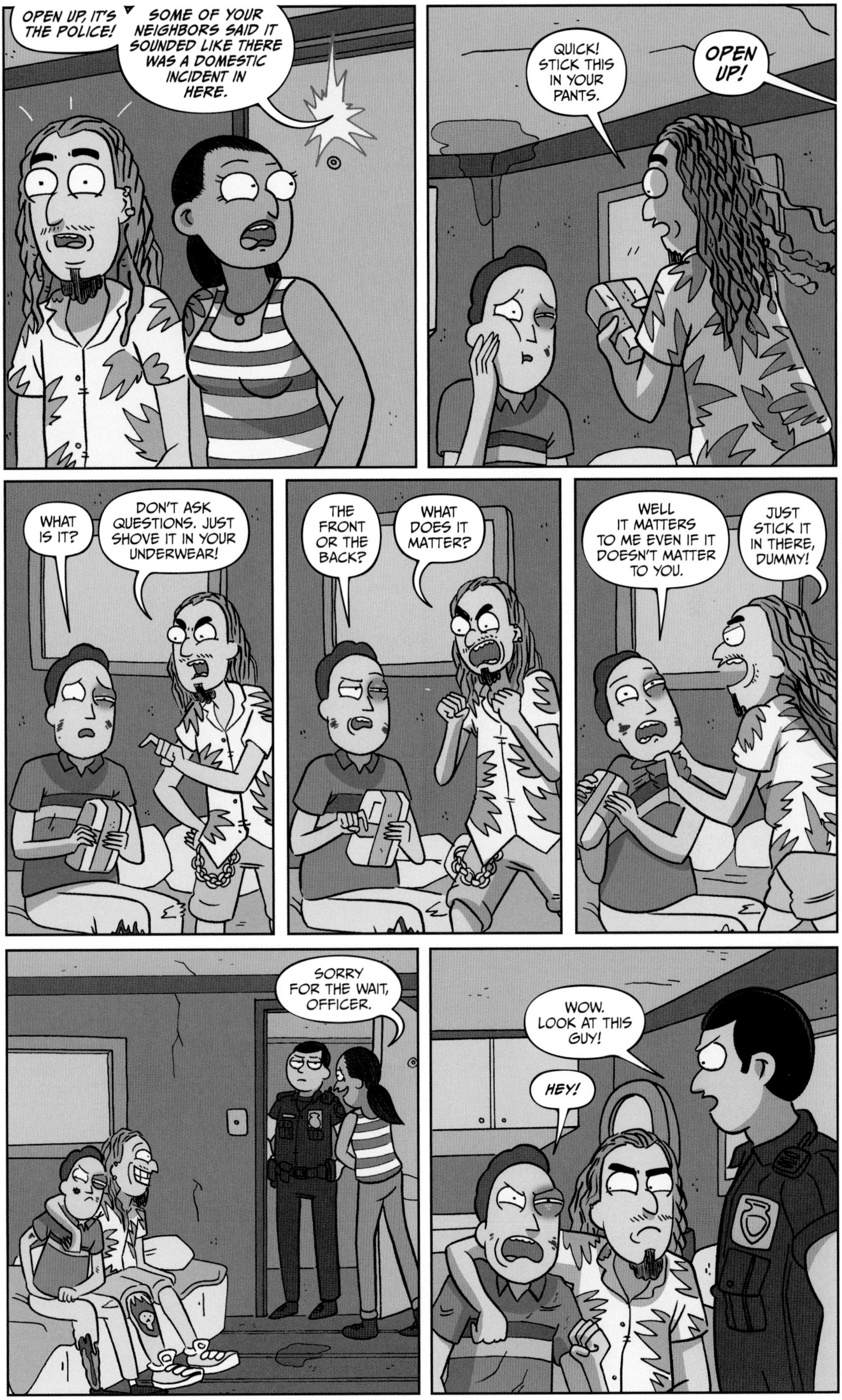
OPEN UP, IT'S THE POLICE!
SOME OF YOUR NEIGHBORS SAID IT SOUNDED LIKE THERE WAS A DOMESTIC INCIDENT IN HERE.
QUICK! STICK THIS IN YOUR PANTS.
OPEN UP!
WHAT IS IT?
DON'T ASK QUESTIONS. JUST SHOVE IT IN YOUR UNDERWEAR!
THE FRONT OR THE BACK?
WHAT DOES IT MATTER?
WELL IT MATTERS TO ME EVEN IF IT DOESN'T MATTER TO YOU.
JUST STICK IT IN THERE, DUMMY!
SORRY FOR THE WAIT, OFFICER.
WOW. LOOK AT THIS GUY!
HEY!

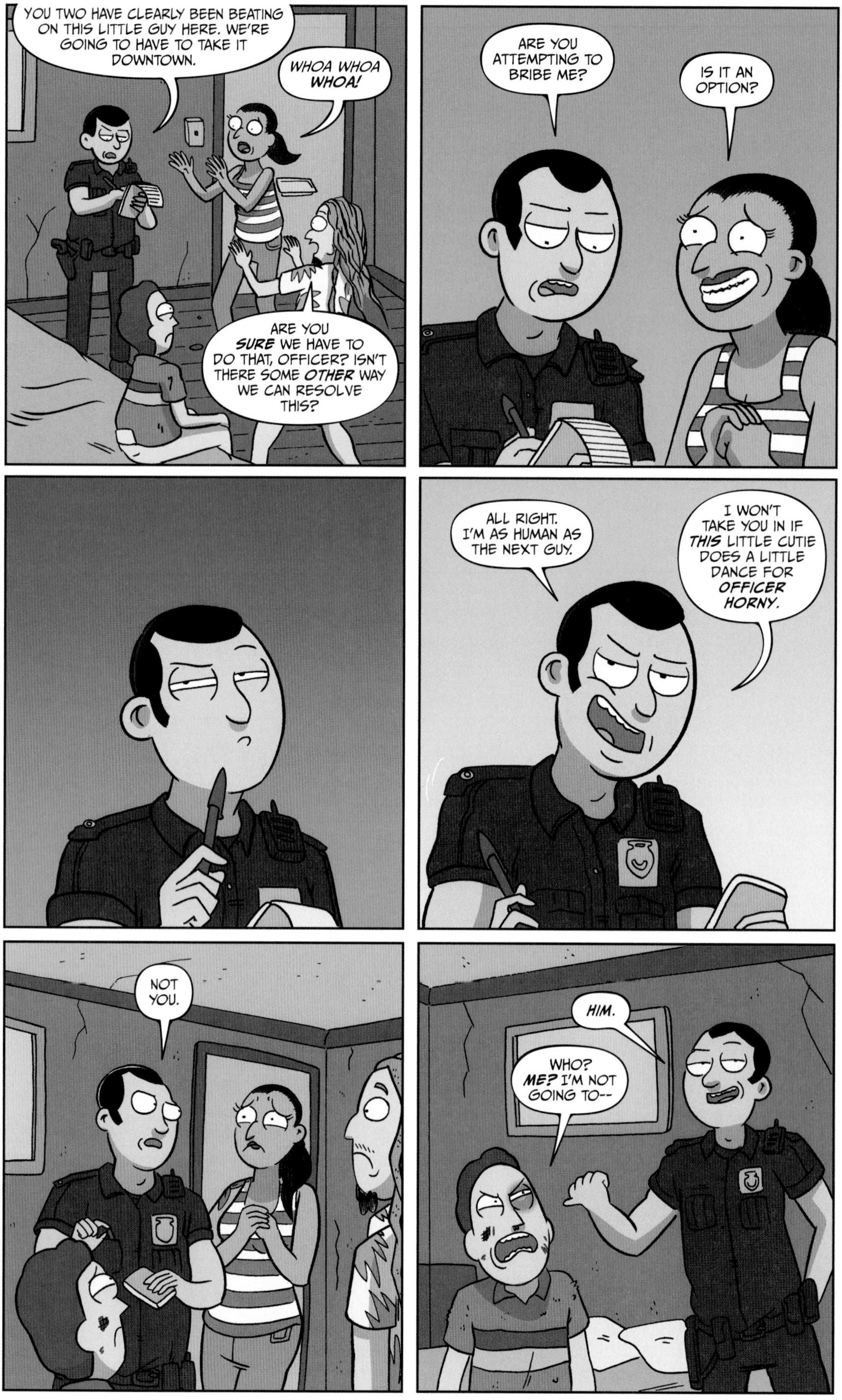
YOU TWO HAVE CLEARLY BEEN BEATING ON THIS LITTLE GUY HERE. WE'RE GOING TO HAVE TO TAKE IT DOWNTOWN.
WHOA WHOA WHOA!
ARE YOU SURE WE HAVE TO DO THAT, OFFICER? ISN'T THERE SOME OTHER WAY WE CAN RESOLVE THIS?
ARE YOU ATTEMPTING TO BRIBE ME?
IS IT AN OPTION?
ALL RIGHT. I'M AS HUMAN AS THE NEXT GUY.
I WON'T TAKE YOU IN IF THIS LITTLE CUTIE DOES A LITTLE DANCE FOR OFFICER HORNY.
NOT YOU.
HIM.
WHO? ME? I'M NOT GOING TO--

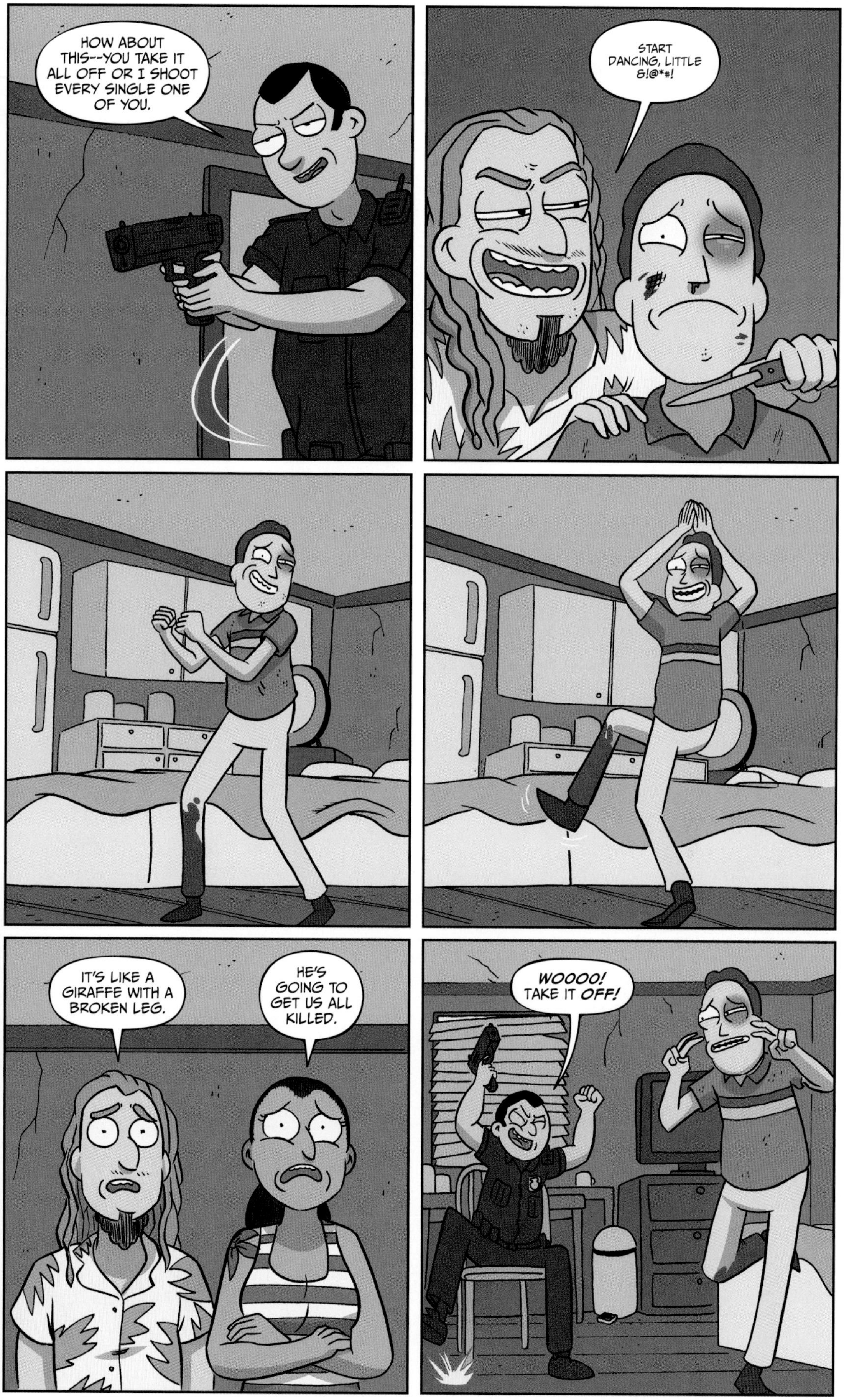
HOW ABOUT THIS--YOU TAKE IT ALL OFF OR I SHOOT EVERY SINGLE ONE OF YOU.
START DANCING, LITTLE &!@*#!
IT'S LIKE A GIRAFFE WITH A BROKEN LEG.
HE'S GOING TO GET US ALL KILLED.
WOOOO! TAKE IT OFF!

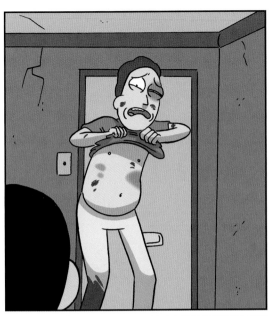

I JUST WANTED A NEW RÉSUMÉ!

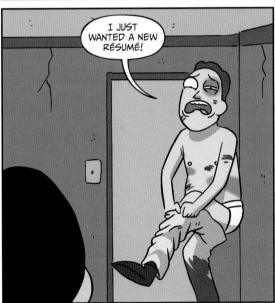

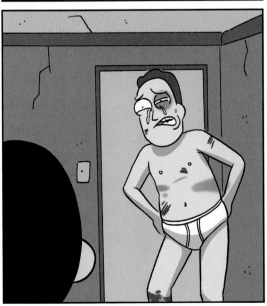

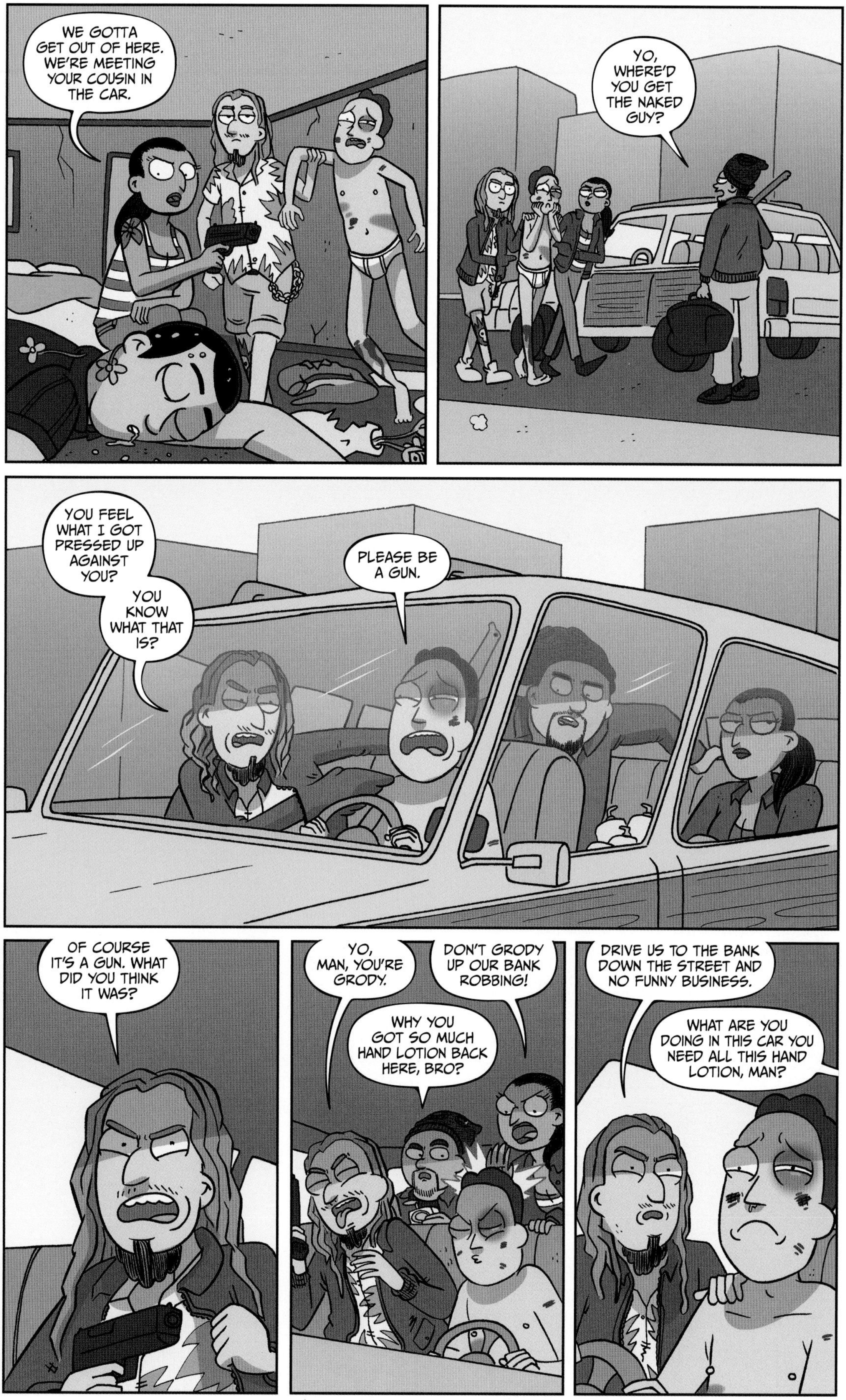
WE GOTTA GET OUT OF HERE. WE'RE MEETING YOUR COUSIN IN THE CAR.
YO, WHERE'D YOU GET THE NAKED GUY?
YOU FEEL WHAT I GOT PRESSED UP AGAINST YOU?
YOU KNOW WHAT THAT IS?
PLEASE BE A GUN.
OF COURSE IT'S A GUN. WHAT DID YOU THINK IT WAS?
YO, MAN, YOU'RE GRODY.
DON'T GRODY UP OUR BANK ROBBING!
WHY YOU GOT SO MUCH HAND LOTION BACK HERE, BRO?
DRIVE US TO THE BANK DOWN THE STREET AND NO FUNNY BUSINESS.
WHAT ARE YOU DOING IN THIS CAR YOU NEED ALL THIS HAND LOTION, MAN?

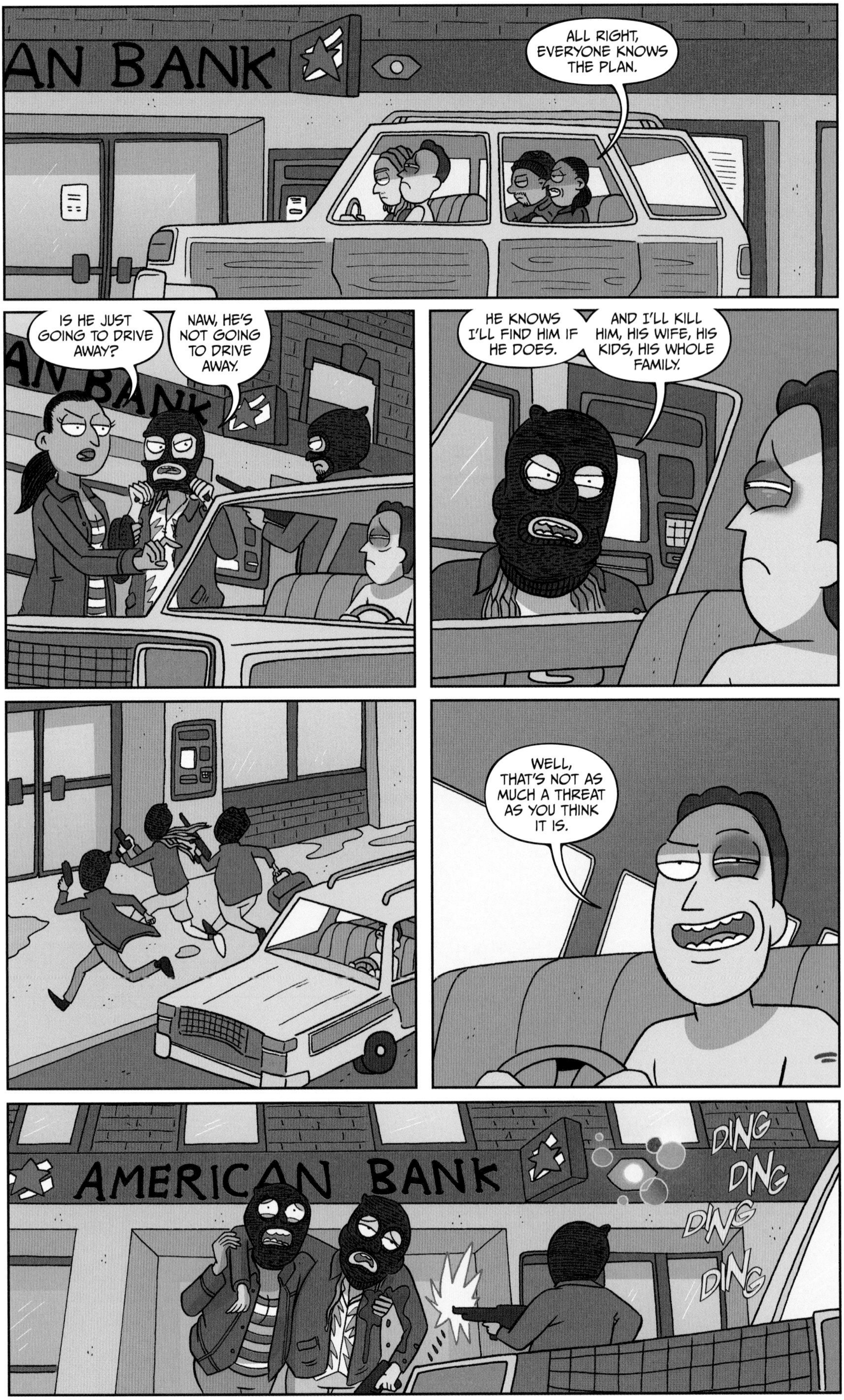
AN BANK
ALL RIGHT, EVERYONE KNOWS THE PLAN.
IS HE JUST GOING TO DRIVE AWAY?
NAW, HE'S NOT GOING TO DRIVE AWAY.
HE KNOWS I'LL FIND HIM IF HE DOES.
AND I'LL KILL HIM, HIS WIFE, HIS KIDS, HIS WHOLE FAMILY.
WELL, THAT'S NOT AS MUCH A THREAT AS YOU THINK IT IS.
AMERICAN BANK
DING
DING
DING
DING

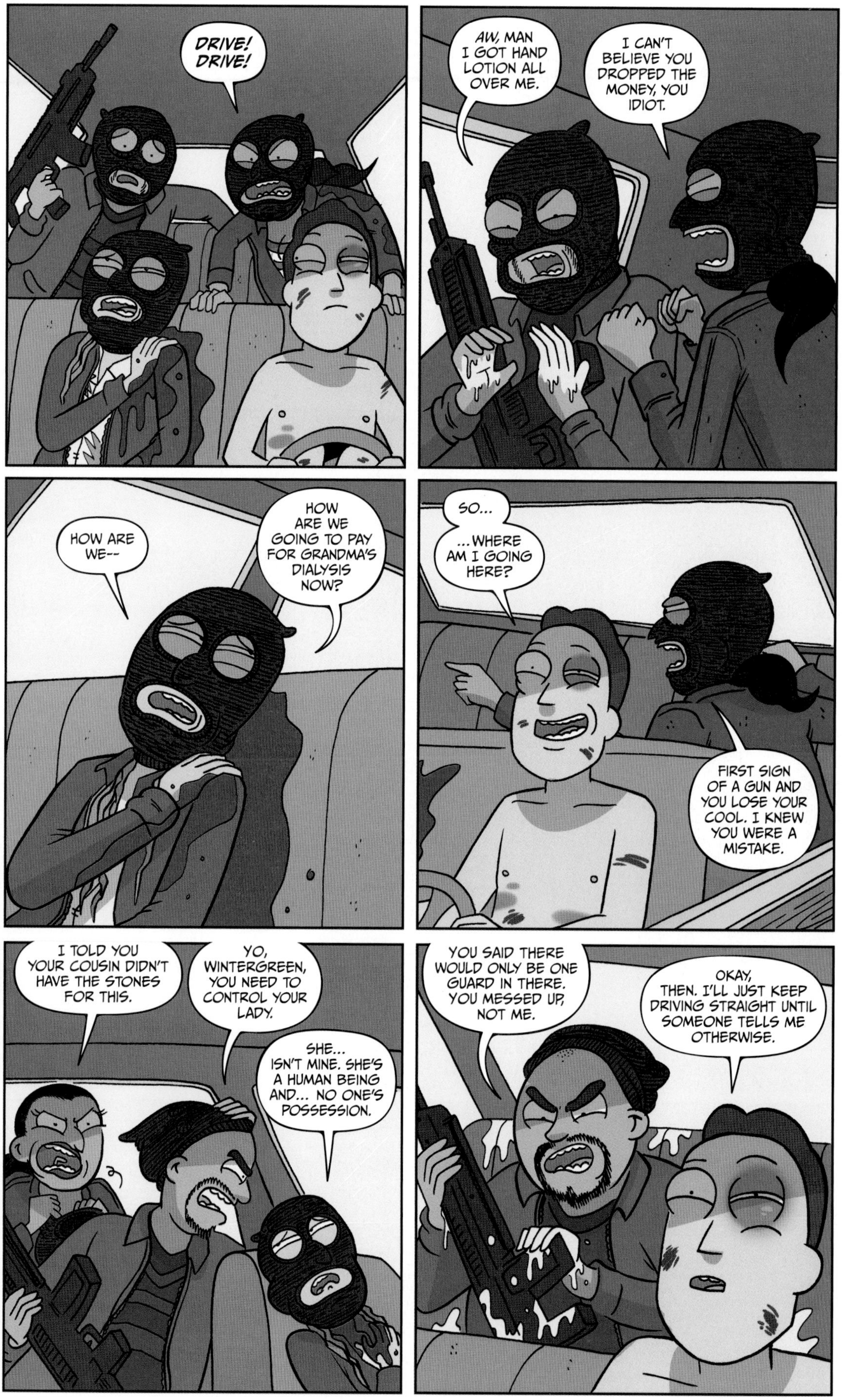
DRIVE! DRIVE!
AW, MAN I GOT HAND LOTION ALL OVER ME.
I CAN'T BELIEVE YOU DROPPED THE MONEY, YOU IDIOT.
HOW ARE WE--
HOW ARE WE GOING TO PAY FOR GRANDMA'S DIALYSIS NOW?
SO...
...WHERE AM I GOING HERE?
FIRST SIGN OF A GUN AND YOU LOSE YOUR COOL. I KNEW YOU WERE A MISTAKE.
I TOLD YOU YOUR COUSIN DIDN'T HAVE THE STONES FOR THIS.
YO, WINTERGREEN, YOU NEED TO CONTROL YOUR LADY.
SHE... ISN'T MINE. SHE'S A HUMAN BEING AND... NO ONE'S POSSESSION.
YOU SAID THERE WOULD ONLY BE ONE GUARD IN THERE. YOU MESSED UP, NOT ME.
OKAY, THEN. I'LL JUST KEEP DRIVING STRAIGHT UNTIL SOMEONE TELLS ME OTHERWISE.

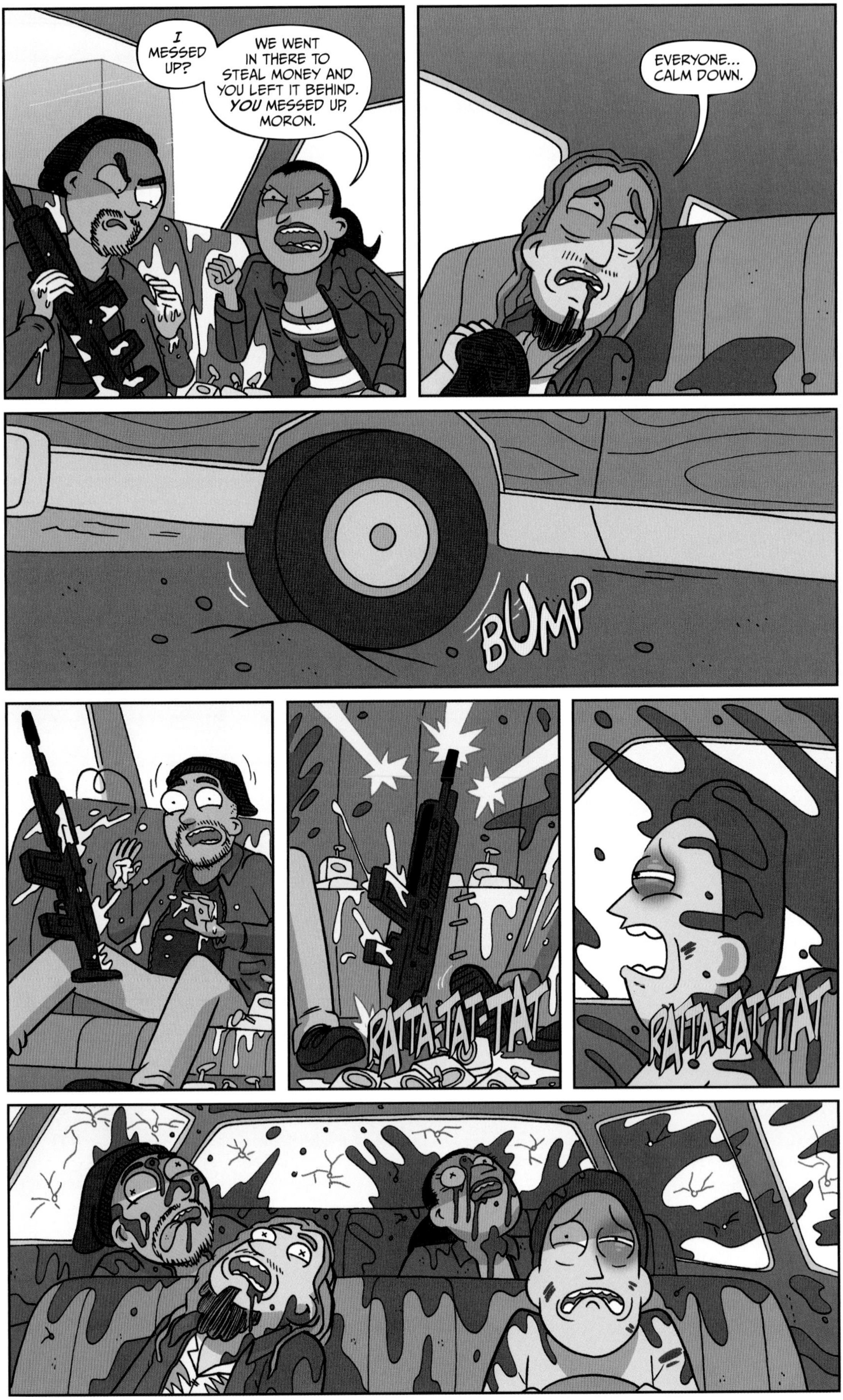
I MESSED UP?
WE WENT IN THERE TO STEAL MONEY AND YOU LEFT IT BEHIND. *YOU* MESSED UP, MORON.
EVERYONE... CALM DOWN.
BUMP
RATTA-TAT-TAT
RATTA-TAT-TAT

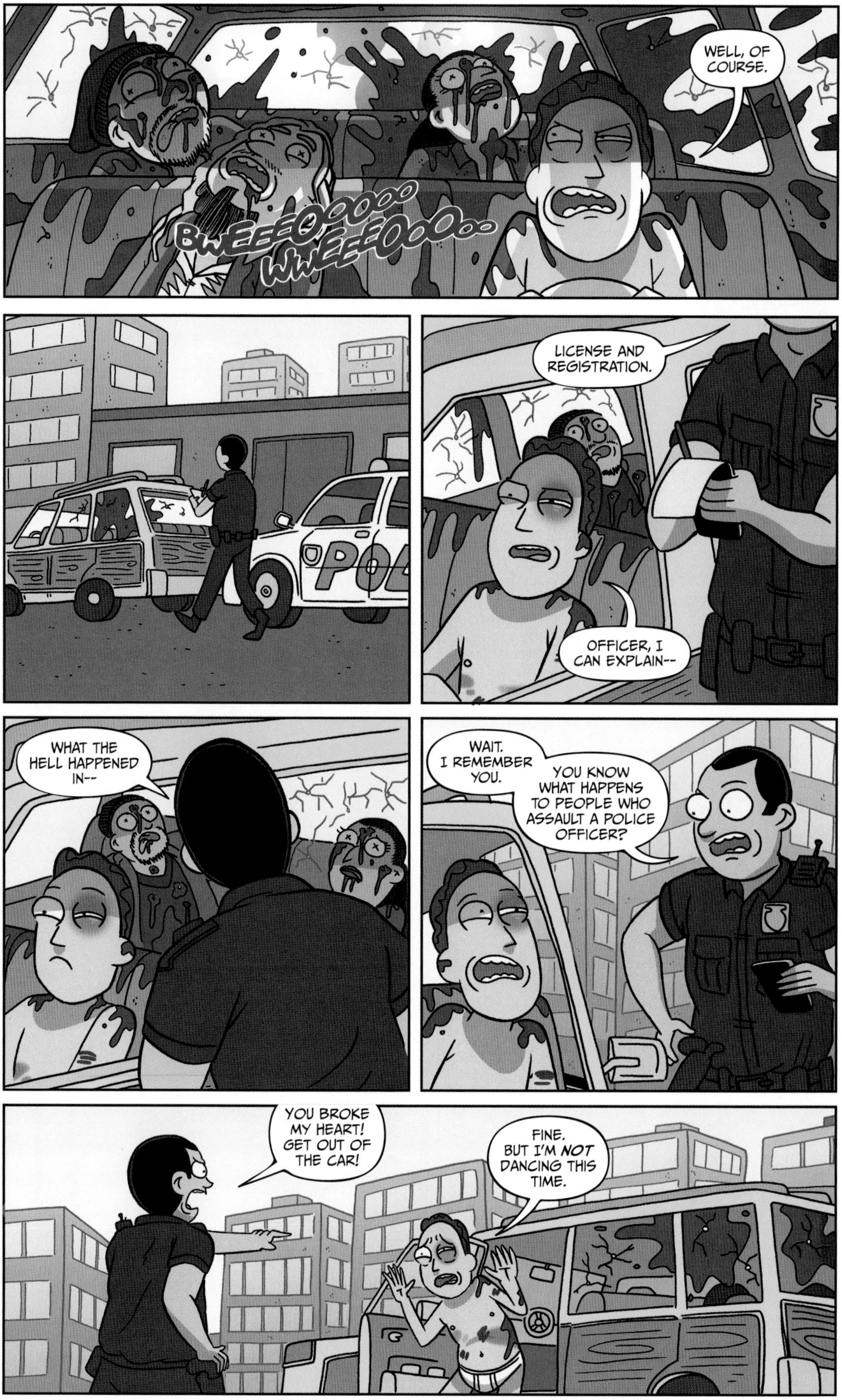
WELL, OF COURSE.
BWEEEOOOOOO
WWEEEOOOOO
LICENSE AND REGISTRATION.
OFFICER, I CAN EXPLAIN--
WHAT THE HELL HAPPENED IN--
WAIT. I REMEMBER YOU.
YOU KNOW WHAT HAPPENS TO PEOPLE WHO ASSAULT A POLICE OFFICER?
YOU BROKE MY HEART! GET OUT OF THE CAR!
FINE. BUT I'M *NOT* DANCING THIS TIME.

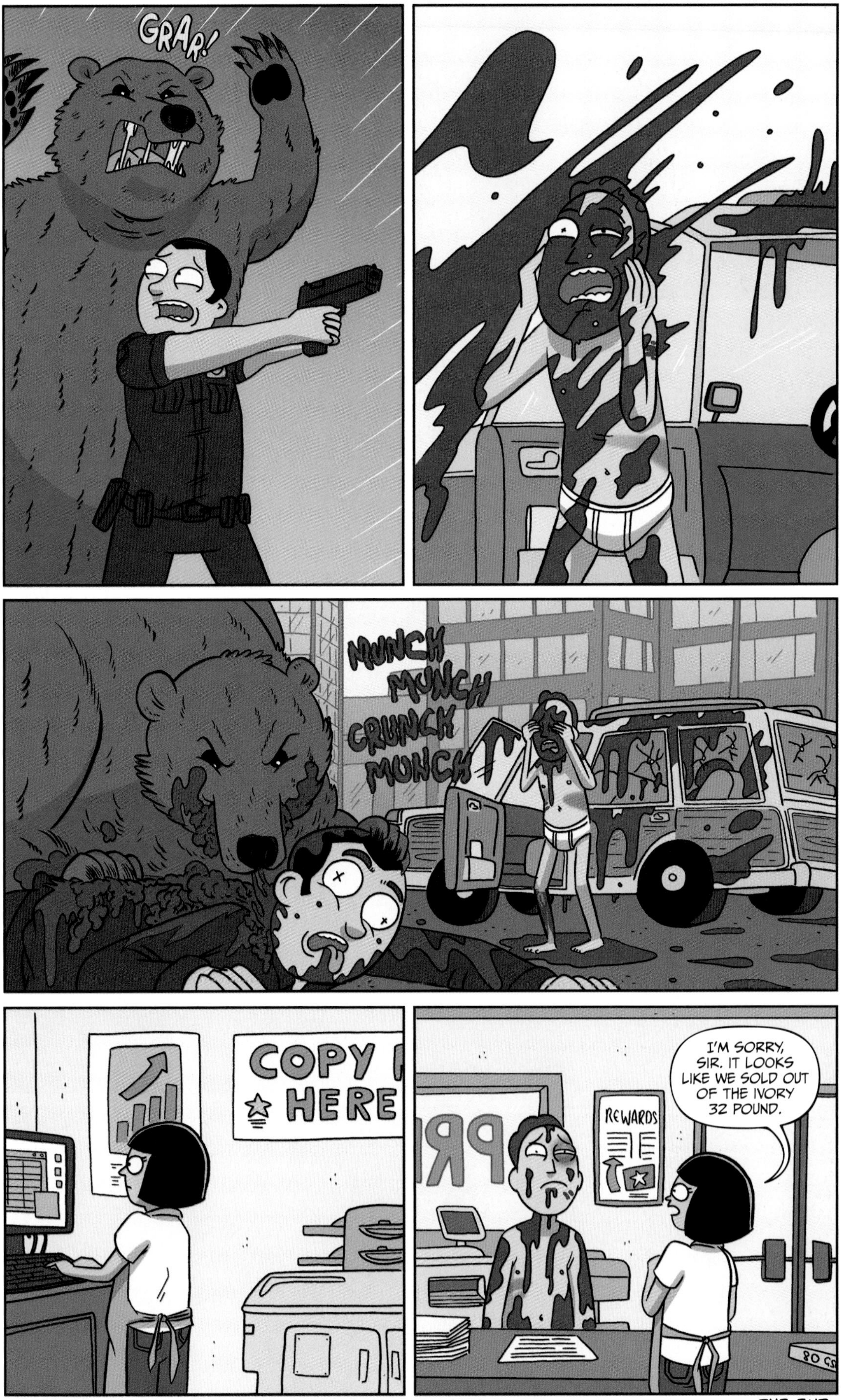
GRAR!
MUNCH
MUNCH
CRUNCH
MUNCH
COPY
HERE
REWARDS
I'M SORRY, SIR. IT LOOKS LIKE WE SOLD OUT OF THE IVORY 32 POUND.

THE END.

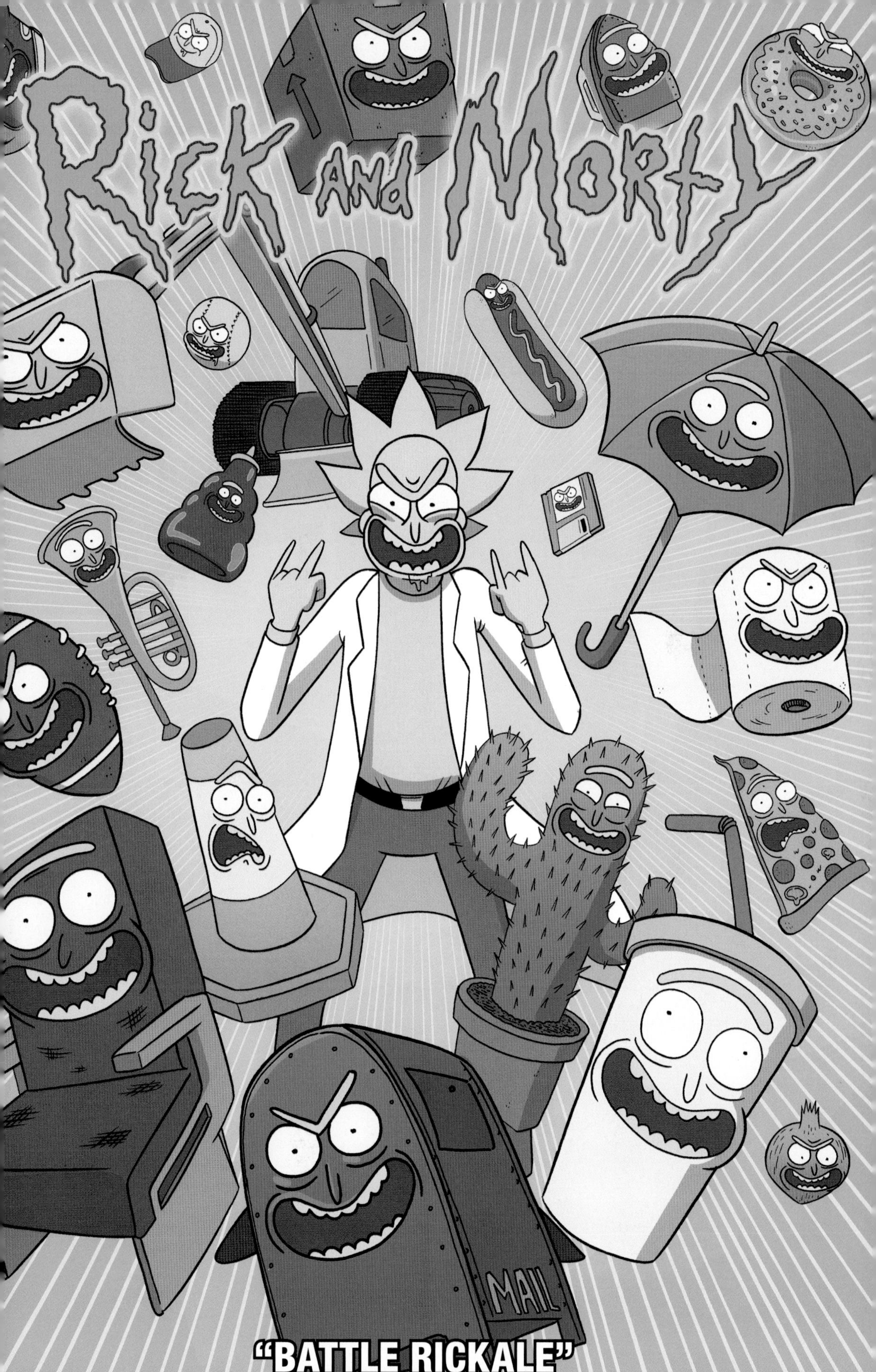
Rick and Morty
MAIL

"BATTLE RICKALE"

WRITTEN BY **KYLE STARKS** ILLUSTRATED BY **MARC ELLERBY** COLORED BY **SARAH STERN** LETTERED BY **CRANK!**

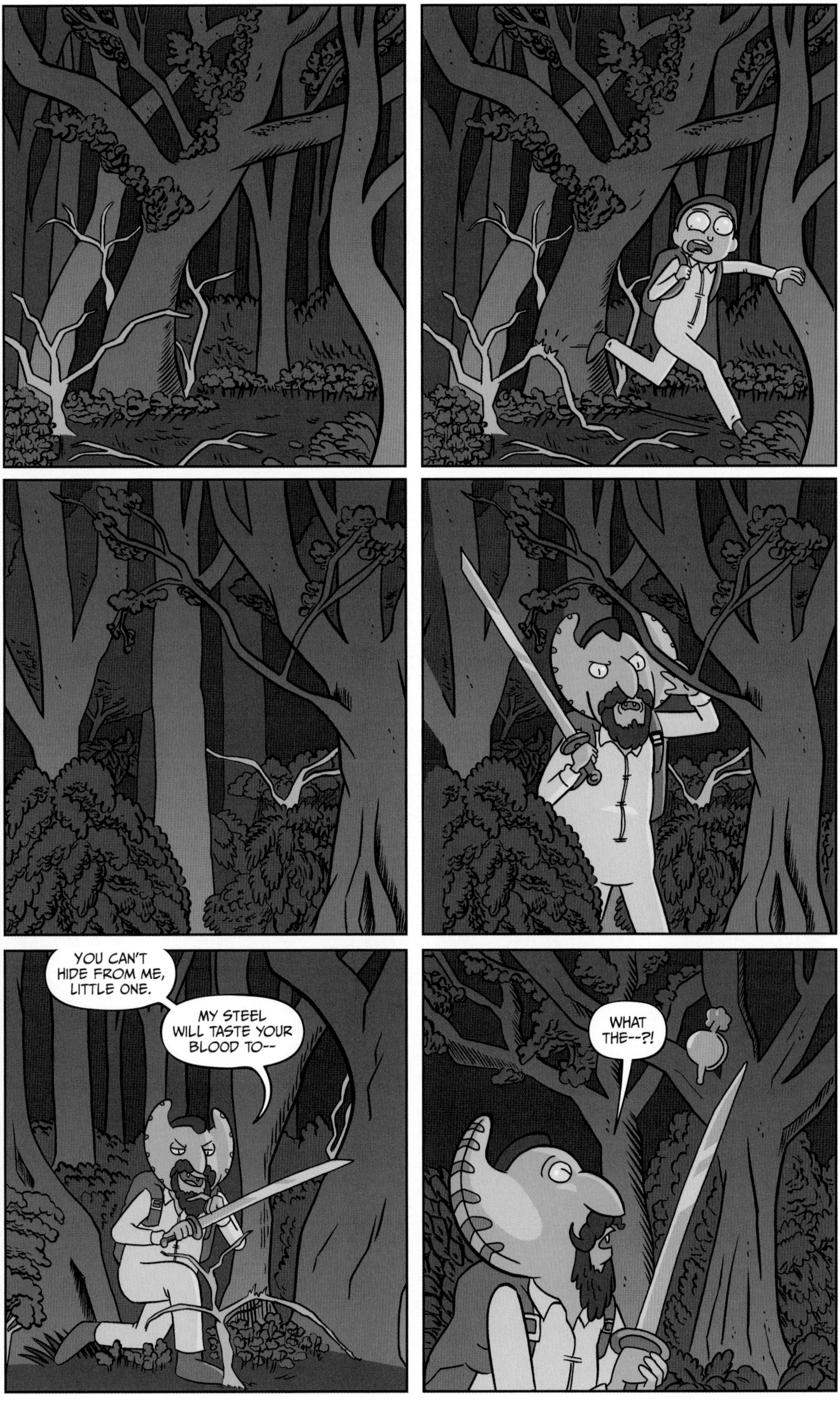
YOU CAN'T HIDE FROM ME, LITTLE ONE.
MY STEEL WILL TASTE YOUR BLOOD TO--
WHAT THE--?!

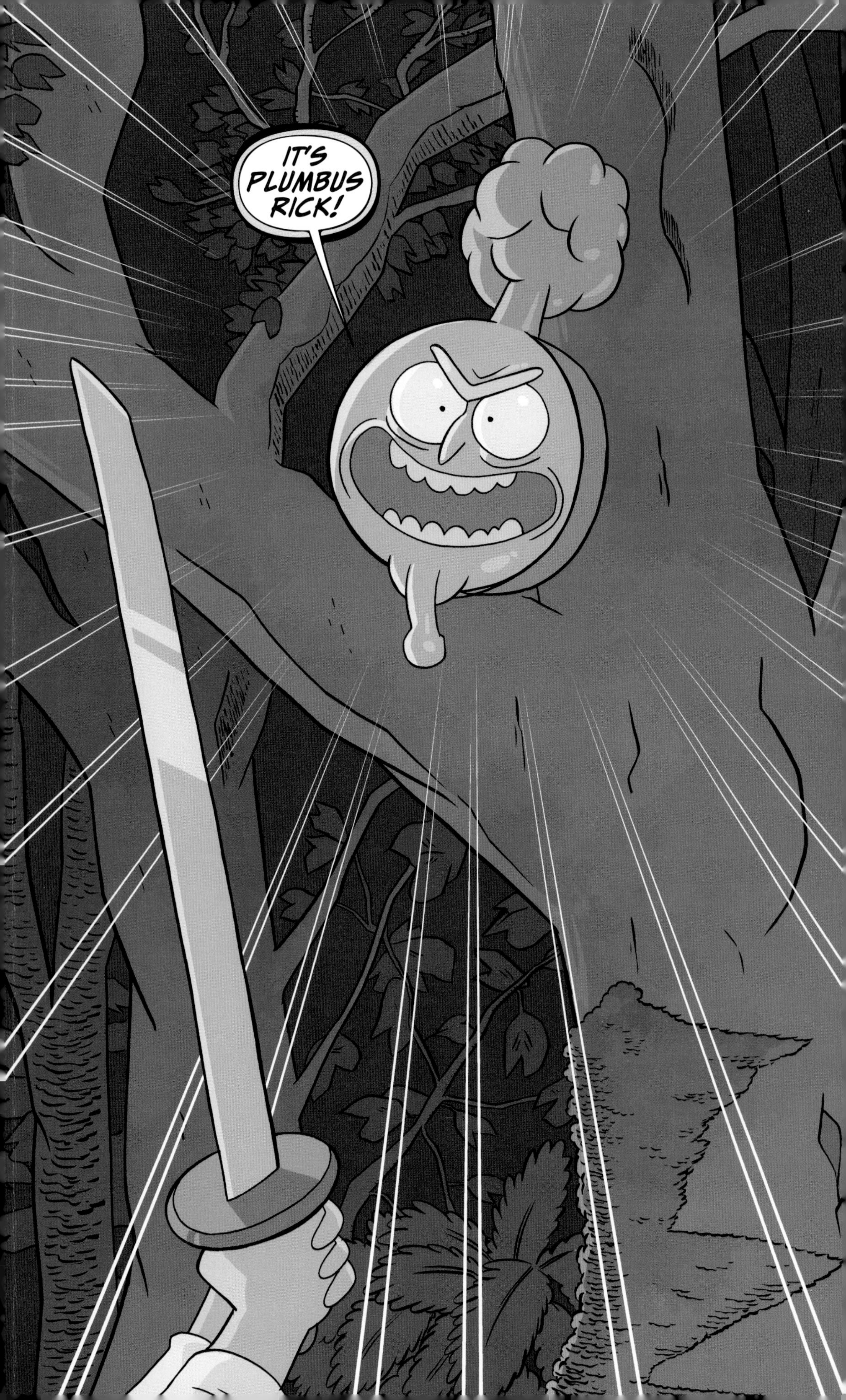
IT'S PLUMBUS RICK!

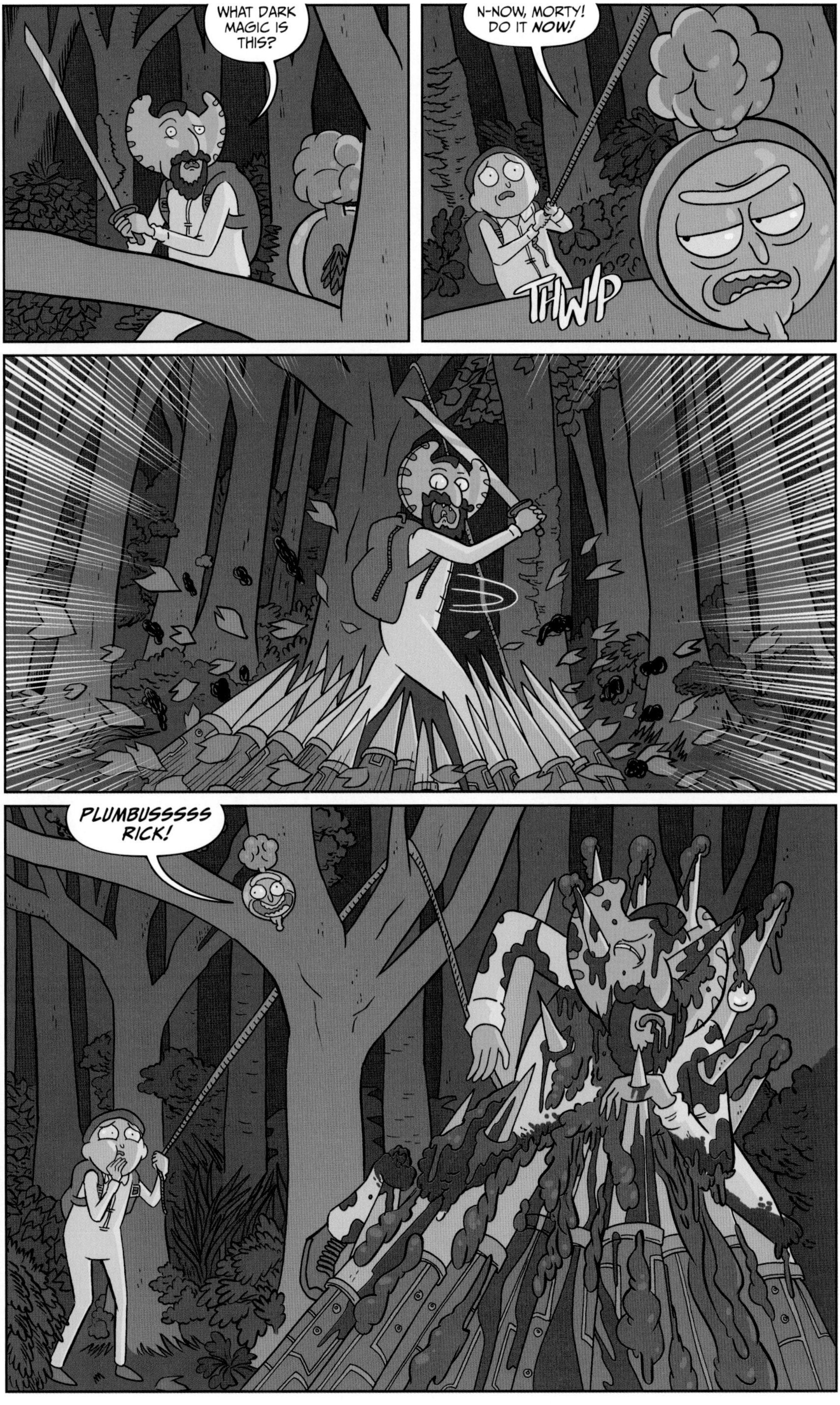
WHAT DARK MAGIC IS THIS?
N-NOW, MORTY! DO IT *NOW!*
THWIP
PLUMBUSSSSS RICK!

NNNNNNGH, OH GEEZ. I CAN'T DO THIS ANYMORE, RICK.

THE KILLINGS? A-A-ALL THE KILLING? THE BLOOD? THE MAYHEM?

I CAN'T TAKE IT ANYMORE.

WH-WHAT NUMBER WAS THAT? I CAN'T EVEN KEEP TRACK. IT'S CHANGING ME, RICK.

RICK?

WH-WHY ARE YOU MAKING ME DO THIS, RICK?

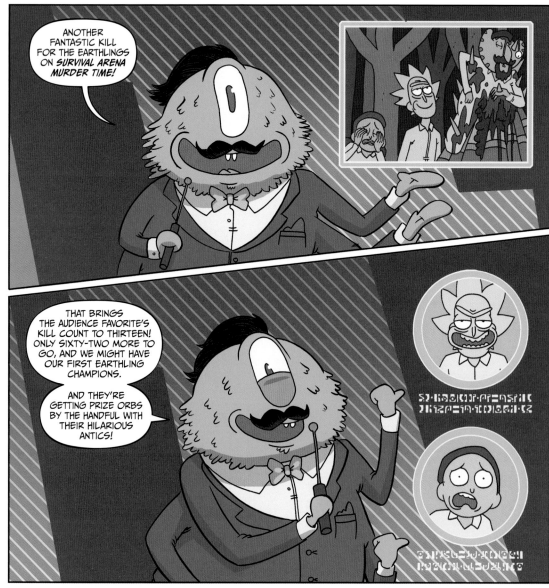

ANOTHER FANTASTIC KILL FOR THE EARTHLINGS ON *SURVIVAL ARENA MURDER TIME!*

THAT BRINGS THE AUDIENCE FAVORITE'S KILL COUNT TO THIRTEEN! ONLY SIXTY-TWO MORE TO GO, AND WE MIGHT HAVE OUR FIRST EARTHLING CHAMPIONS.

AND THEY'RE GETTING PRIZE ORBS BY THE HANDFUL WITH THEIR HILARIOUS ANTICS!

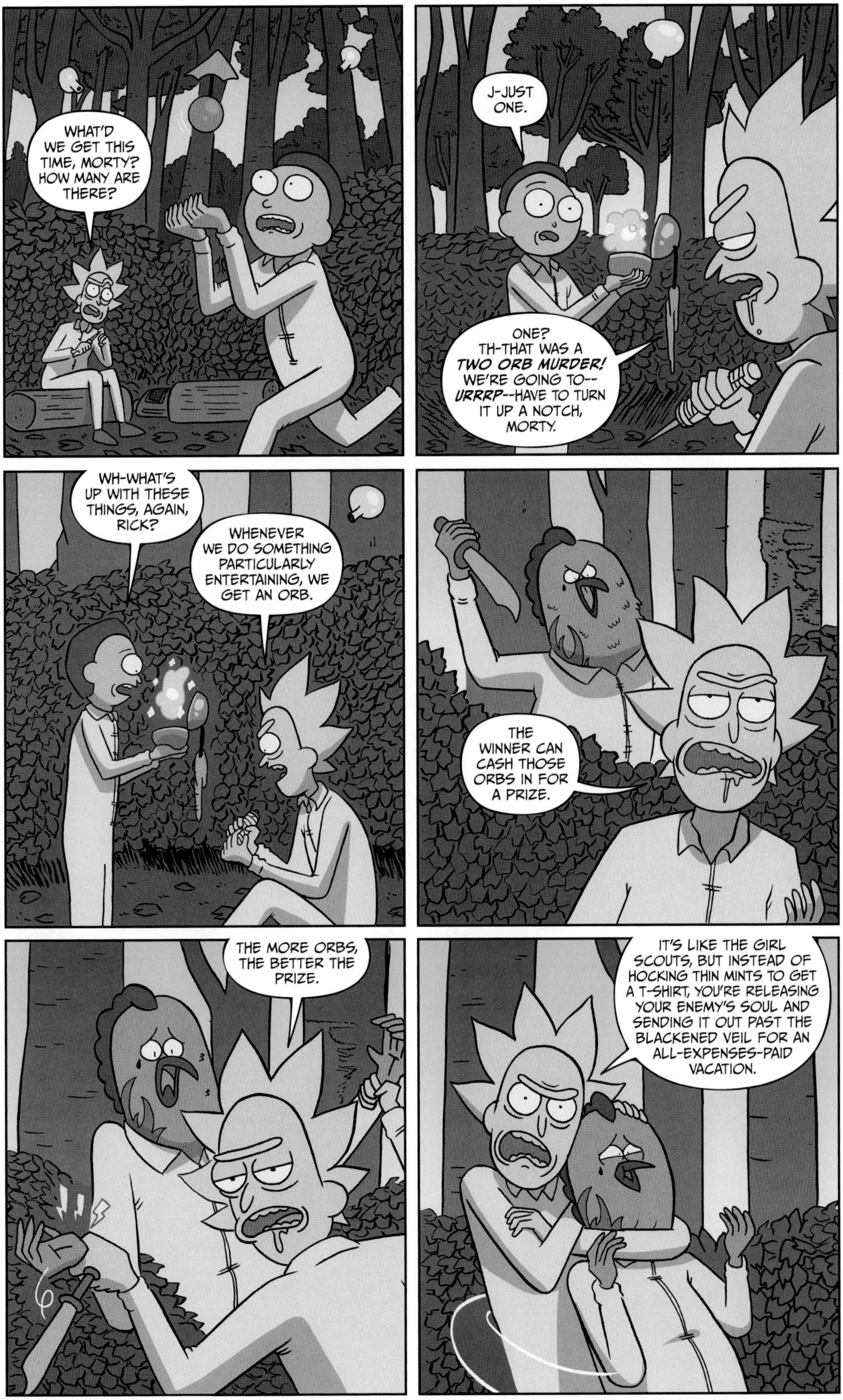
WHAT'D WE GET THIS TIME, MORTY? HOW MANY ARE THERE?
J-JUST ONE.
ONE? TH-THAT WAS A TWO ORB MURDER! WE'RE GOING TO--URRRP--HAVE TO TURN IT UP A NOTCH, MORTY.
WH-WHAT'S UP WITH THESE THINGS, AGAIN, RICK?
WHENEVER WE DO SOMETHING PARTICULARLY ENTERTAINING, WE GET AN ORB.
THE WINNER CAN CASH THOSE ORBS IN FOR A PRIZE.
THE MORE ORBS, THE BETTER THE PRIZE.
IT'S LIKE THE GIRL SCOUTS, BUT INSTEAD OF HOCKING THIN MINTS TO GET A T-SHIRT, YOU'RE RELEASING YOUR ENEMY'S SOUL AND SENDING IT OUT PAST THE BLACKENED VEIL FOR AN ALL-EXPENSES-PAID VACATION.

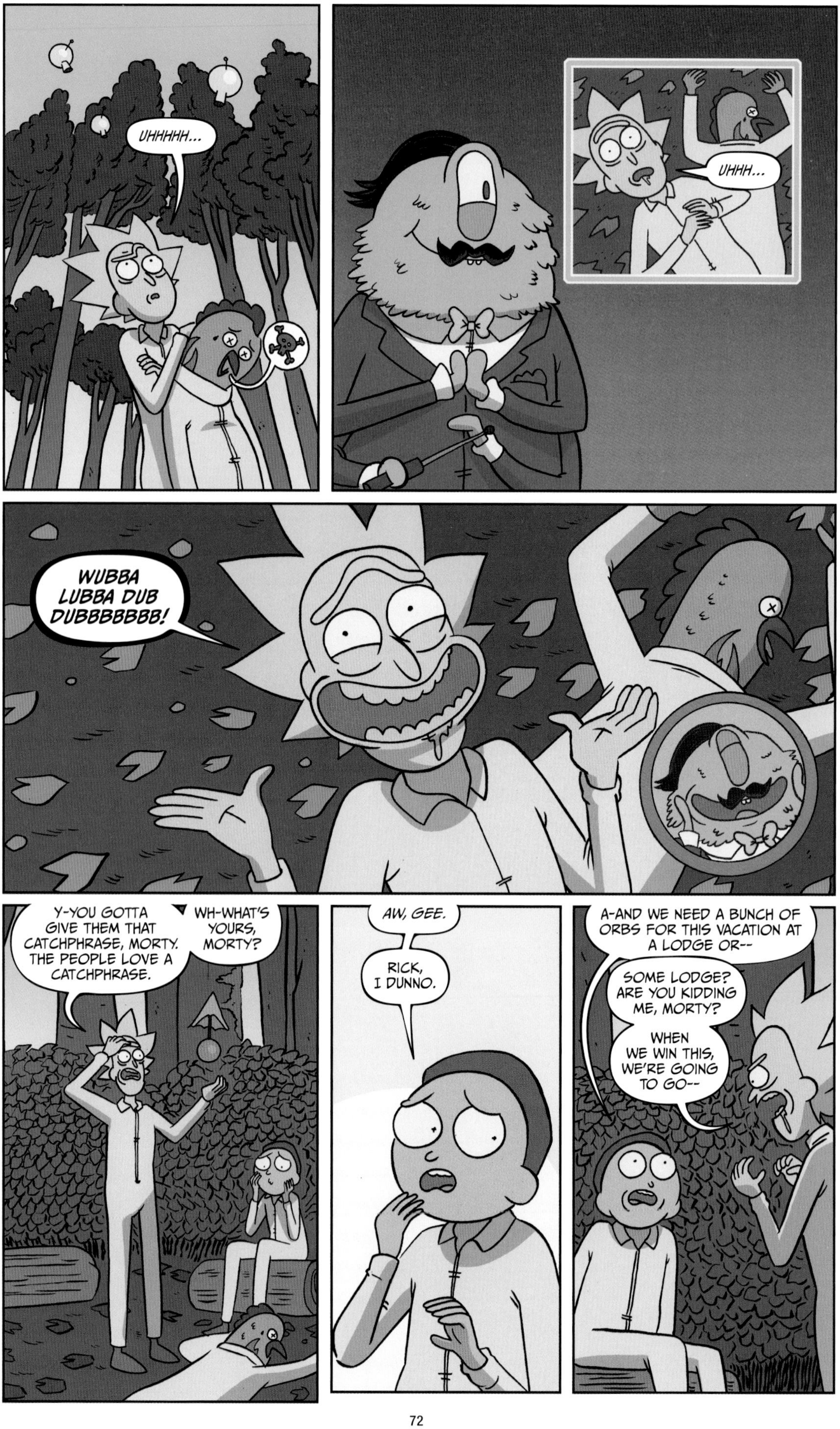
UHHHHH...
UHHH...
WUBBA LUBBA DUB DUBBBBBBB!
Y-YOU GOTTA GIVE THEM THAT CATCHPHRASE, MORTY. THE PEOPLE LOVE A CATCHPHRASE.
WH-WHAT'S YOURS, MORTY?
AW, GEE.
RICK, I DUNNO.
A-AND WE NEED A BUNCH OF ORBS FOR THIS VACATION AT A LODGE OR--
SOME LODGE? ARE YOU KIDDING ME, MORTY?
WHEN WE WIN THIS, WE'RE GOING TO GO--

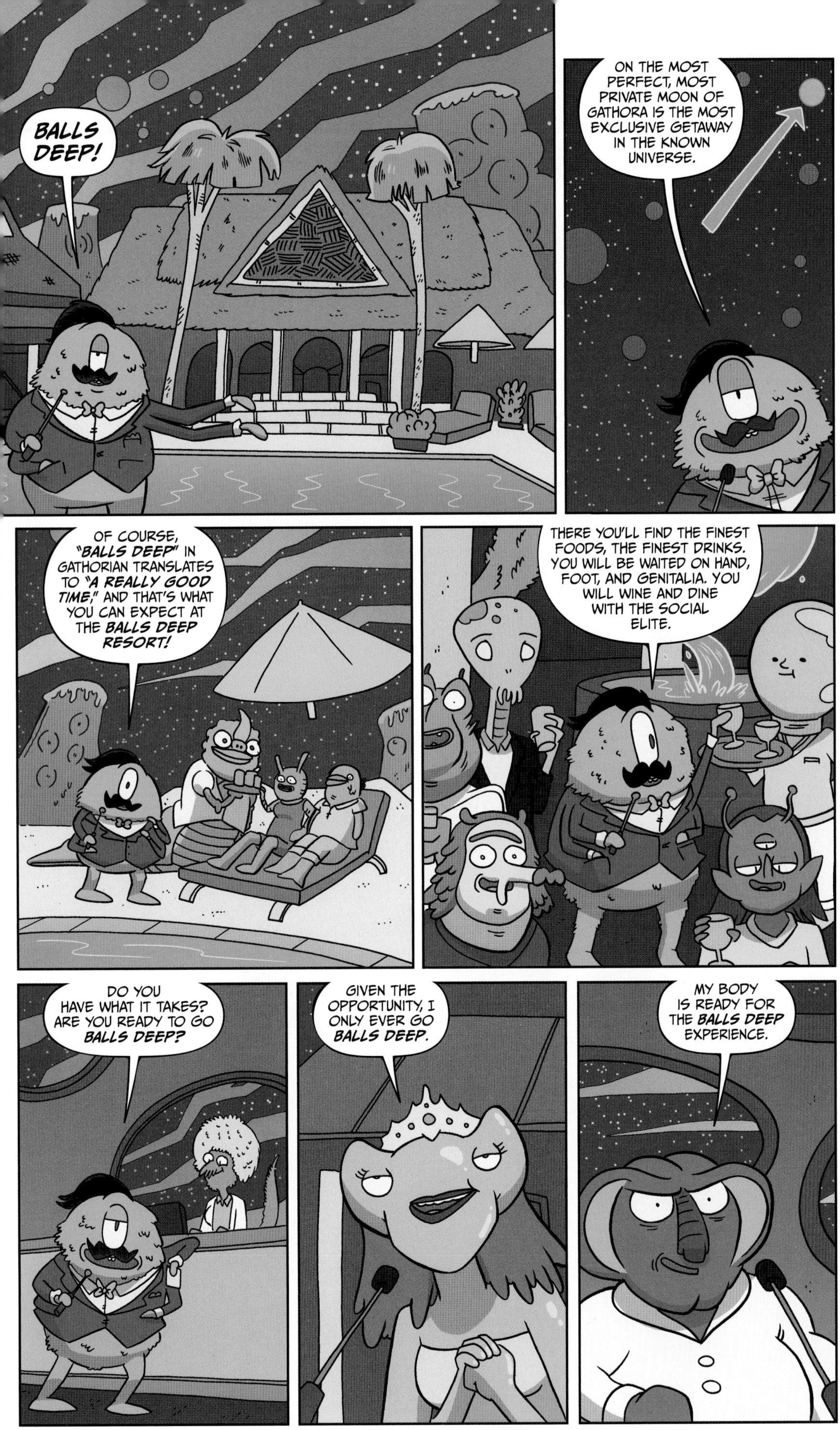
BALLS DEEP!
ON THE MOST PERFECT, MOST PRIVATE MOON OF GATHORA IS THE MOST EXCLUSIVE GETAWAY IN THE KNOWN UNIVERSE.
OF COURSE, "BALLS DEEP" IN GATHORIAN TRANSLATES TO "A REALLY GOOD TIME," AND THAT'S WHAT YOU CAN EXPECT AT THE BALLS DEEP RESORT!
THERE YOU'LL FIND THE FINEST FOODS, THE FINEST DRINKS. YOU WILL BE WAITED ON HAND, FOOT, AND GENITALIA. YOU WILL WINE AND DINE WITH THE SOCIAL ELITE.
DO YOU HAVE WHAT IT TAKES? ARE YOU READY TO GO BALLS DEEP?
GIVEN THE OPPORTUNITY, I ONLY EVER GO BALLS DEEP.
MY BODY IS READY FOR THE BALLS DEEP EXPERIENCE.

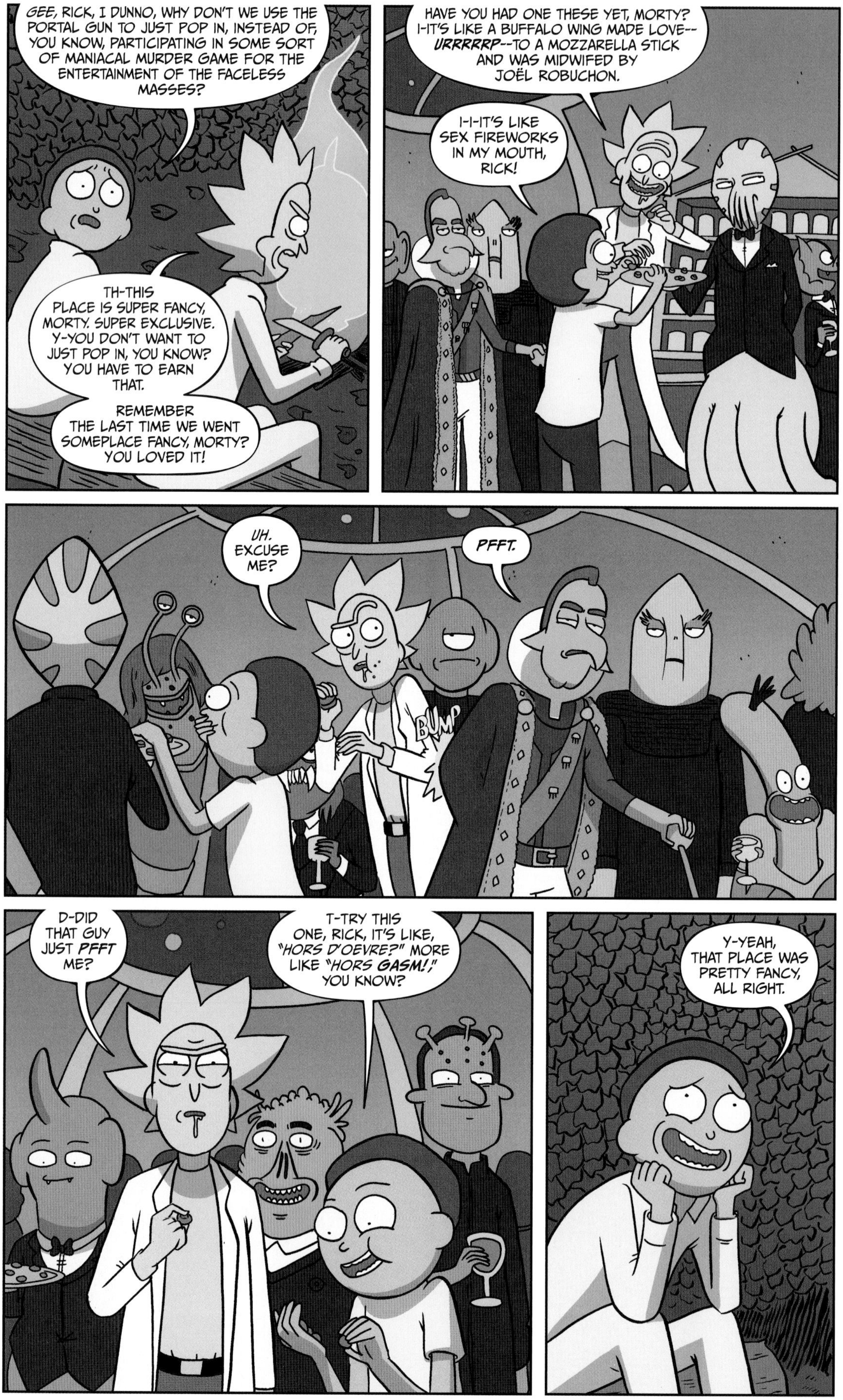
GEE, RICK, I DUNNO, WHY DON'T WE USE THE PORTAL GUN TO JUST POP IN, INSTEAD OF, YOU KNOW, PARTICIPATING IN SOME SORT OF MANIACAL MURDER GAME FOR THE ENTERTAINMENT OF THE FACELESS MASSES?
TH-THIS PLACE IS SUPER FANCY, MORTY. SUPER EXCLUSIVE. Y-YOU DON'T WANT TO JUST POP IN, YOU KNOW? YOU HAVE TO EARN THAT.
REMEMBER THE LAST TIME WE WENT SOMEPLACE FANCY, MORTY? YOU LOVED IT!
HAVE YOU HAD ONE THESE YET, MORTY? I-IT'S LIKE A BUFFALO WING MADE LOVE-- URRRRRP--TO A MOZZARELLA STICK AND WAS MIDWIFED BY JOËL ROBUCHON.
I-I-IT'S LIKE SEX FIREWORKS IN MY MOUTH, RICK!
UH. EXCUSE ME?
PFFT.
BUMP
D-DID THAT GUY JUST PFFT ME?
T-TRY THIS ONE, RICK, IT'S LIKE, "HORS D'OEVRE?" MORE LIKE "HORS GASM!," YOU KNOW?
Y-YEAH, THAT PLACE WAS PRETTY FANCY, ALL RIGHT.

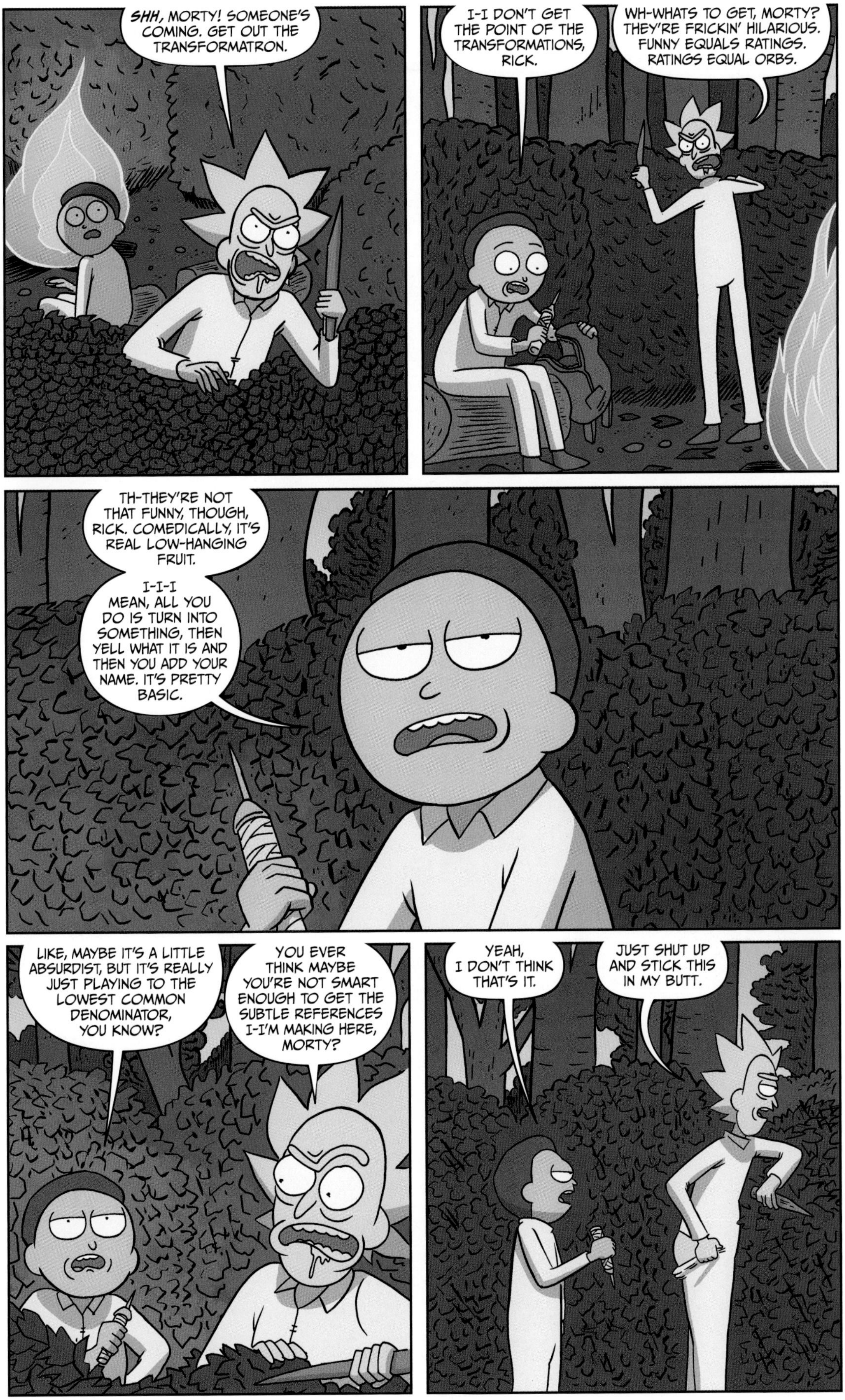
SHH, MORTY! SOMEONE'S COMING. GET OUT THE TRANSFORMATRON.
I-I DON'T GET THE POINT OF THE TRANSFORMATIONS, RICK.
WH-WHATS TO GET, MORTY? THEY'RE FRICKIN' HILARIOUS. FUNNY EQUALS RATINGS. RATINGS EQUAL ORBS.
TH-THEY'RE NOT THAT FUNNY, THOUGH, RICK. COMEDICALLY, IT'S REAL LOW-HANGING FRUIT.
I-I-I MEAN, ALL YOU DO IS TURN INTO SOMETHING, THEN YELL WHAT IT IS AND THEN YOU ADD YOUR NAME. IT'S PRETTY BASIC.
LIKE, MAYBE IT'S A LITTLE ABSURDIST, BUT IT'S REALLY JUST PLAYING TO THE LOWEST COMMON DENOMINATOR, YOU KNOW?
YOU EVER THINK MAYBE YOU'RE NOT SMART ENOUGH TO GET THE SUBTLE REFERENCES I-I'M MAKING HERE, MORTY?
YEAH, I DON'T THINK THAT'S IT.
JUST SHUT UP AND STICK THIS IN MY BUTT.

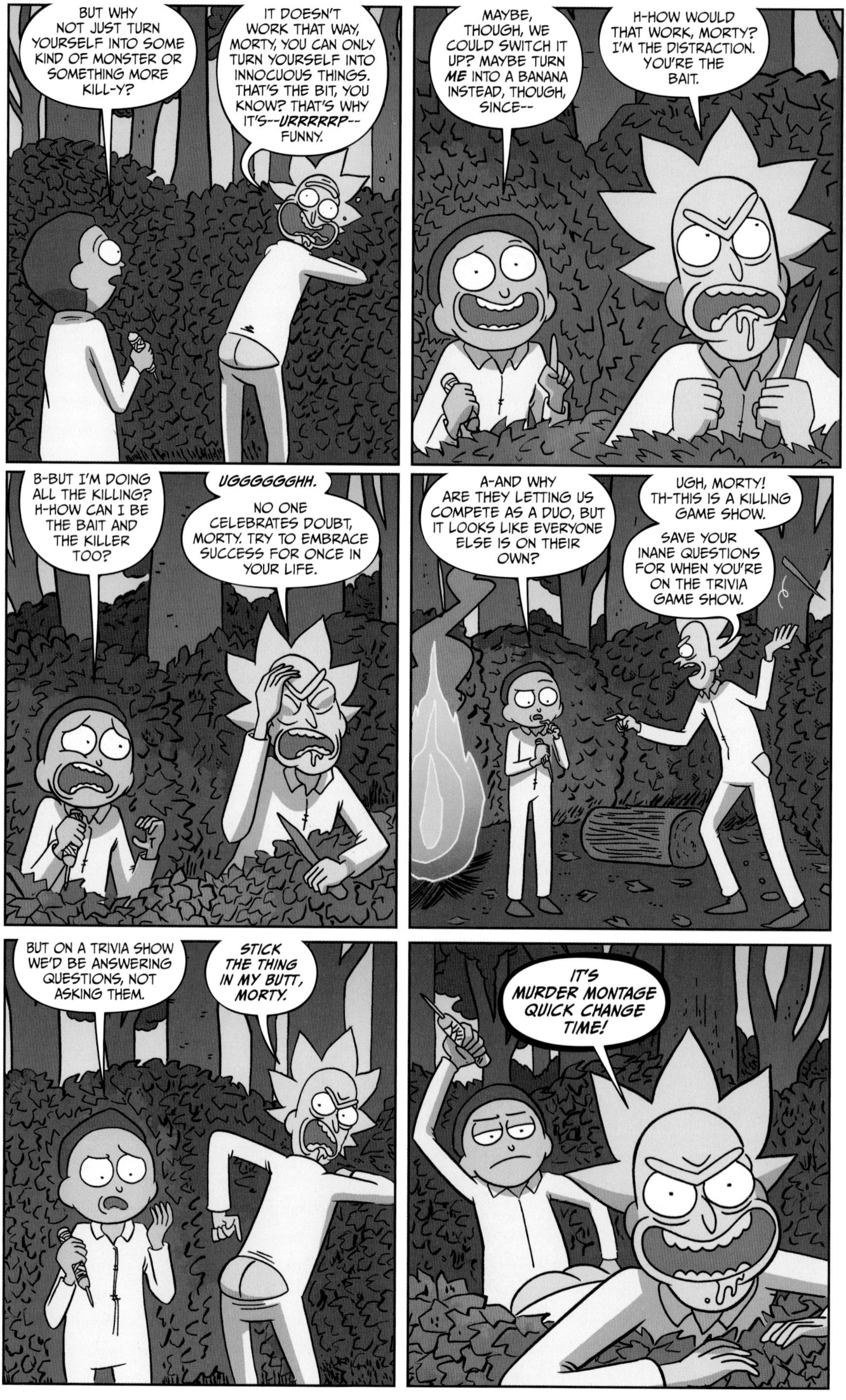
BUT WHY NOT JUST TURN YOURSELF INTO SOME KIND OF MONSTER OR SOMETHING MORE KILL-Y?
IT DOESN'T WORK THAT WAY, MORTY, YOU CAN ONLY TURN YOURSELF INTO INNOCUOUS THINGS. THAT'S THE BIT, YOU KNOW? THAT'S WHY IT'S--URRRRRP--FUNNY.
MAYBE, THOUGH, WE COULD SWITCH IT UP? MAYBE TURN ME INTO A BANANA INSTEAD, THOUGH, SINCE--
H-HOW WOULD THAT WORK, MORTY? I'M THE DISTRACTION. YOU'RE THE BAIT.
B-BUT I'M DOING ALL THE KILLING? H-HOW CAN I BE THE BAIT AND THE KILLER TOO?
UGGGGGGHH.
NO ONE CELEBRATES DOUBT, MORTY. TRY TO EMBRACE SUCCESS FOR ONCE IN YOUR LIFE.
A-AND WHY ARE THEY LETTING US COMPETE AS A DUO, BUT IT LOOKS LIKE EVERYONE ELSE IS ON THEIR OWN?
UGH, MORTY! TH-THIS IS A KILLING GAME SHOW.
SAVE YOUR INANE QUESTIONS FOR WHEN YOU'RE ON THE TRIVIA GAME SHOW.
BUT ON A TRIVIA SHOW WE'D BE ANSWERING QUESTIONS, NOT ASKING THEM.
STICK THE THING IN MY BUTT, MORTY.
IT'S MURDER MONTAGE QUICK CHANGE TIME!

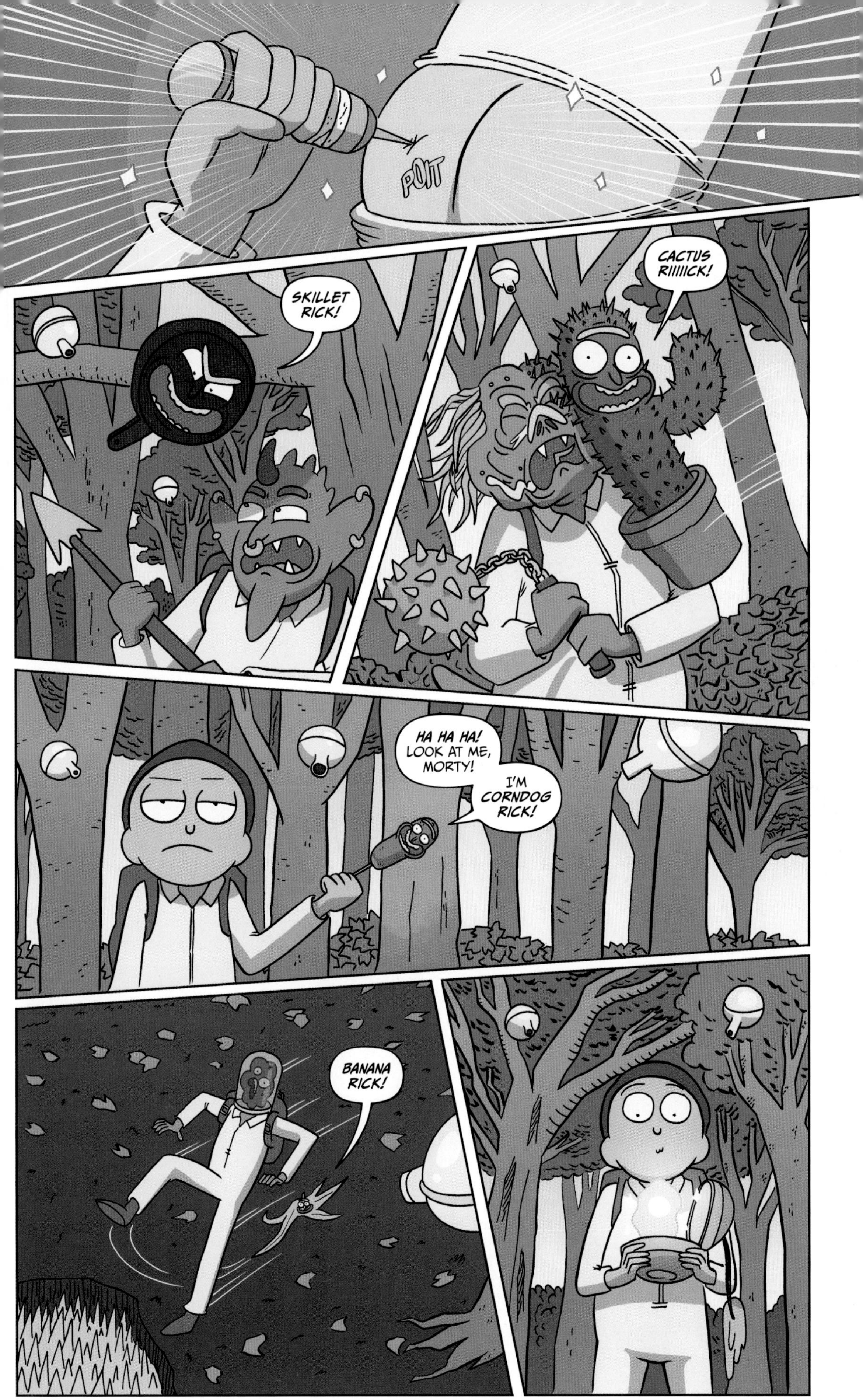
POIT
SKILLET RICK!
CACTUS RIIIIICK!
HA HA HA! LOOK AT ME, MORTY!
I'M CORNDOG RICK!
BANANA RICK!

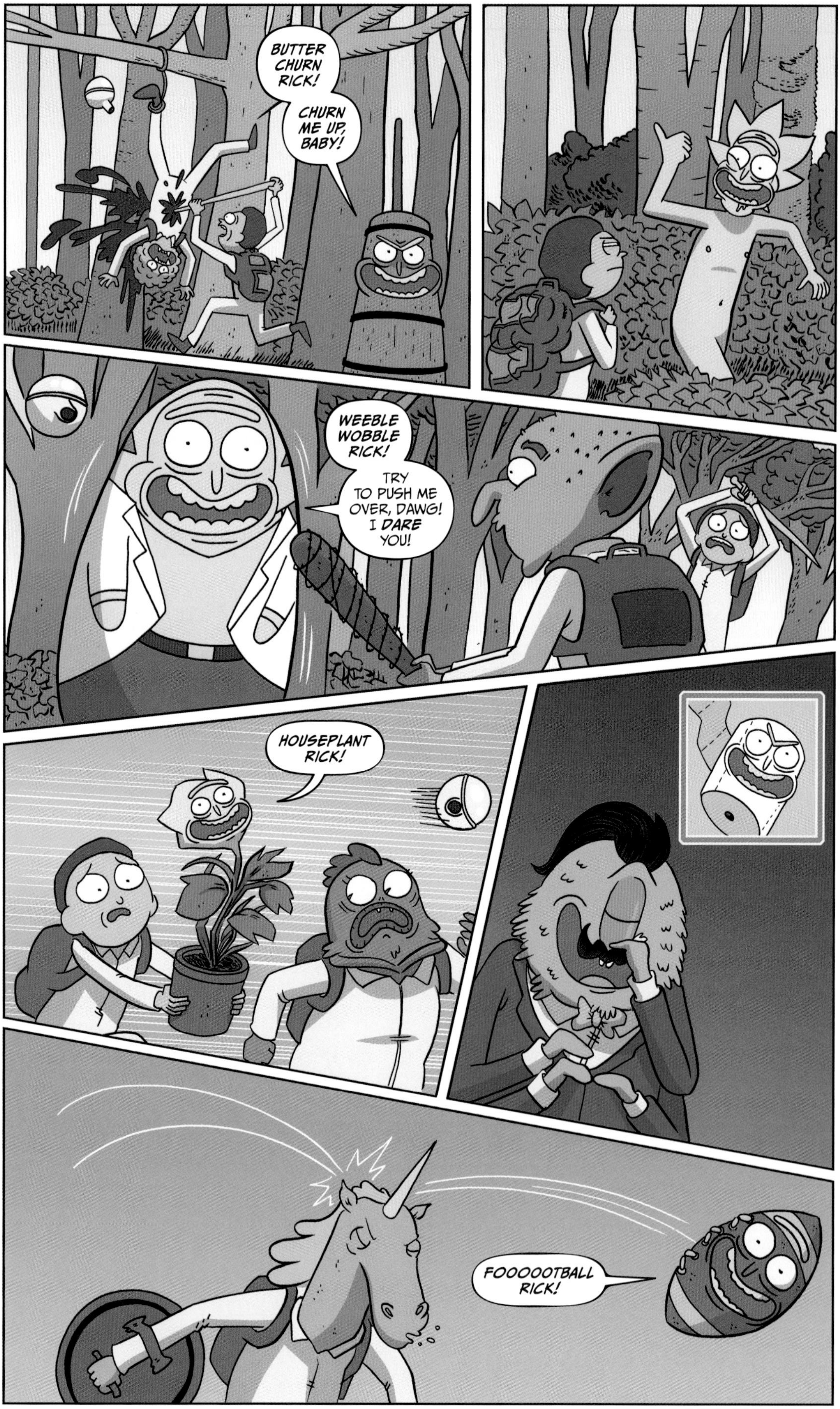

BUTTER CHURN RICK!
CHURN ME UP, BABY!
WEEBLE WOBBLE RICK!
TRY TO PUSH ME OVER, DAWG! I DARE YOU!
HOUSEPLANT RICK!
FOOOOOTBALL RICK!

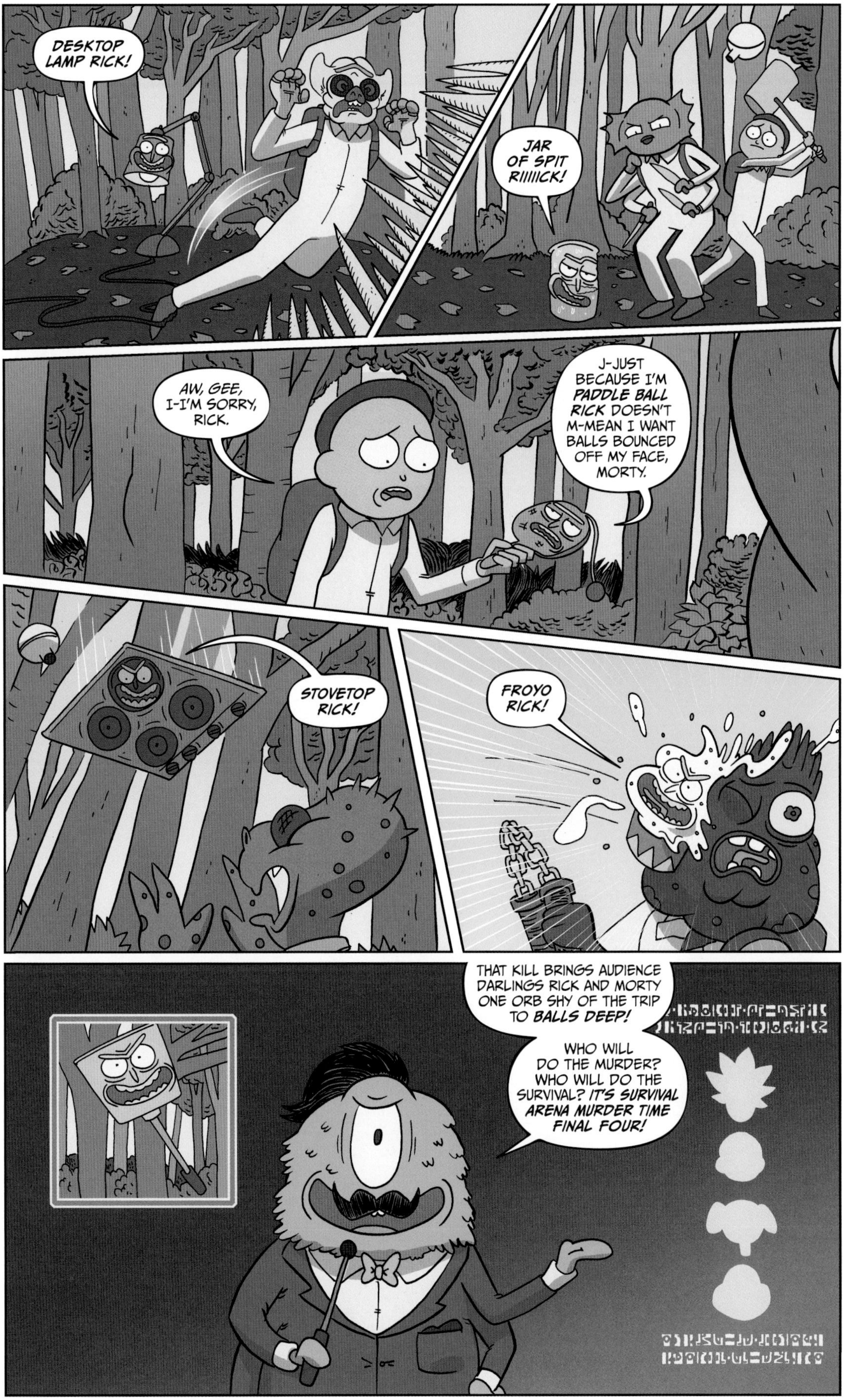
DESKTOP LAMP RICK!
JAR OF SPIT RIIIICK!
AW, GEE, I-I'M SORRY, RICK.
J-JUST BECAUSE I'M **PADDLE BALL RICK** DOESN'T M-MEAN I WANT BALLS BOUNCED OFF MY FACE, MORTY.
STOVETOP RICK!
FROYO RICK!
THAT KILL BRINGS AUDIENCE DARLINGS RICK AND MORTY ONE ORB SHY OF THE TRIP TO **BALLS DEEP!**
WHO WILL DO THE MURDER? WHO WILL DO THE SURVIVAL? ***IT'S SURVIVAL ARENA MURDER TIME FINAL FOUR!***

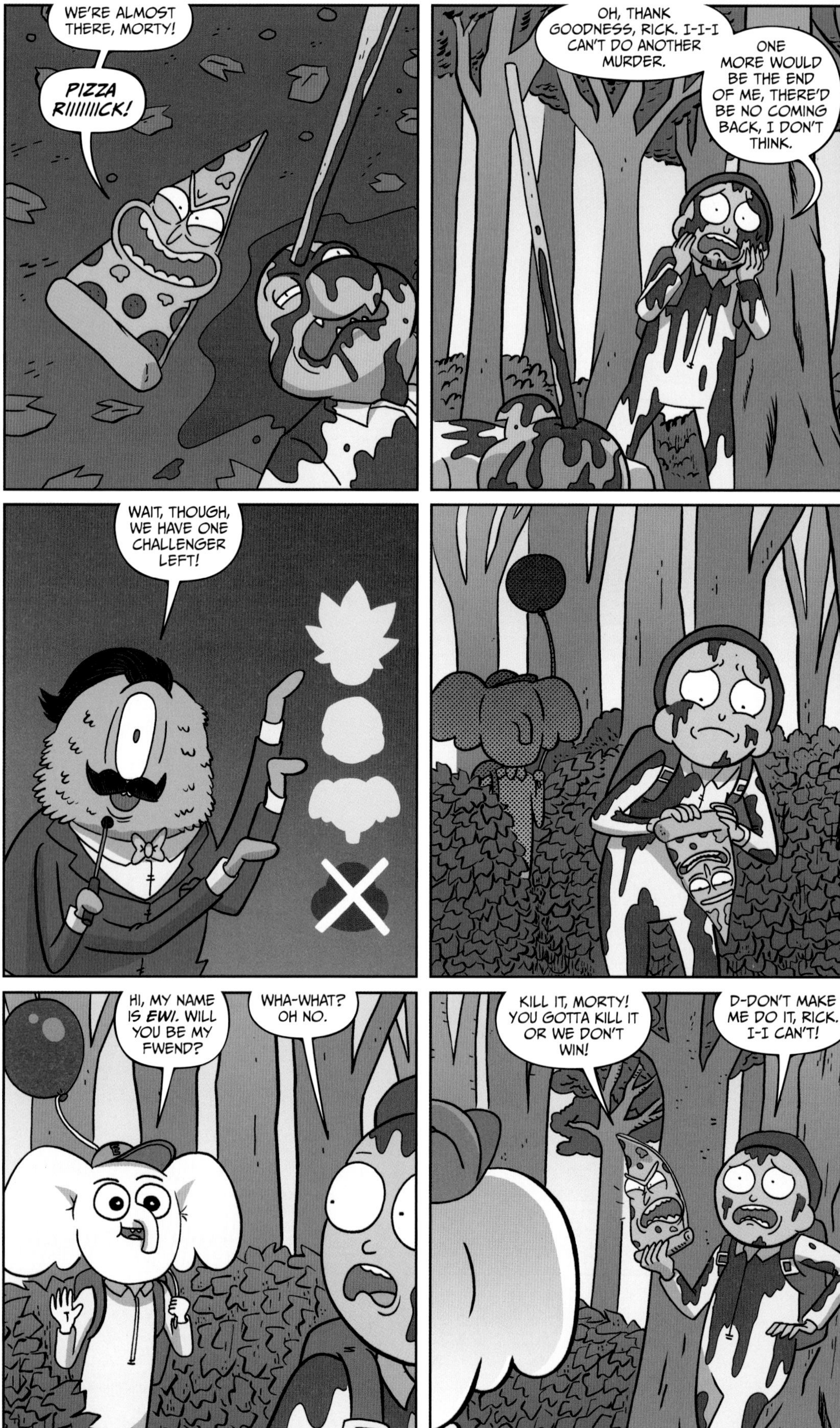
WE'RE ALMOST THERE, MORTY!
PIZZA RIIIIIICK!
OH, THANK GOODNESS, RICK. I-I-I CAN'T DO ANOTHER MURDER.
ONE MORE WOULD BE THE END OF ME, THERE'D BE NO COMING BACK, I DON'T THINK.
WAIT, THOUGH, WE HAVE ONE CHALLENGER LEFT!
HI, MY NAME IS EWI. WILL YOU BE MY FWEND?
WHA-WHAT? OH NO.
KILL IT, MORTY! YOU GOTTA KILL IT OR WE DON'T WIN!
D-DON'T MAKE ME DO IT, RICK. I-I CAN'T!

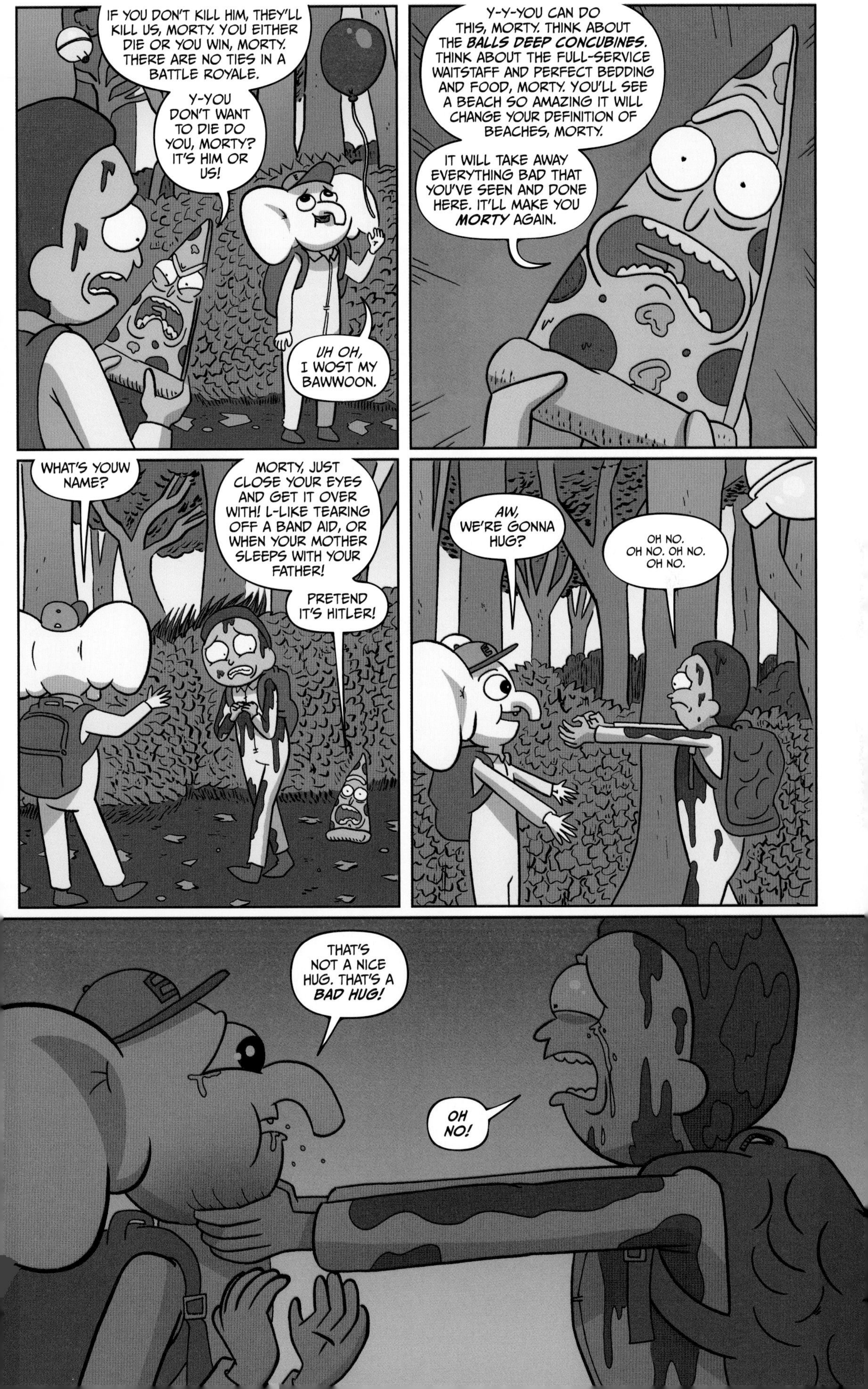
IF YOU DON'T KILL HIM, THEY'LL KILL US, MORTY. YOU EITHER DIE OR YOU WIN, MORTY. THERE ARE NO TIES IN A BATTLE ROYALE.
Y-YOU DON'T WANT TO DIE DO YOU, MORTY? IT'S HIM OR US!
UH OH, I WOST MY BAWWOON.
Y-Y-YOU CAN DO THIS, MORTY. THINK ABOUT THE BALLS DEEP CONCUBINES. THINK ABOUT THE FULL-SERVICE WAITSTAFF AND PERFECT BEDDING AND FOOD, MORTY. YOU'LL SEE A BEACH SO AMAZING IT WILL CHANGE YOUR DEFINITION OF BEACHES, MORTY.
IT WILL TAKE AWAY EVERYTHING BAD THAT YOU'VE SEEN AND DONE HERE. IT'LL MAKE YOU MORTY AGAIN.
WHAT'S YOUW NAME?
MORTY, JUST CLOSE YOUR EYES AND GET IT OVER WITH! L-LIKE TEARING OFF A BAND AID, OR WHEN YOUR MOTHER SLEEPS WITH YOUR FATHER!
PRETEND IT'S HITLER!
AW, WE'RE GONNA HUG?
OH NO. OH NO. OH NO. OH NO.
THAT'S NOT A NICE HUG. THAT'S A BAD HUG!
OH NO!

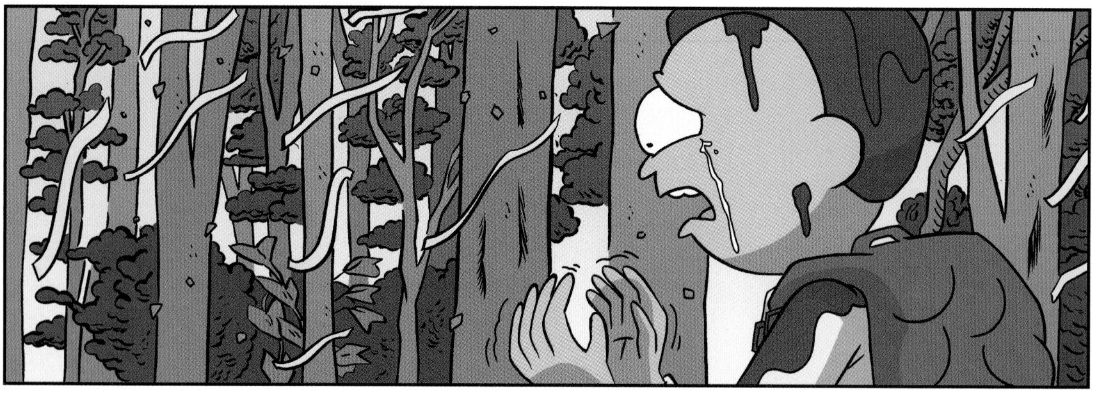

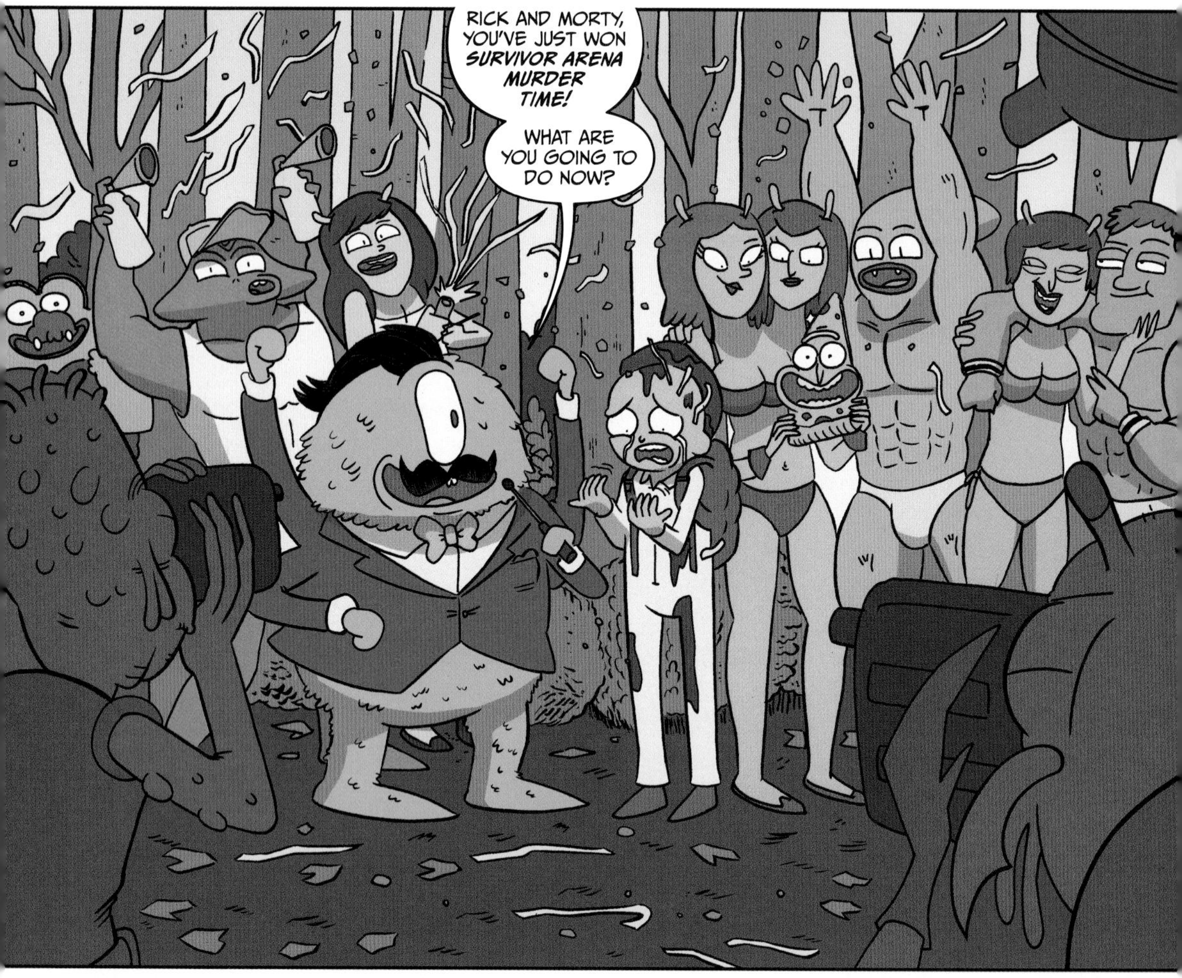
RICK AND MORTY, YOU'VE JUST WON *SURVIVOR ARENA MURDER TIME!*
WHAT ARE YOU GOING TO DO NOW?

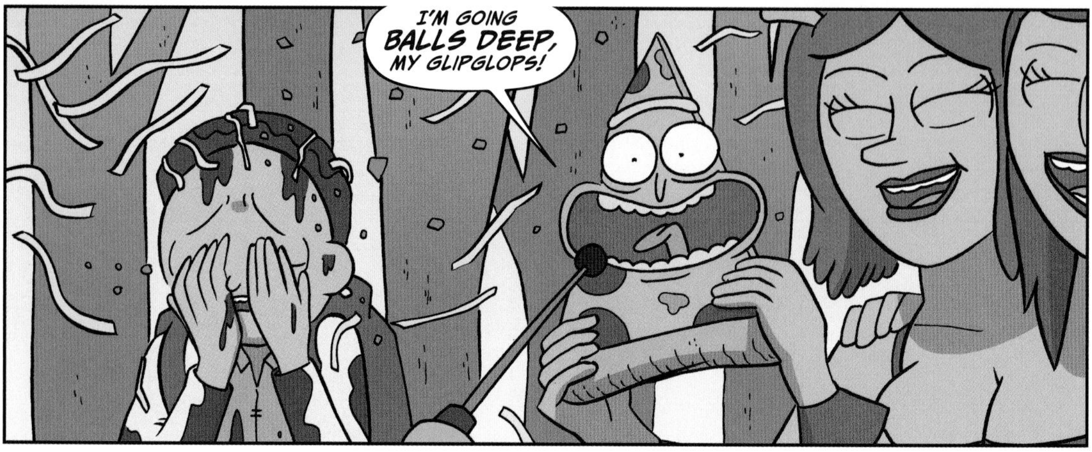
I'M GOING ***BALLS DEEP,*** *MY GLIPGLOPS!*

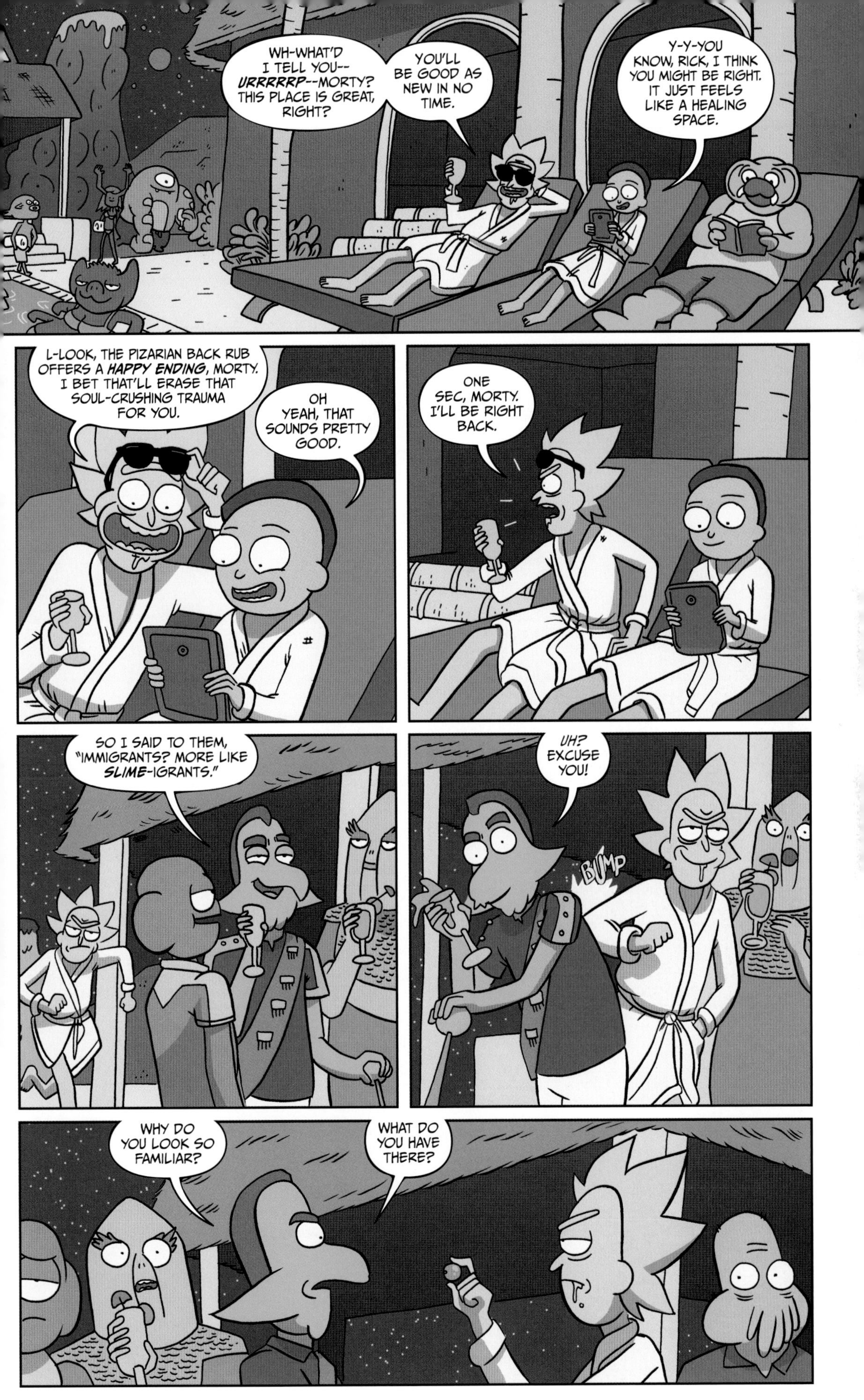
WH-WHAT'D I TELL YOU-- URRRRRP--MORTY? THIS PLACE IS GREAT, RIGHT?
YOU'LL BE GOOD AS NEW IN NO TIME.
Y-Y-YOU KNOW, RICK, I THINK YOU MIGHT BE RIGHT. IT JUST FEELS LIKE A HEALING SPACE.
L-LOOK, THE PIZARIAN BACK RUB OFFERS A *HAPPY ENDING*, MORTY. I BET THAT'LL ERASE THAT SOUL-CRUSHING TRAUMA FOR YOU.
OH YEAH, THAT SOUNDS PRETTY GOOD.
ONE SEC, MORTY. I'LL BE RIGHT BACK.
SO I SAID TO THEM, "IMMIGRANTS? MORE LIKE *SLIME*-IGRANTS."
UH? EXCUSE YOU!
BUMP
WHY DO YOU LOOK SO FAMILIAR?
WHAT DO YOU HAVE THERE?

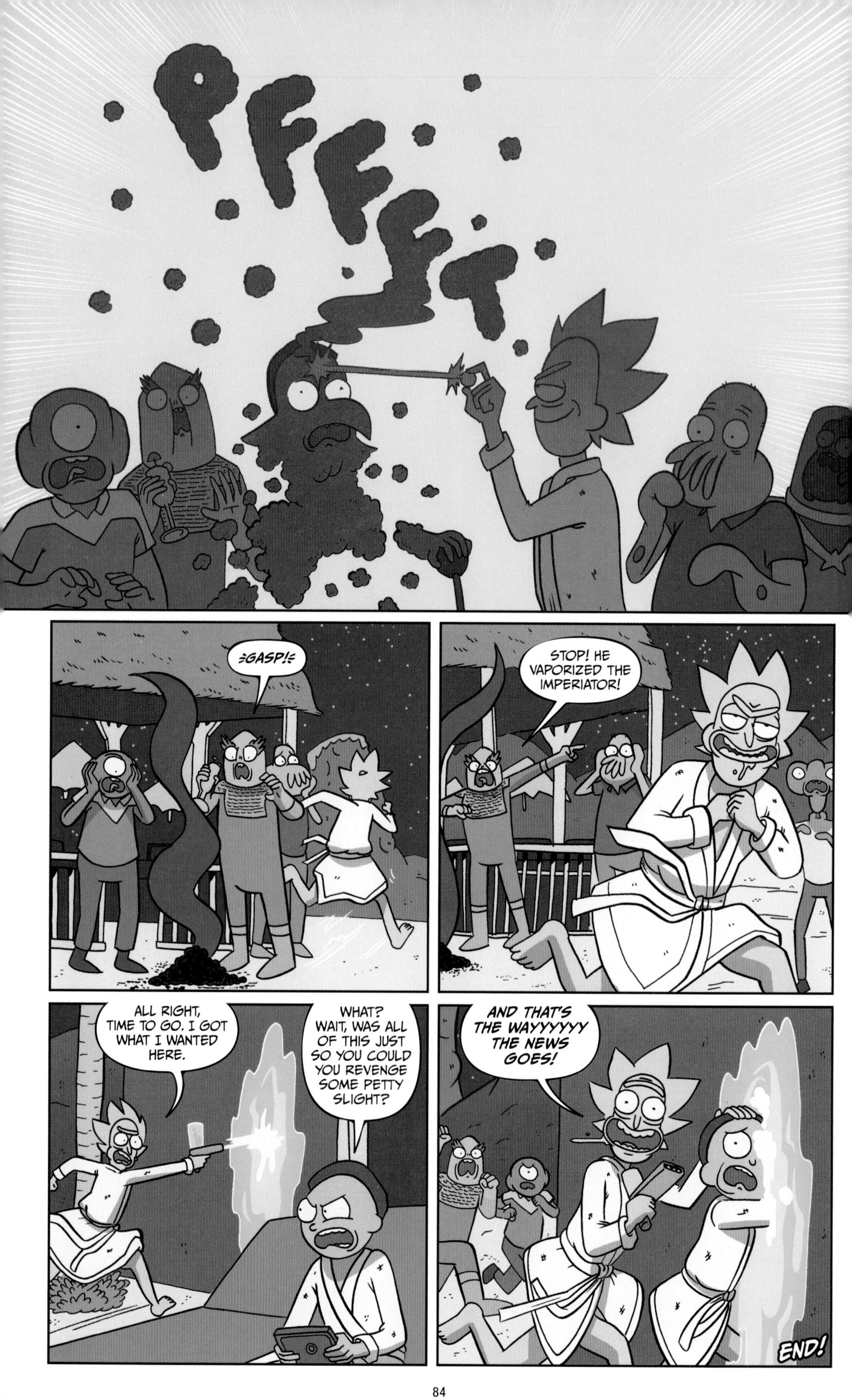
PFFFT
GASP!
STOP! HE VAPORIZED THE IMPERIATOR!
ALL RIGHT, TIME TO GO. I GOT WHAT I WANTED HERE.
WHAT? WAIT, WAS ALL OF THIS JUST SO YOU COULD YOU REVENGE SOME PETTY SLIGHT?
AND THAT'S THE WAYYYYYY THE NEWS GOES!
END!

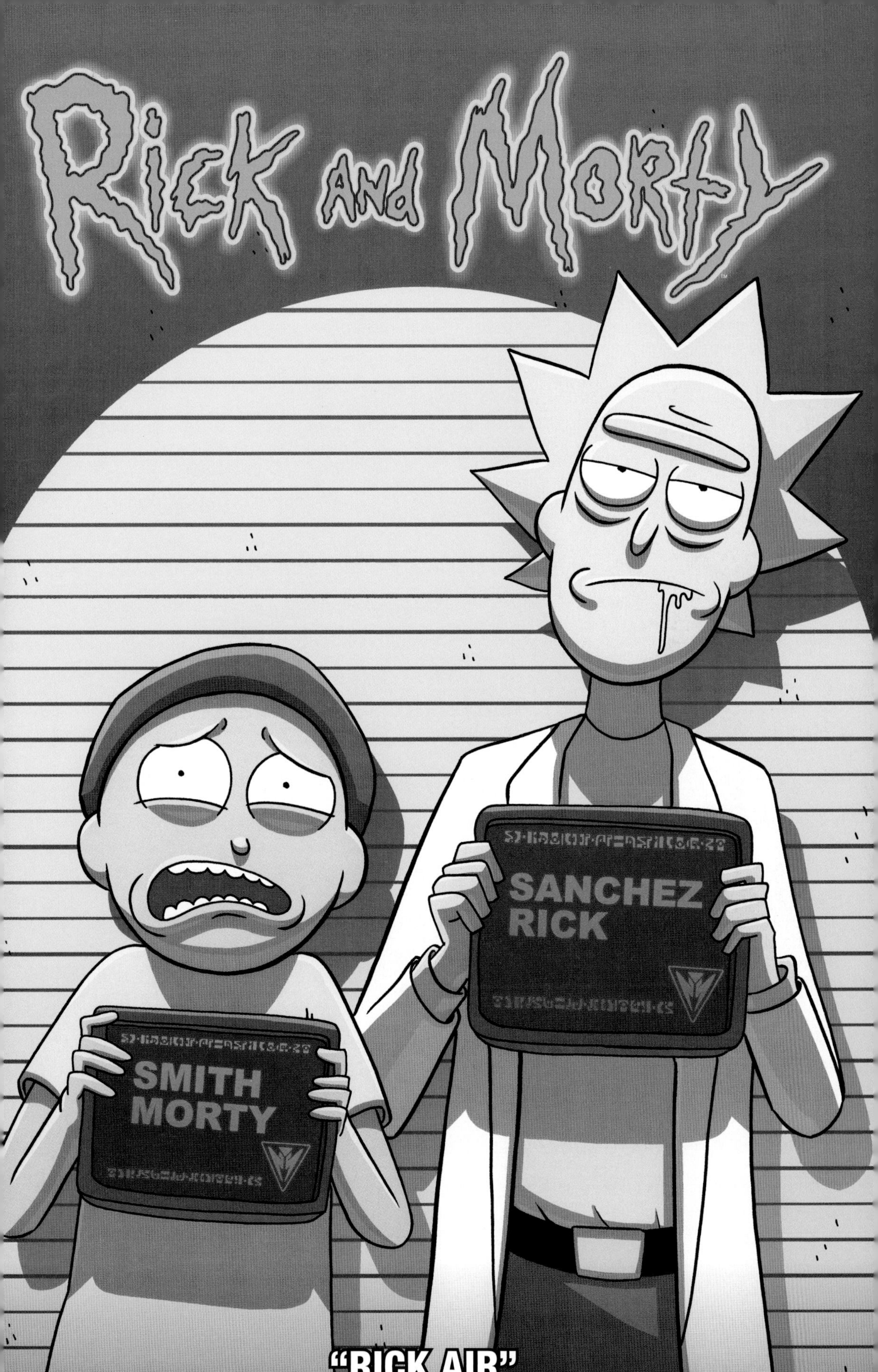
Rick and Morty
SANCHEZ
RICK
SMITH
MORTY

"RICK AIR"

WRITTEN BY **KYLE STARKS** ILLUSTRATED BY **KATY FARINA** COLORED BY **RIAN SYGH** LETTERED BY **CRANK!**

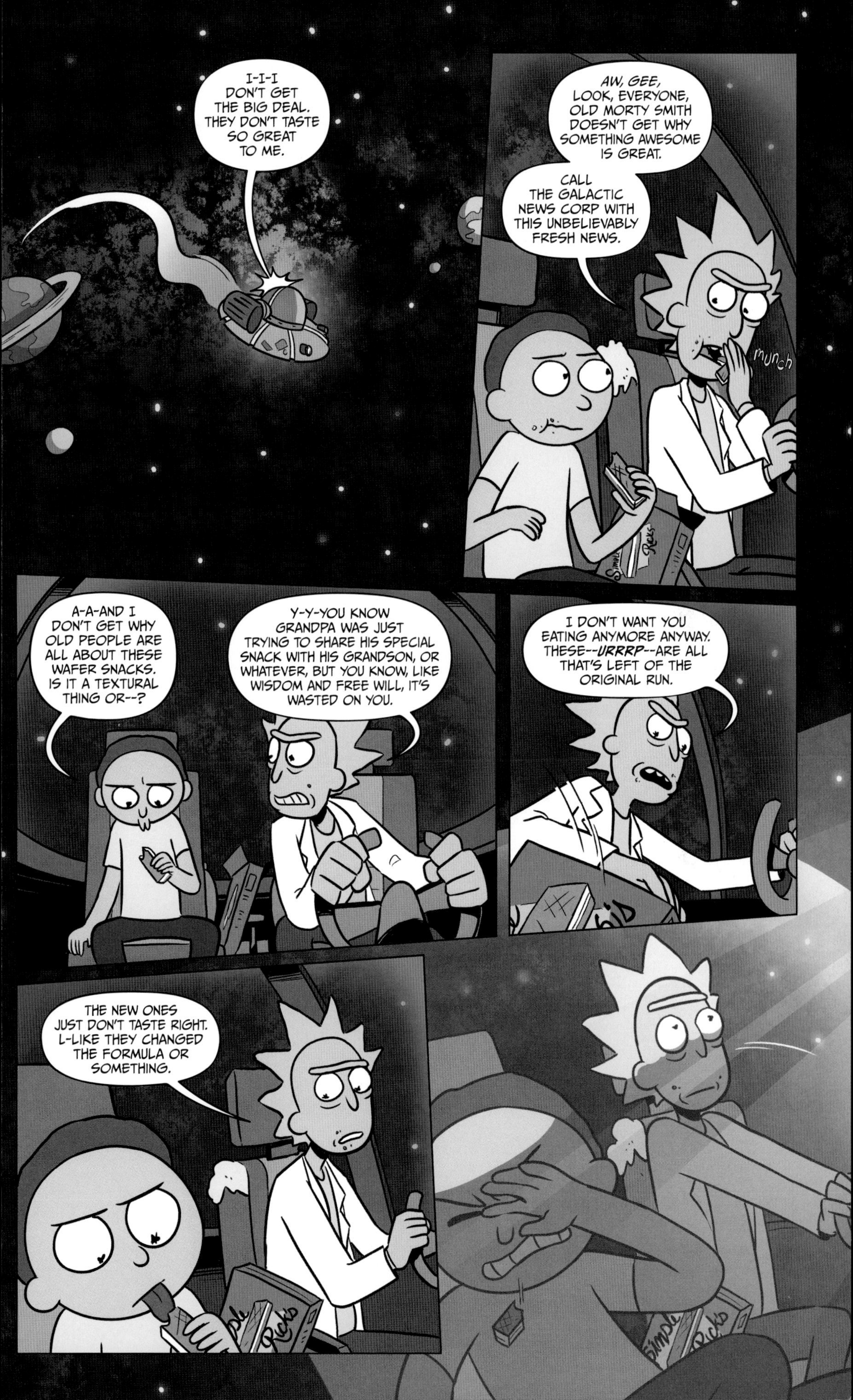
I-I-I DON'T GET THE BIG DEAL. THEY DON'T TASTE SO GREAT TO ME.
AW, GEE, LOOK, EVERYONE, OLD MORTY SMITH DOESN'T GET WHY SOMETHING AWESOME IS GREAT.
CALL THE GALACTIC NEWS CORP WITH THIS UNBELIEVABLY FRESH NEWS.
munch
A-A-AND I DON'T GET WHY OLD PEOPLE ARE ALL ABOUT THESE WAFER SNACKS. IS IT A TEXTURAL THING OR--?
Y-Y-YOU KNOW GRANDPA WAS JUST TRYING TO SHARE HIS SPECIAL SNACK WITH HIS GRANDSON, OR WHATEVER, BUT YOU KNOW, LIKE WISDOM AND FREE WILL, IT'S WASTED ON YOU.
I DON'T WANT YOU EATING ANYMORE ANYWAY. THESE--URRRP--ARE ALL THAT'S LEFT OF THE ORIGINAL RUN.
THE NEW ONES JUST DON'T TASTE RIGHT. L-LIKE THEY CHANGED THE FORMULA OR SOMETHING.
Simple Ricks

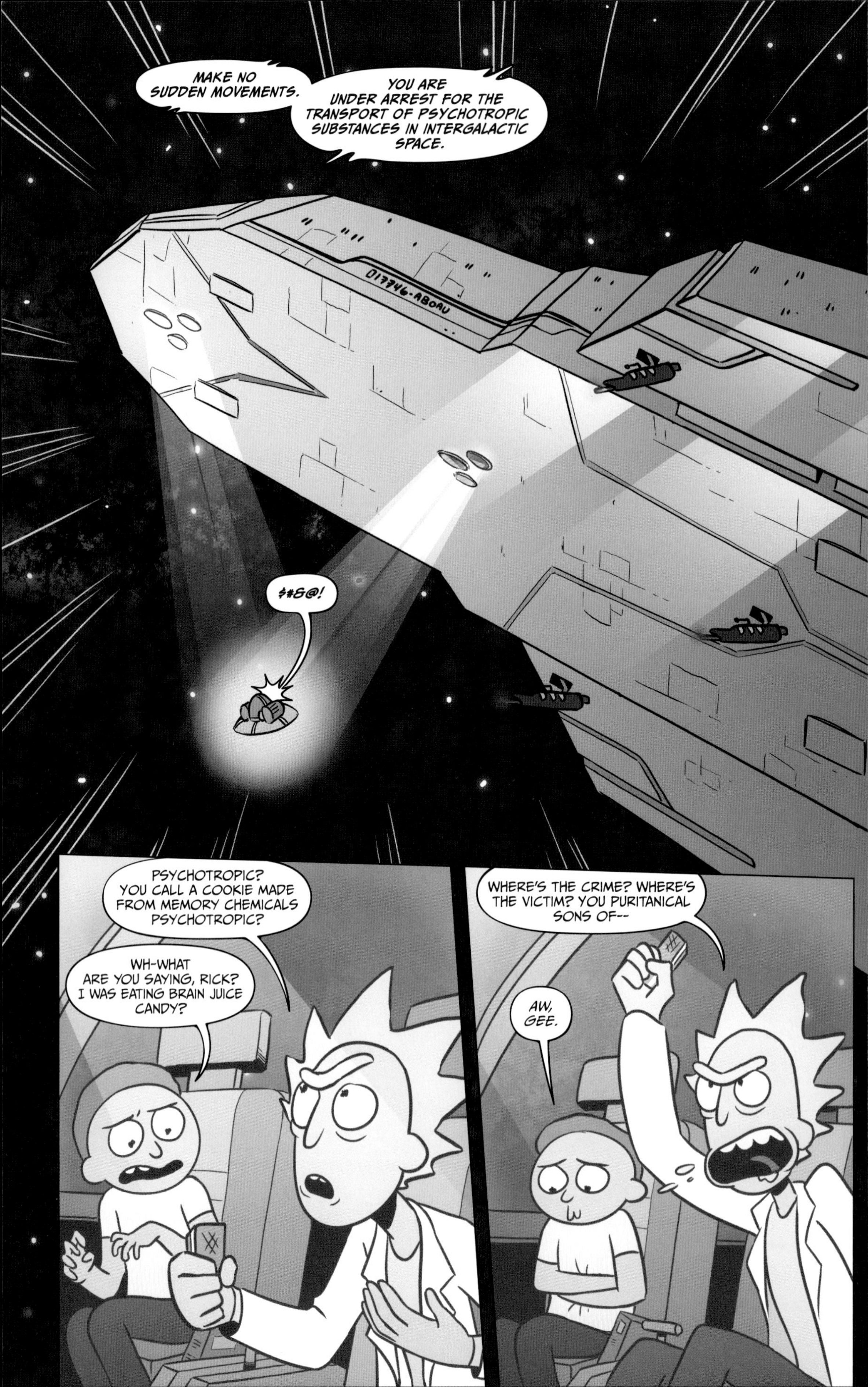
MAKE NO SUDDEN MOVEMENTS.
YOU ARE UNDER ARREST FOR THE TRANSPORT OF PSYCHOTROPIC SUBSTANCES IN INTERGALACTIC SPACE.
017746-ABOAU
$#&@!
PSYCHOTROPIC? YOU CALL A COOKIE MADE FROM MEMORY CHEMICALS PSYCHOTROPIC?
WH-WHAT ARE YOU SAYING, RICK? I WAS EATING BRAIN JUICE CANDY?
WHERE'S THE CRIME? WHERE'S THE VICTIM? YOU PURITANICAL SONS OF--
AW, GEE.

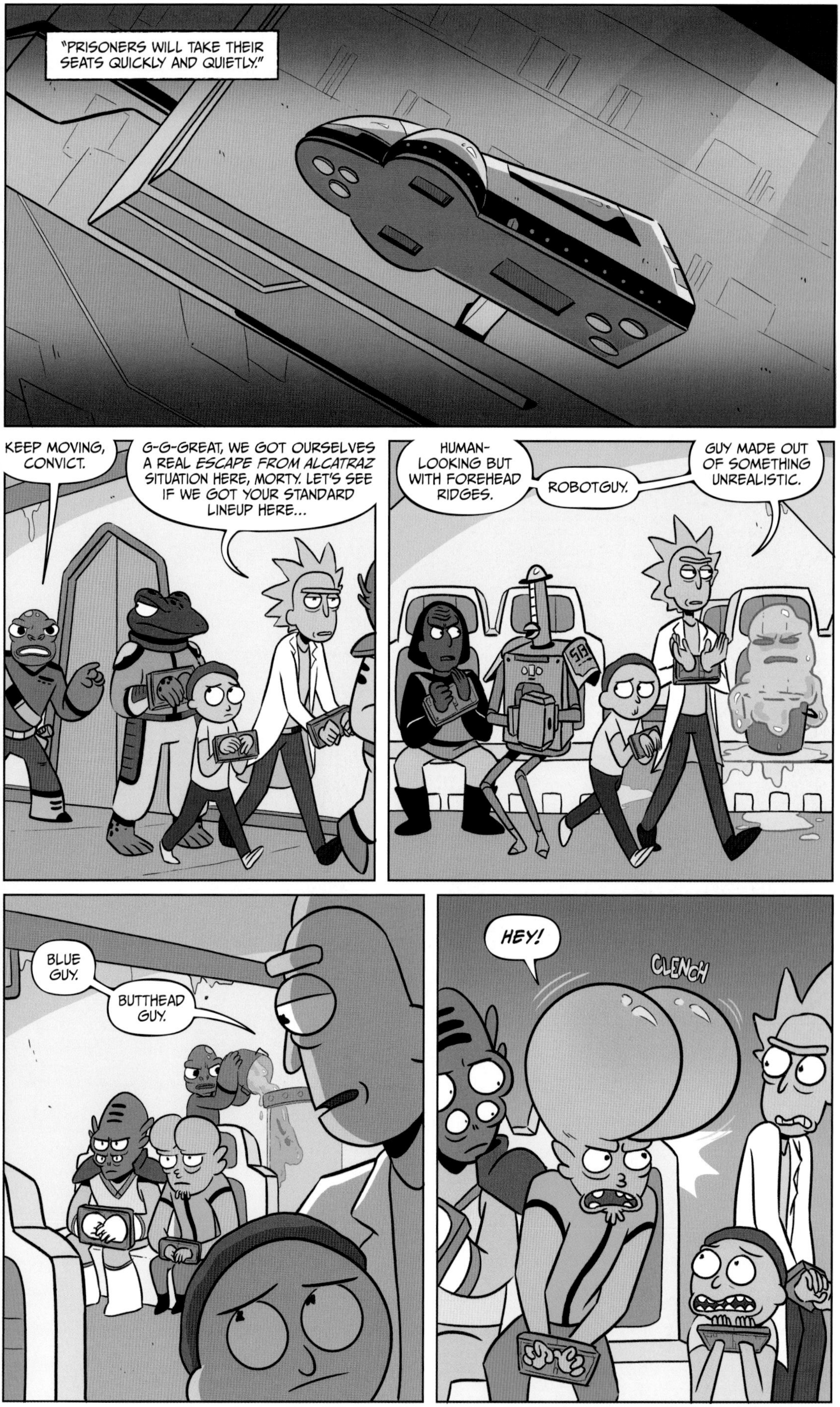
"PRISONERS WILL TAKE THEIR SEATS QUICKLY AND QUIETLY."
KEEP MOVING, CONVICT.
G-G-GREAT, WE GOT OURSELVES A REAL *ESCAPE FROM ALCATRAZ* SITUATION HERE, MORTY. LET'S SEE IF WE GOT YOUR STANDARD LINEUP HERE...
HUMAN-LOOKING BUT WITH FOREHEAD RIDGES.
ROBOTGUY.
GUY MADE OUT OF SOMETHING UNREALISTIC.
BLUE GUY.
BUTTHEAD GUY.
HEY!
CLENCH

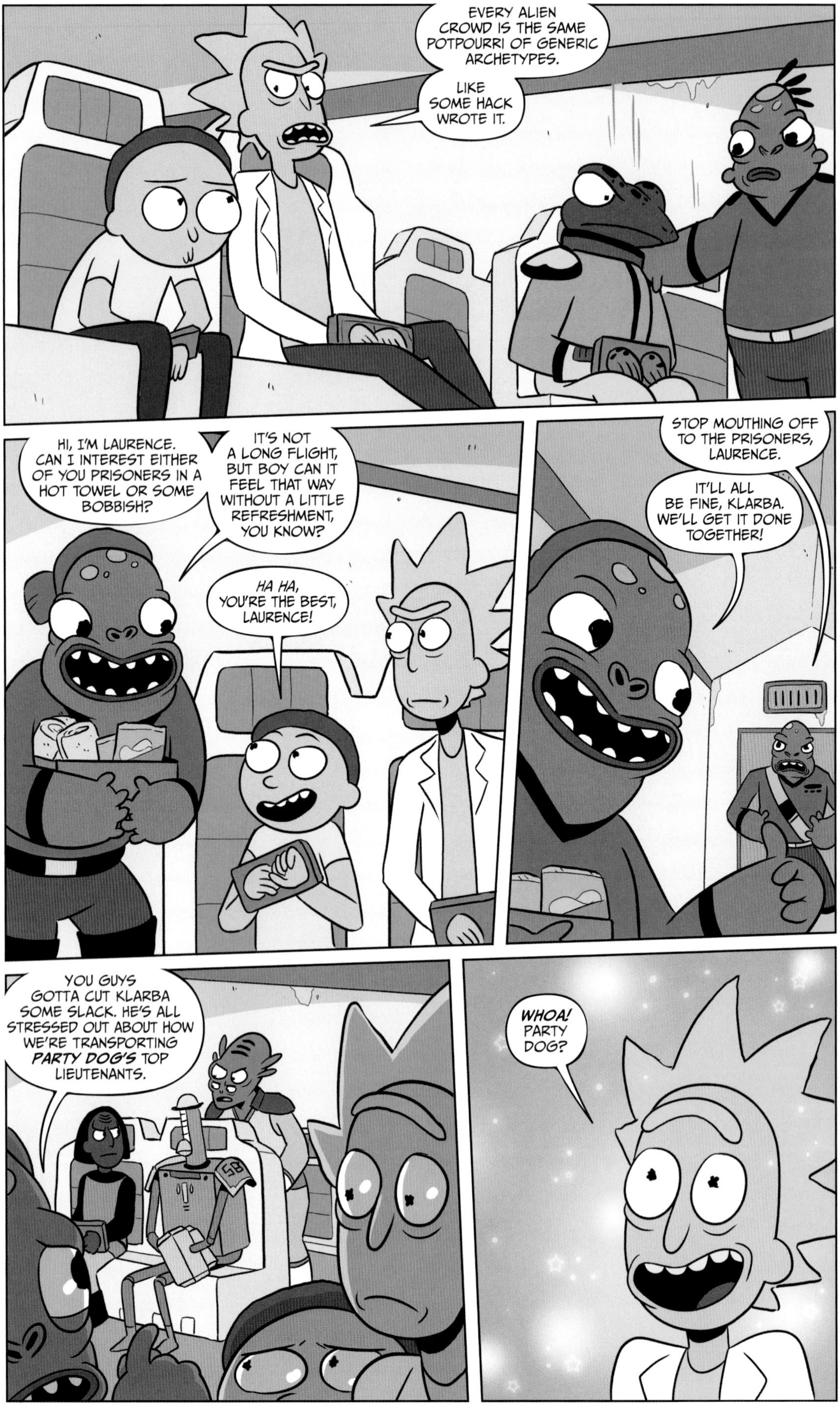

EVERY ALIEN CROWD IS THE SAME POTPOURRI OF GENERIC ARCHETYPES.
LIKE SOME HACK WROTE IT.
HI, I'M LAURENCE. CAN I INTEREST EITHER OF YOU PRISONERS IN A HOT TOWEL OR SOME BOBBISH?
IT'S NOT A LONG FLIGHT, BUT BOY CAN IT FEEL THAT WAY WITHOUT A LITTLE REFRESHMENT, YOU KNOW?
HA HA, YOU'RE THE BEST, LAURENCE!
STOP MOUTHING OFF TO THE PRISONERS, LAURENCE.
IT'LL ALL BE FINE, KLARBA. WE'LL GET IT DONE TOGETHER!
YOU GUYS GOTTA CUT KLARBA SOME SLACK. HE'S ALL STRESSED OUT ABOUT HOW WE'RE TRANSPORTING ***PARTY DOG'S*** TOP LIEUTENANTS.
WHOA! PARTY DOG?

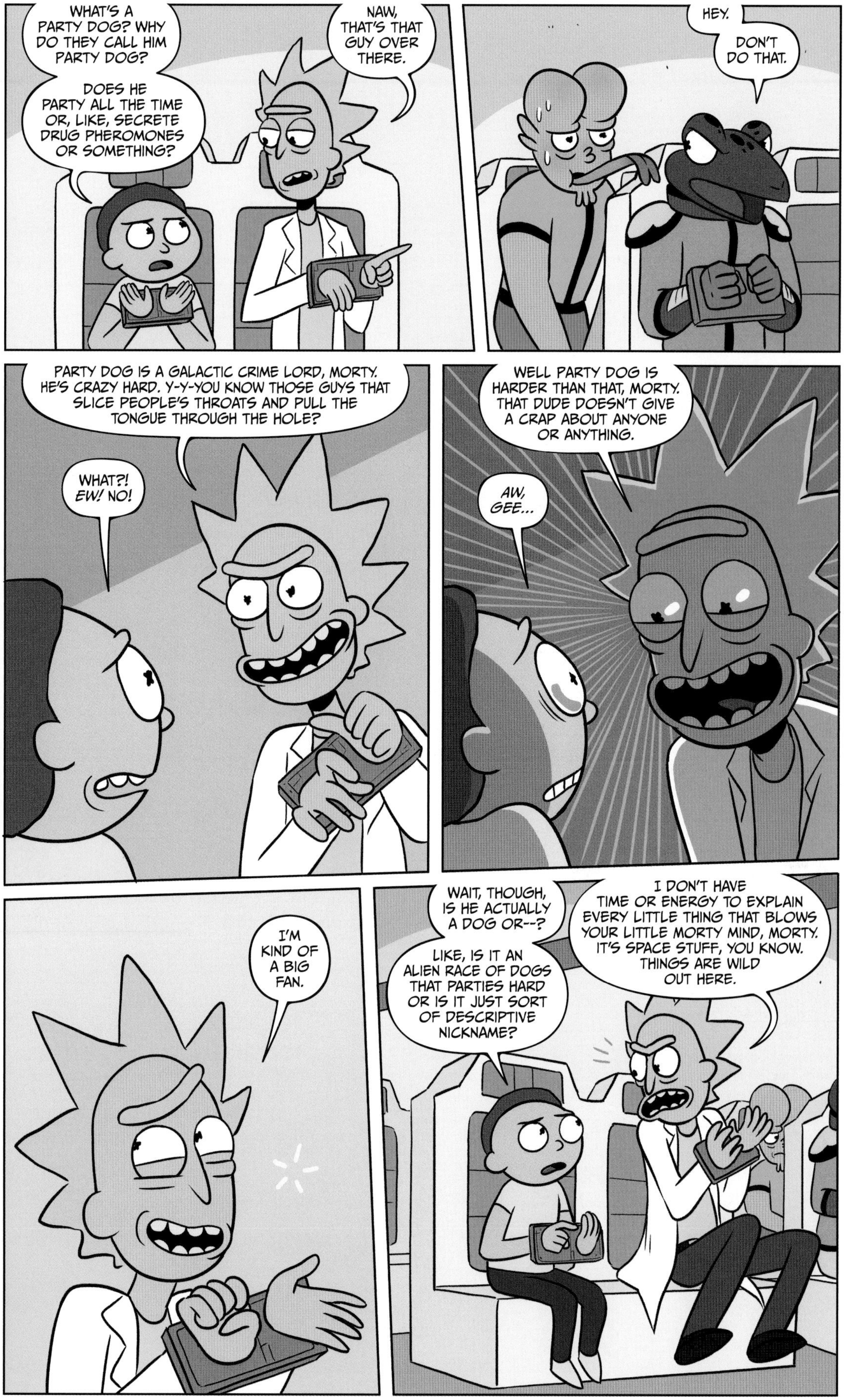
WHAT'S A PARTY DOG? WHY DO THEY CALL HIM PARTY DOG?
DOES HE PARTY ALL THE TIME OR, LIKE, SECRETE DRUG PHEROMONES OR SOMETHING?
NAW, THAT'S THAT GUY OVER THERE.
HEY.
DON'T DO THAT.
PARTY DOG IS A GALACTIC CRIME LORD, MORTY. HE'S CRAZY HARD. Y-Y-YOU KNOW THOSE GUYS THAT SLICE PEOPLE'S THROATS AND PULL THE TONGUE THROUGH THE HOLE?
WHAT?! EW! NO!
WELL PARTY DOG IS HARDER THAN THAT, MORTY. THAT DUDE DOESN'T GIVE A CRAP ABOUT ANYONE OR ANYTHING.
AW, GEE...
I'M KIND OF A BIG FAN.
WAIT, THOUGH, IS HE ACTUALLY A DOG OR--?
LIKE, IS IT AN ALIEN RACE OF DOGS THAT PARTIES HARD OR IS IT JUST SORT OF DESCRIPTIVE NICKNAME?
I DON'T HAVE TIME OR ENERGY TO EXPLAIN EVERY LITTLE THING THAT BLOWS YOUR LITTLE MORTY MIND, MORTY. IT'S SPACE STUFF, YOU KNOW. THINGS ARE WILD OUT HERE.

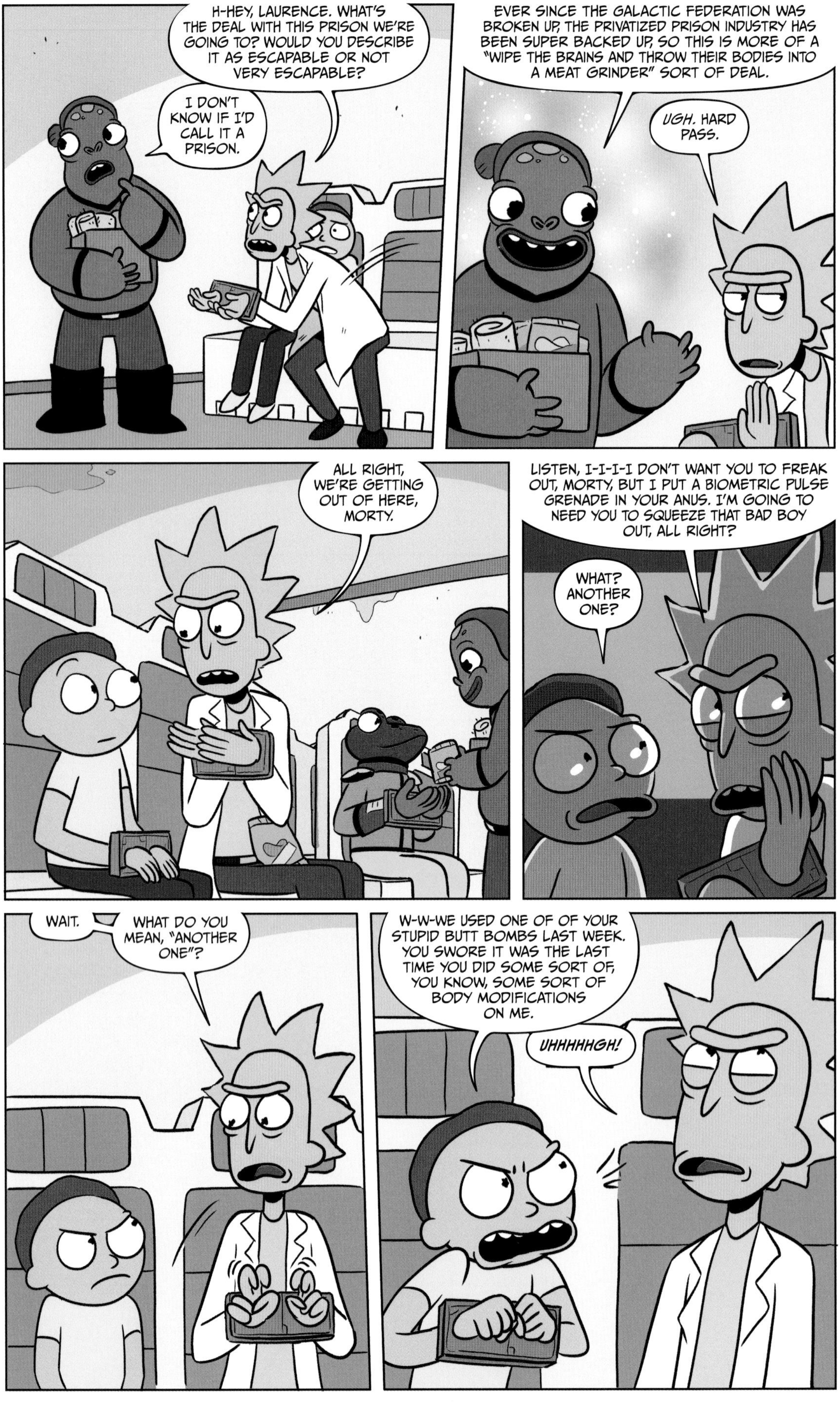
H-HEY, LAURENCE. WHAT'S THE DEAL WITH THIS PRISON WE'RE GOING TO? WOULD YOU DESCRIBE IT AS ESCAPABLE OR NOT VERY ESCAPABLE?
I DON'T KNOW IF I'D CALL IT A PRISON.
EVER SINCE THE GALACTIC FEDERATION WAS BROKEN UP, THE PRIVATIZED PRISON INDUSTRY HAS BEEN SUPER BACKED UP, SO THIS IS MORE OF A "WIPE THE BRAINS AND THROW THEIR BODIES INTO A MEAT GRINDER" SORT OF DEAL.
UGH. HARD PASS.
ALL RIGHT, WE'RE GETTING OUT OF HERE, MORTY.
LISTEN, I-I-I-I DON'T WANT YOU TO FREAK OUT, MORTY, BUT I PUT A BIOMETRIC PULSE GRENADE IN YOUR ANUS. I'M GOING TO NEED YOU TO SQUEEZE THAT BAD BOY OUT, ALL RIGHT?
WHAT? ANOTHER ONE?
WAIT.
WHAT DO YOU MEAN, "ANOTHER ONE"?
W-W-WE USED ONE OF OF YOUR STUPID BUTT BOMBS LAST WEEK. YOU SWORE IT WAS THE LAST TIME YOU DID SOME SORT OF, YOU KNOW, SOME SORT OF BODY MODIFICATIONS ON ME.
UHHHHHGH!

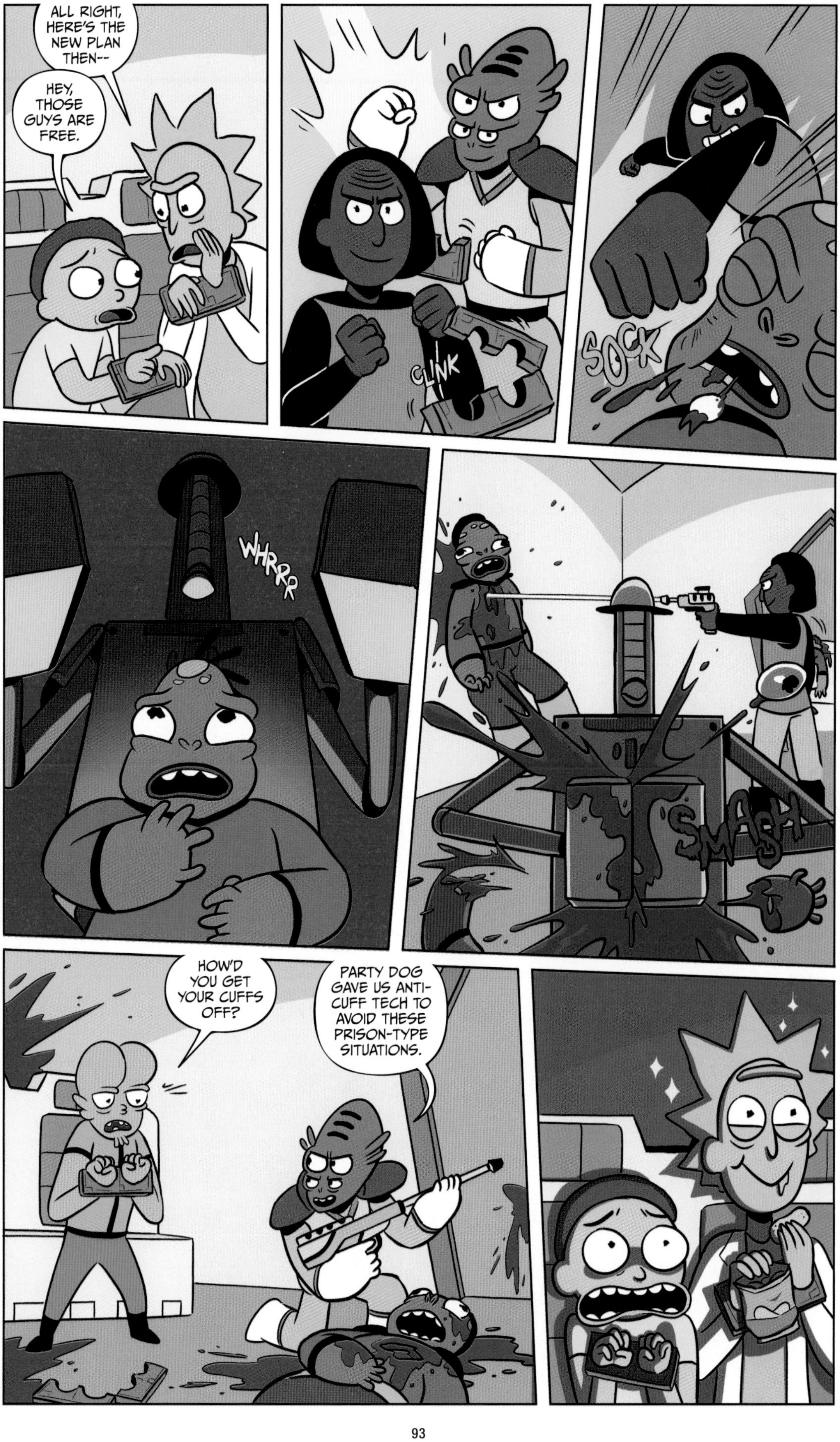
ALL RIGHT, HERE'S THE NEW PLAN THEN--
HEY, THOSE GUYS ARE FREE.
CLINK
SOCK
WHRRR
SMASH
HOW'D YOU GET YOUR CUFFS OFF?
PARTY DOG GAVE US ANTI-CUFF TECH TO AVOID THESE PRISON-TYPE SITUATIONS.

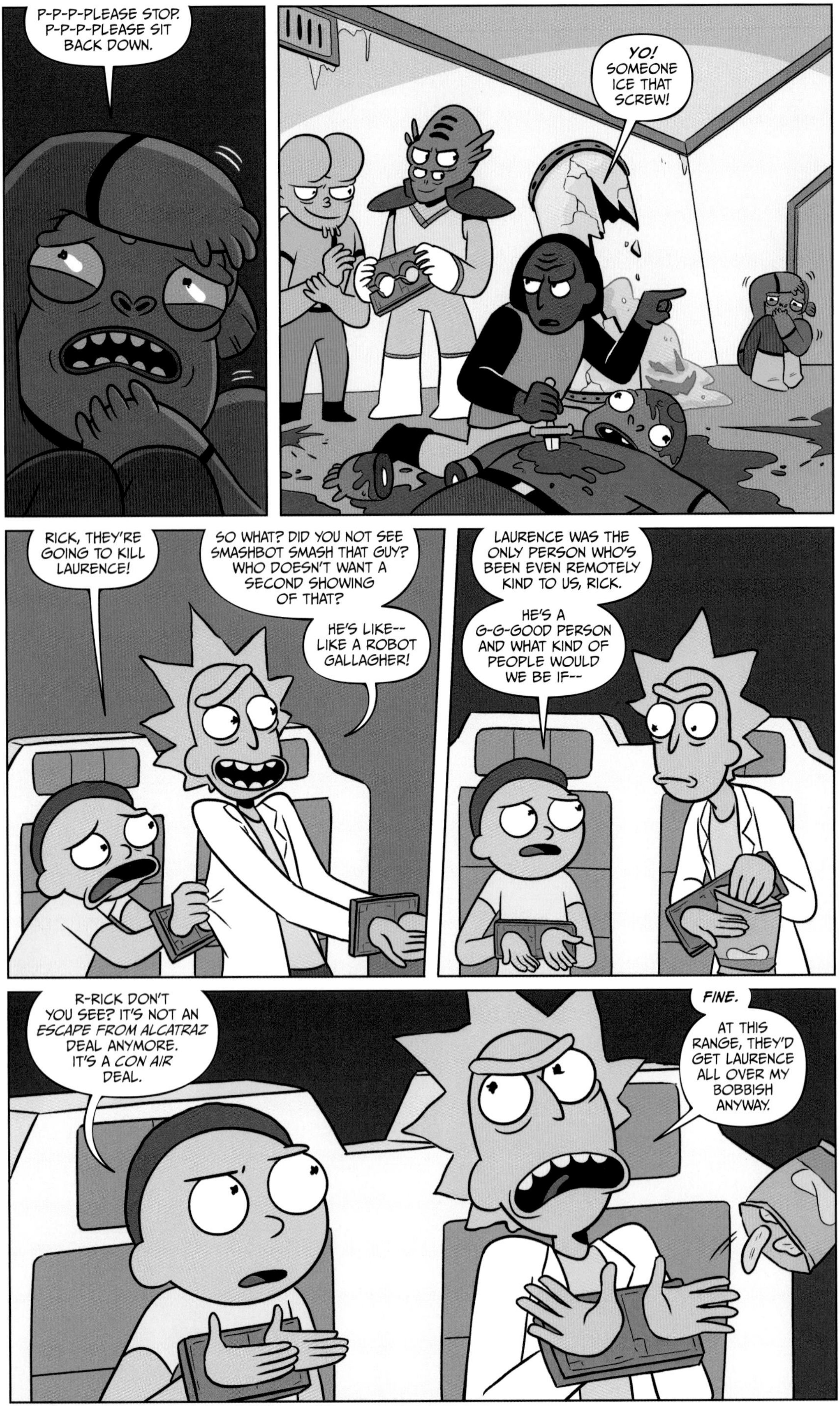

P-P-P-PLEASE STOP. P-P-P-PLEASE SIT BACK DOWN.
YO! SOMEONE ICE THAT SCREW!
RICK, THEY'RE GOING TO KILL LAURENCE!
SO WHAT? DID YOU NOT SEE SMASHBOT SMASH THAT GUY? WHO DOESN'T WANT A SECOND SHOWING OF THAT?
HE'S LIKE-- LIKE A ROBOT GALLAGHER!
LAURENCE WAS THE ONLY PERSON WHO'S BEEN EVEN REMOTELY KIND TO US, RICK.
HE'S A G-G-GOOD PERSON AND WHAT KIND OF PEOPLE WOULD WE BE IF--
R-RICK DON'T YOU SEE? IT'S NOT AN *ESCAPE FROM ALCATRAZ* DEAL ANYMORE. IT'S A *CON AIR* DEAL.
FINE.
AT THIS RANGE, THEY'D GET LAURENCE ALL OVER MY BOBBISH ANYWAY.

HOLD UP, FELLAS. YOU'RE GOING TO NEED TWO THINGS IF YOU WANT TO GET OUT OF THIS SITUATION.

A HOSTAGE TO KEEP ANY INEVITABLE AUTHORITIES OFF YOUR BUTT.

AND SINCE YOU KILLED ONE ALREADY, A PILOT.

UNLESS THAT THING CAN DO IT.

CAN YOU FLY THIS THING?

WHY IS EVERYONE LOOKING AT ME? WHY WOULD I BE ABLE TO PILOT ANYTHING?

BECAUSE-- YOU KNOW? YOU'RE, LIKE, A COMPUTER, RIGHT? CAN'T YOU HACK INTO IT?

THAT'S RACIST.

YOU KNOW ALL I CAN DO IS SMASH.

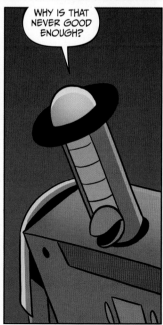

WHY IS THAT NEVER GOOD ENOUGH?

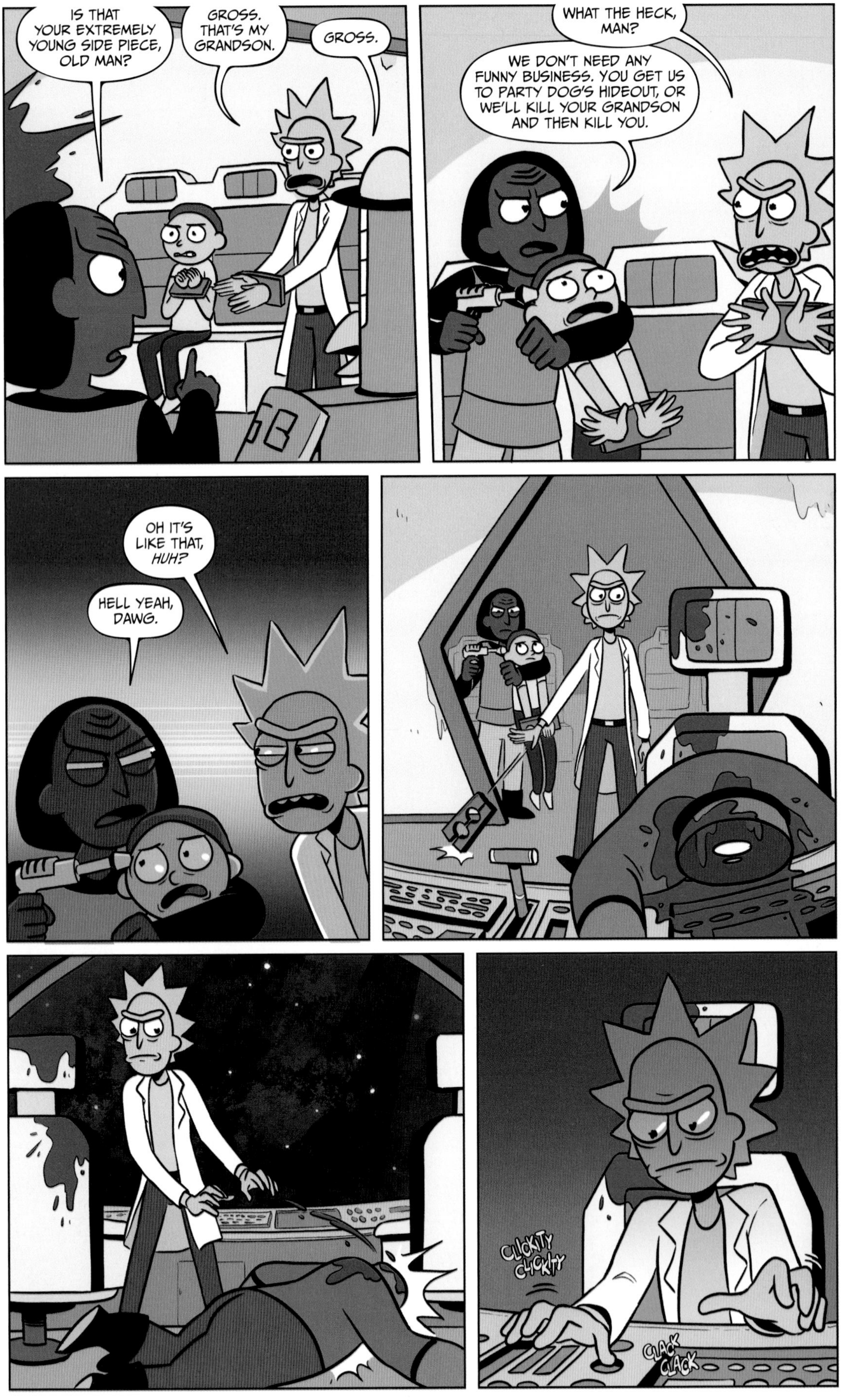
IS THAT YOUR EXTREMELY YOUNG SIDE PIECE, OLD MAN?
GROSS. THAT'S MY GRANDSON.
GROSS.
WHAT THE HECK, MAN?
WE DON'T NEED ANY FUNNY BUSINESS. YOU GET US TO PARTY DOG'S HIDEOUT, OR WE'LL KILL YOUR GRANDSON AND THEN KILL YOU.
OH IT'S LIKE THAT, *HUH?*
HELL YEAH, DAWG.
CLICKITY CLICKITY
CLACK CLACK

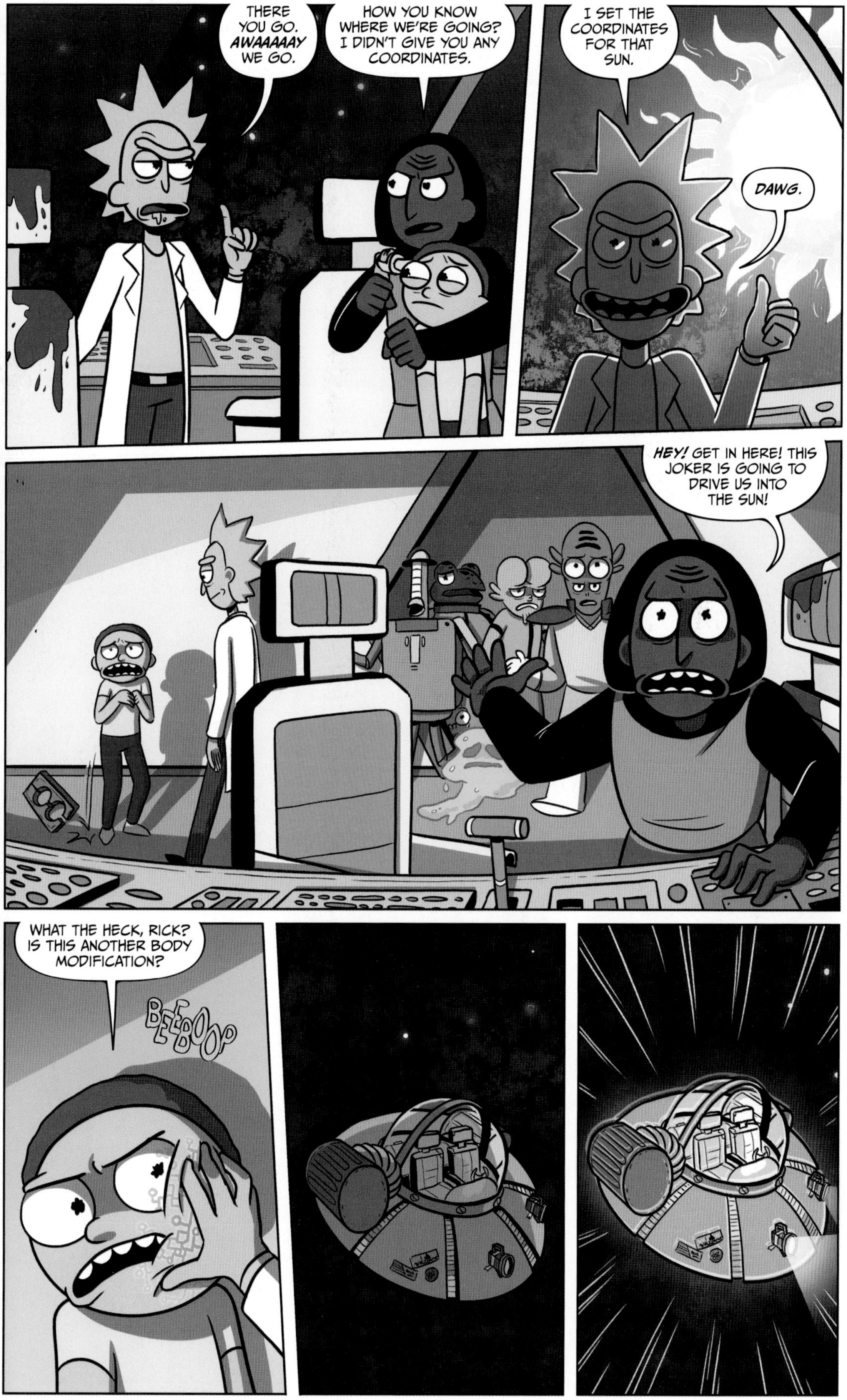
THERE YOU GO. AWAAAAAY WE GO.
HOW YOU KNOW WHERE WE'RE GOING? I DIDN'T GIVE YOU ANY COORDINATES.
I SET THE COORDINATES FOR THAT SUN.
DAWG.
HEY! GET IN HERE! THIS JOKER IS GOING TO DRIVE US INTO THE SUN!
WHAT THE HECK, RICK? IS THIS ANOTHER BODY MODIFICATION?
BEEBOOP

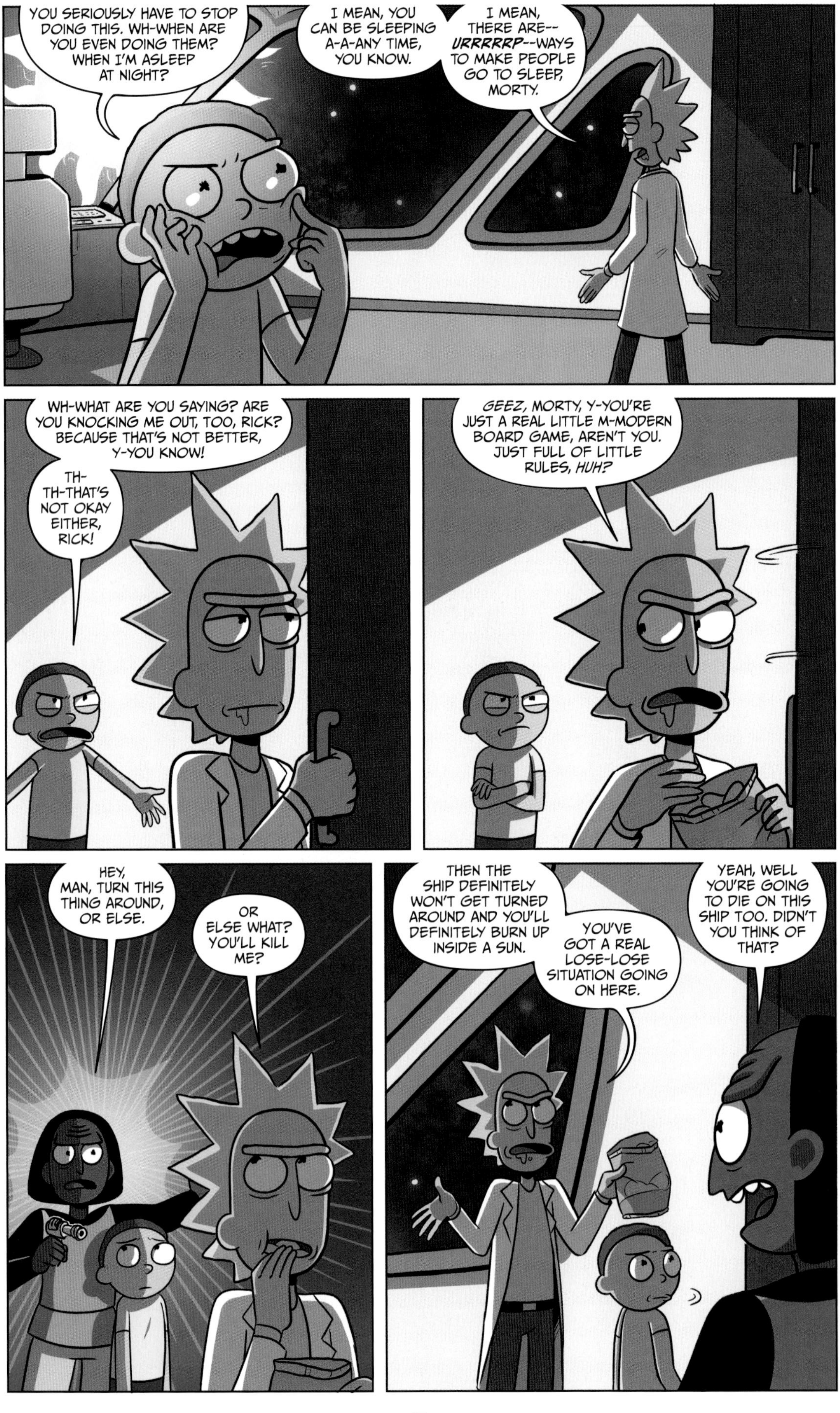
YOU SERIOUSLY HAVE TO STOP DOING THIS. WH-WHEN ARE YOU EVEN DOING THEM? WHEN I'M ASLEEP AT NIGHT?
I MEAN, YOU CAN BE SLEEPING A-A-ANY TIME, YOU KNOW.
I MEAN, THERE ARE-- URRRRRP--WAYS TO MAKE PEOPLE GO TO SLEEP, MORTY.
WH-WHAT ARE YOU SAYING? ARE YOU KNOCKING ME OUT, TOO, RICK? BECAUSE THAT'S NOT BETTER, Y-YOU KNOW!
TH- TH-THAT'S NOT OKAY EITHER, RICK!
GEEZ, MORTY, Y-YOU'RE JUST A REAL LITTLE M-MODERN BOARD GAME, AREN'T YOU. JUST FULL OF LITTLE RULES, HUH?
HEY, MAN, TURN THIS THING AROUND, OR ELSE.
OR ELSE WHAT? YOU'LL KILL ME?
THEN THE SHIP DEFINITELY WON'T GET TURNED AROUND AND YOU'LL DEFINITELY BURN UP INSIDE A SUN.
YOU'VE GOT A REAL LOSE-LOSE SITUATION GOING ON HERE.
YEAH, WELL YOU'RE GOING TO DIE ON THIS SHIP TOO. DIDN'T YOU THINK OF THAT?

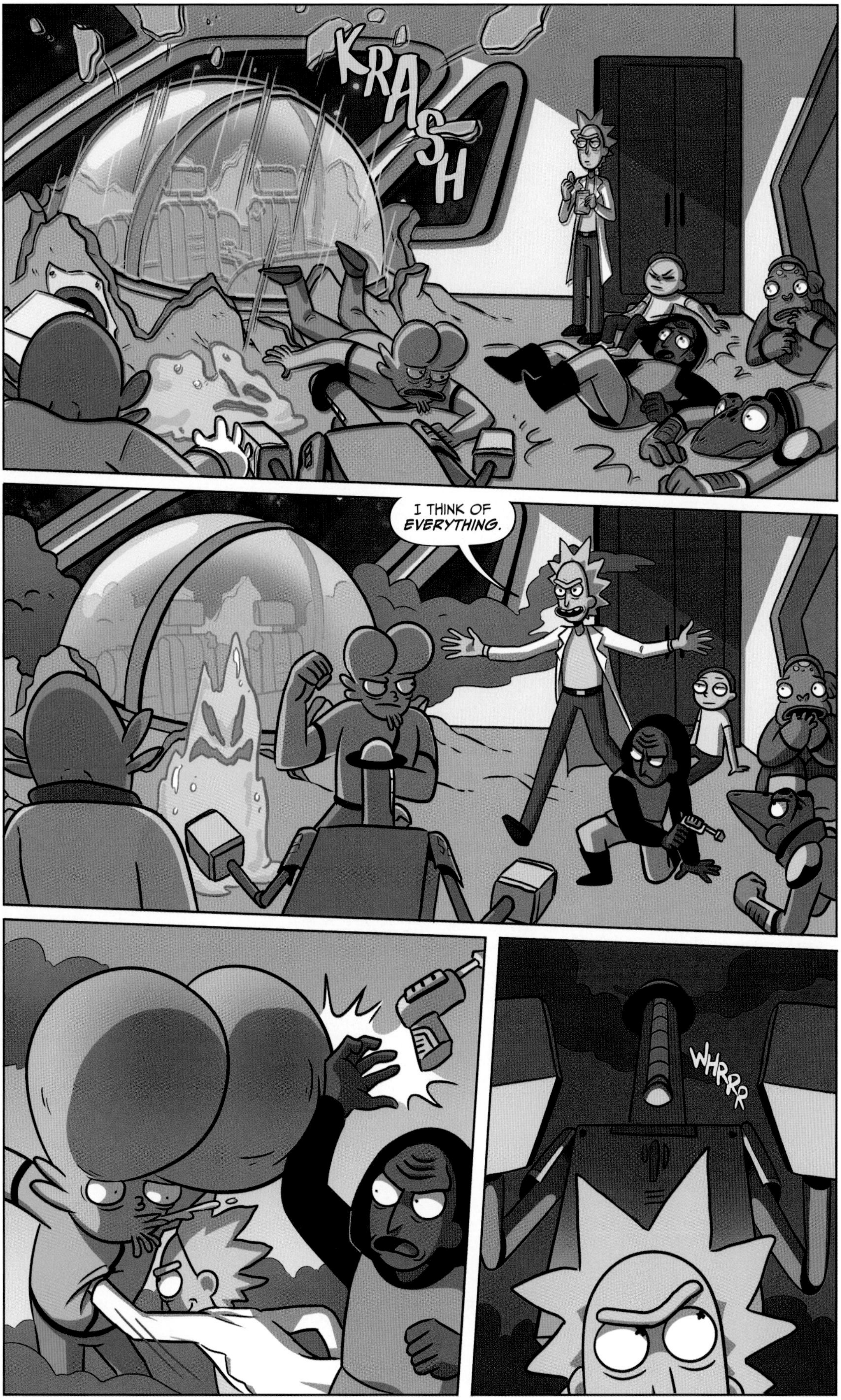
KRASH
I THINK OF EVERYTHING.
WHRRR

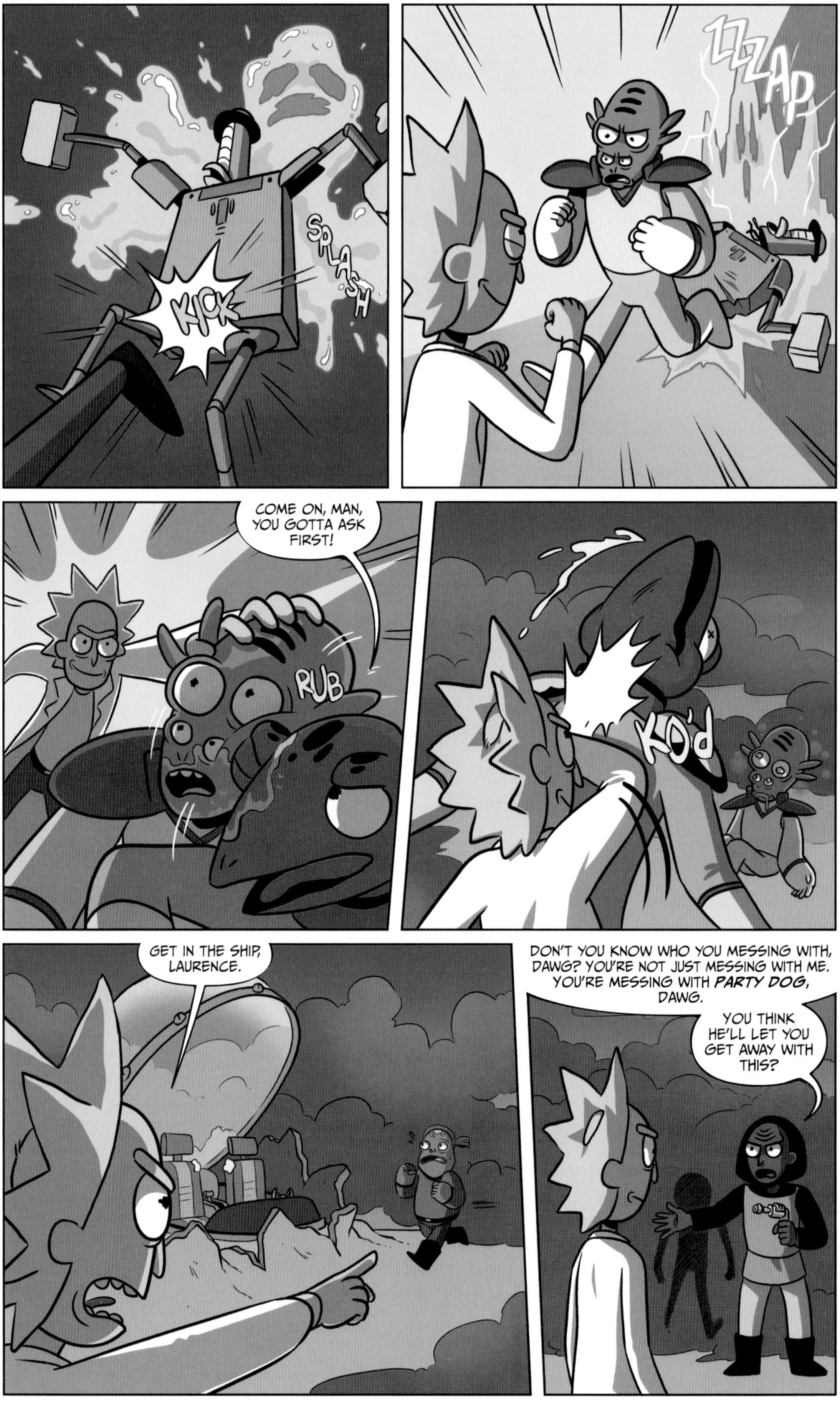
SPLASH
KICK
ZZZAP
COME ON, MAN, YOU GOTTA ASK FIRST!
RUB
KO'd
GET IN THE SHIP, LAURENCE.
DON'T YOU KNOW WHO YOU MESSING WITH, DAWG? YOU'RE NOT JUST MESSING WITH ME. YOU'RE MESSING WITH PARTY DOG, DAWG.
YOU THINK HE'LL LET YOU GET AWAY WITH THIS?

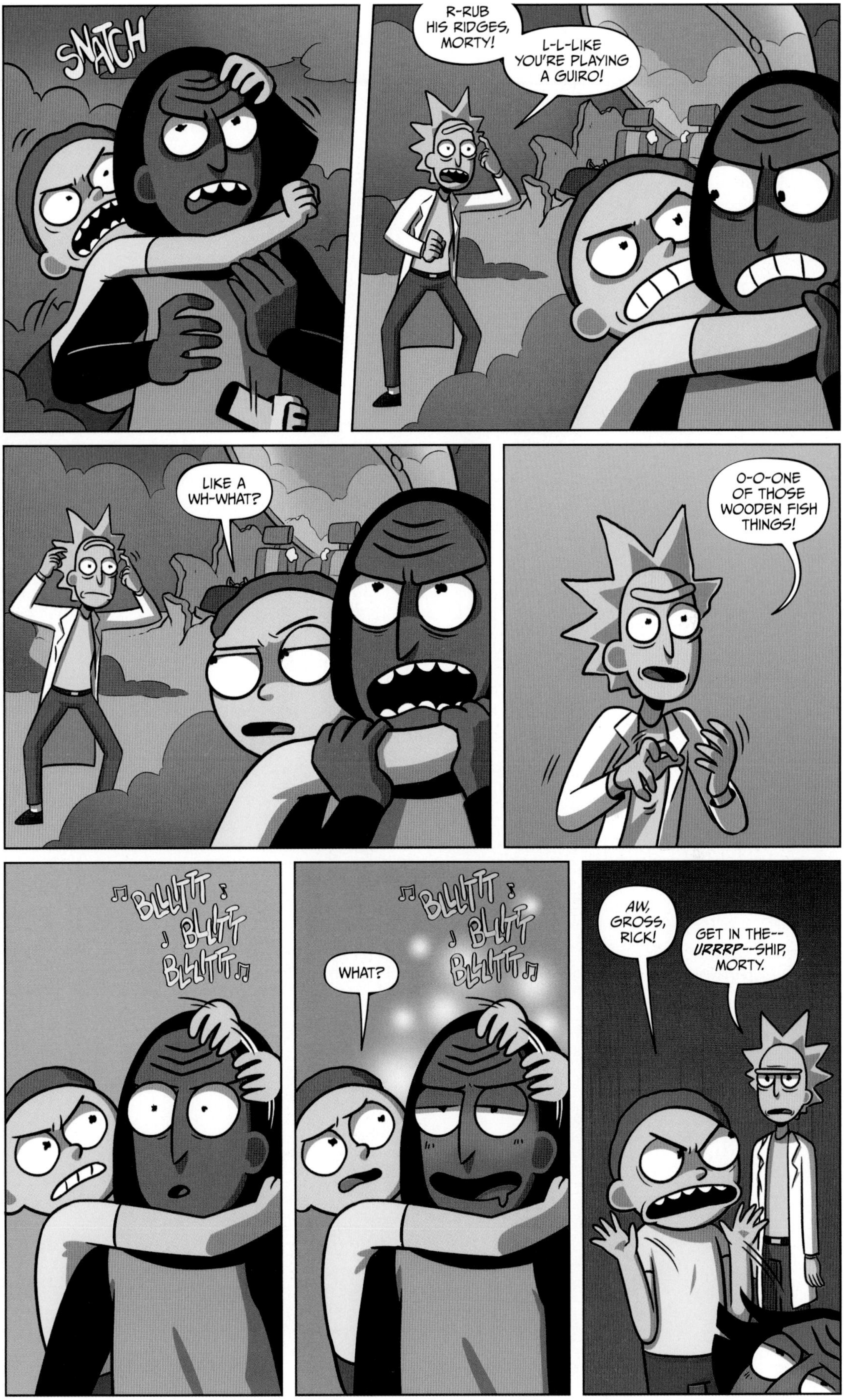
SNATCH
R-RUB HIS RIDGES, MORTY!
L-L-LIKE YOU'RE PLAYING A GUIRO!
LIKE A WH-WHAT?
O-O-ONE OF THOSE WOODEN FISH THINGS!
BLLLTTT BLLTTT BLLLTTT
WHAT?
BLLLTTT BLLTTT BLLLTTT
AW, GROSS, RICK!
GET IN THE-- *URRRP*--SHIP, MORTY.

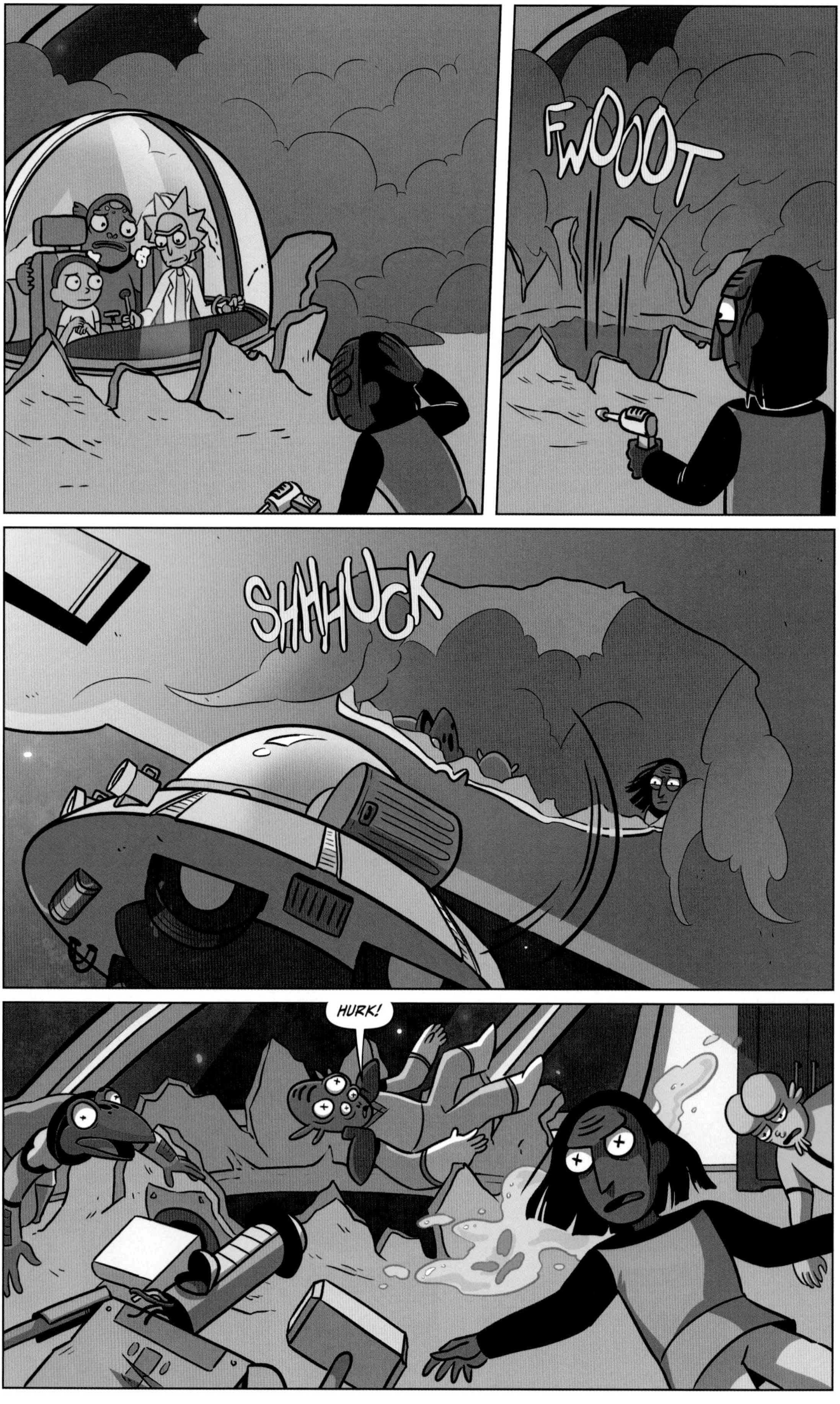

FWOOOT
SHHHUCK
HURK!

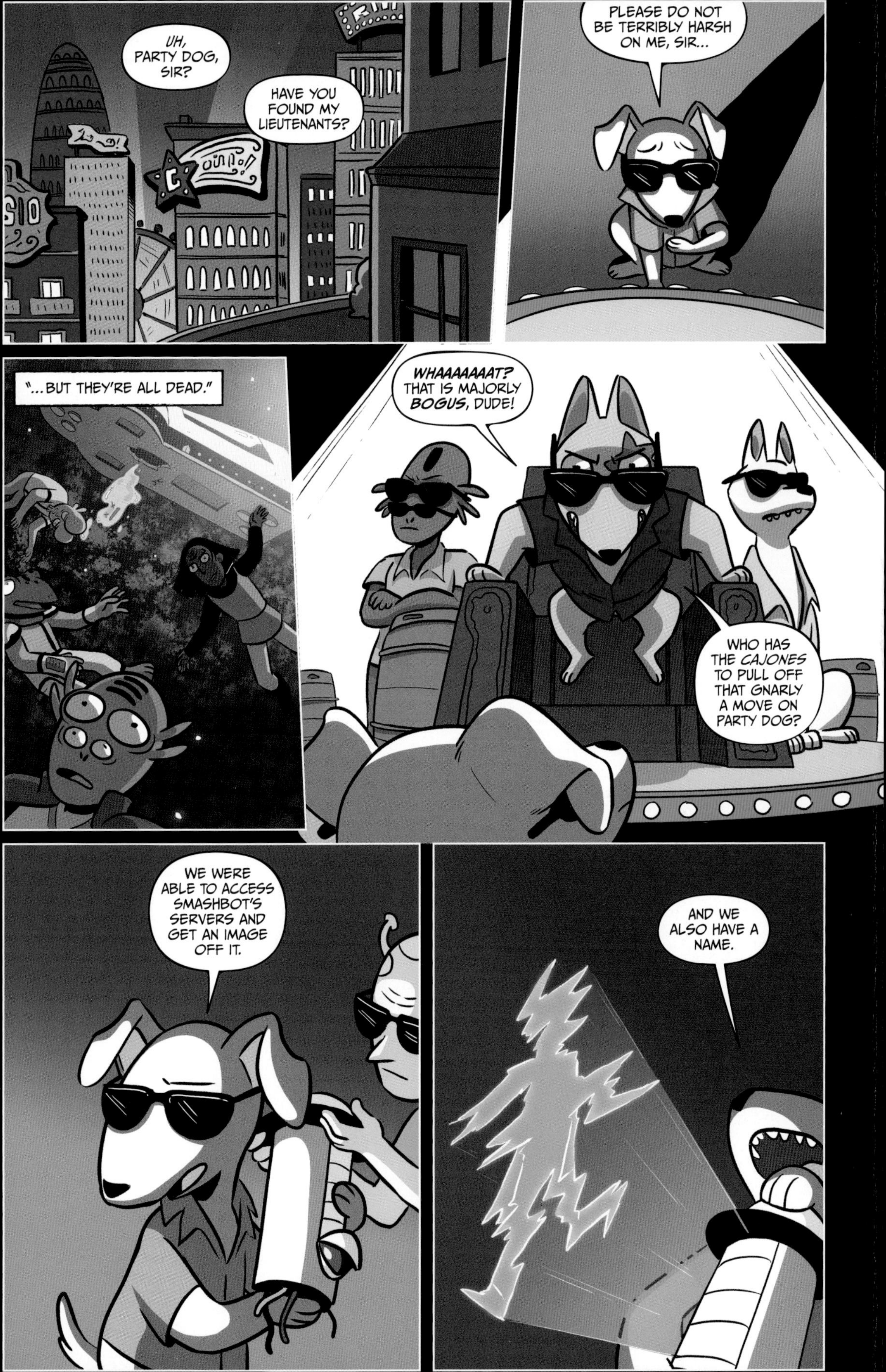
UH, PARTY DOG, SIR?
HAVE YOU FOUND MY LIEUTENANTS?
PLEASE DO NOT BE TERRIBLY HARSH ON ME, SIR...
"...BUT THEY'RE ALL DEAD."
WHAAAAAAAT? THAT IS MAJORLY BOGUS, DUDE!
WHO HAS THE CAJONES TO PULL OFF THAT GNARLY A MOVE ON PARTY DOG?
WE WERE ABLE TO ACCESS SMASHBOT'S SERVERS AND GET AN IMAGE OFF IT.
AND WE ALSO HAVE A NAME.

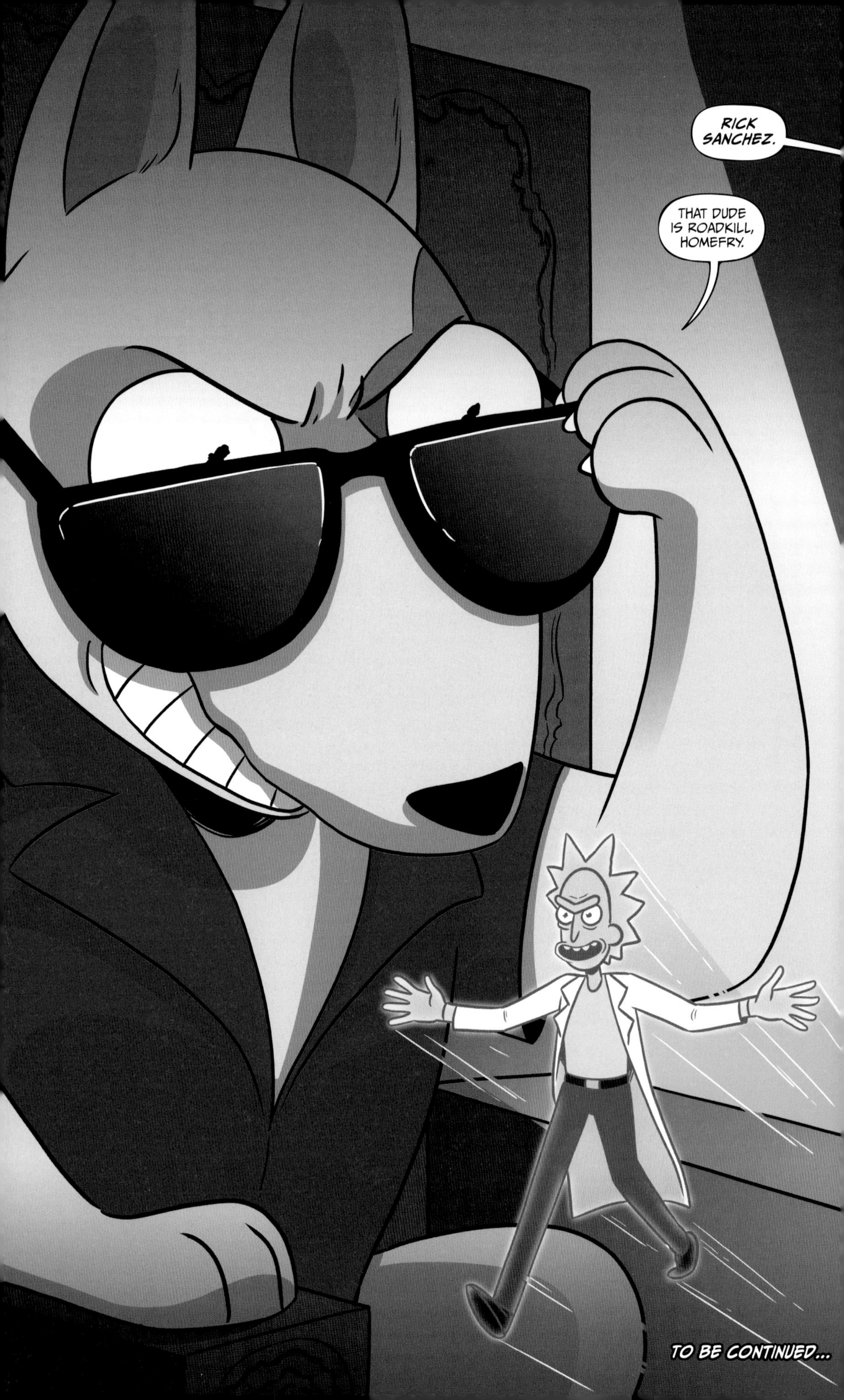
RICK SANCHEZ.
THAT DUDE IS ROADKILL, HOMEFRY.
TO BE CONTINUED...

BONUS SHORTS

WRITTEN BY **JOSH TRUJILLO**   ILLUSTRATED BY **RII ABREGO**
COLORED BY **SARAH STERN**   LETTERED BY **CRANK!**

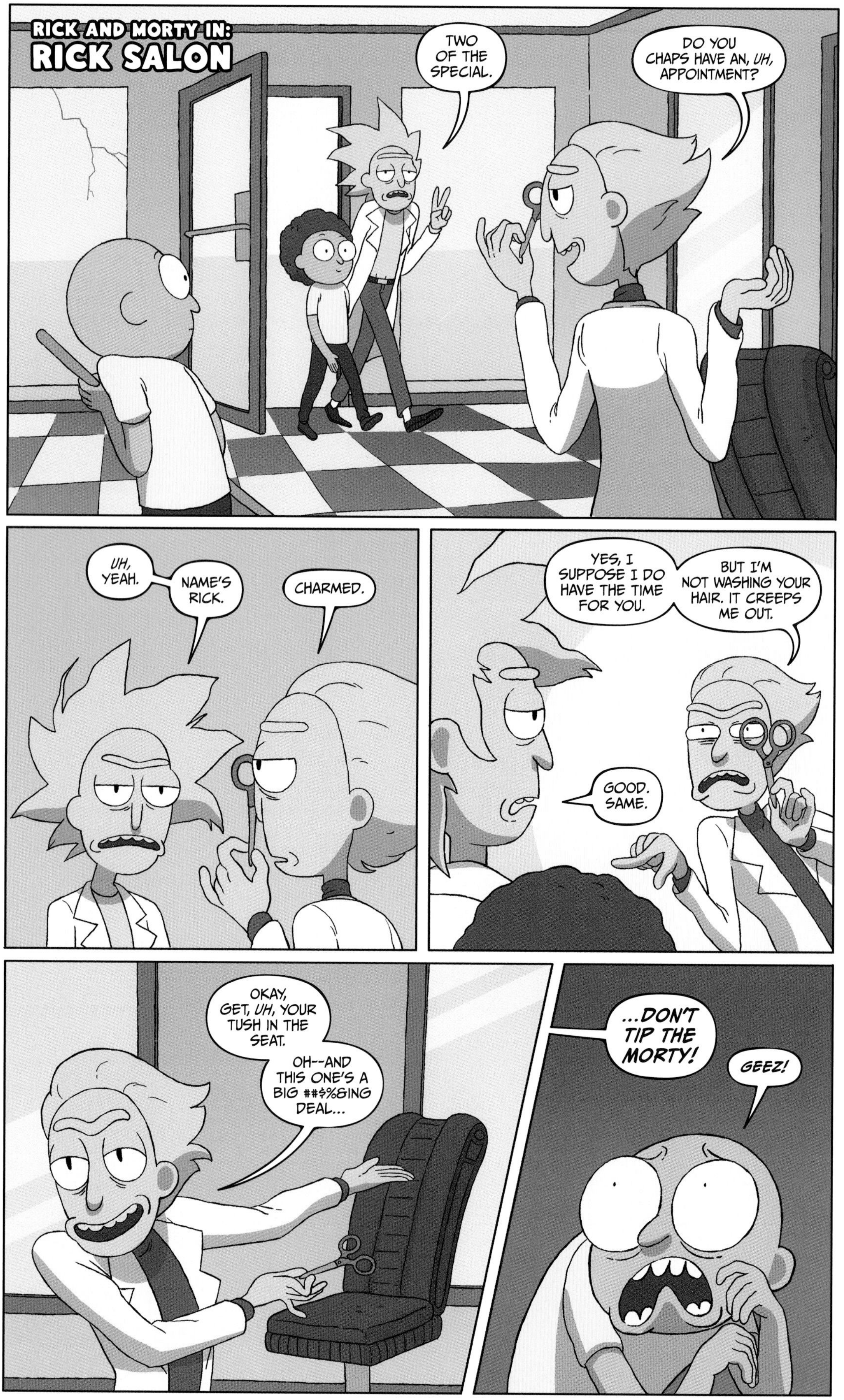
RICK AND MORTY IN:
RICK SALON
TWO OF THE SPECIAL.
DO YOU CHAPS HAVE AN, UH, APPOINTMENT?
UH, YEAH.
NAME'S RICK.
CHARMED.
YES, I SUPPOSE I DO HAVE THE TIME FOR YOU.
BUT I'M NOT WASHING YOUR HAIR. IT CREEPS ME OUT.
GOOD. SAME.
OKAY, GET, UH, YOUR TUSH IN THE SEAT.
OH--AND THIS ONE'S A BIG ##$%&ING DEAL...
...DON'T TIP THE MORTY!
GEEZ!

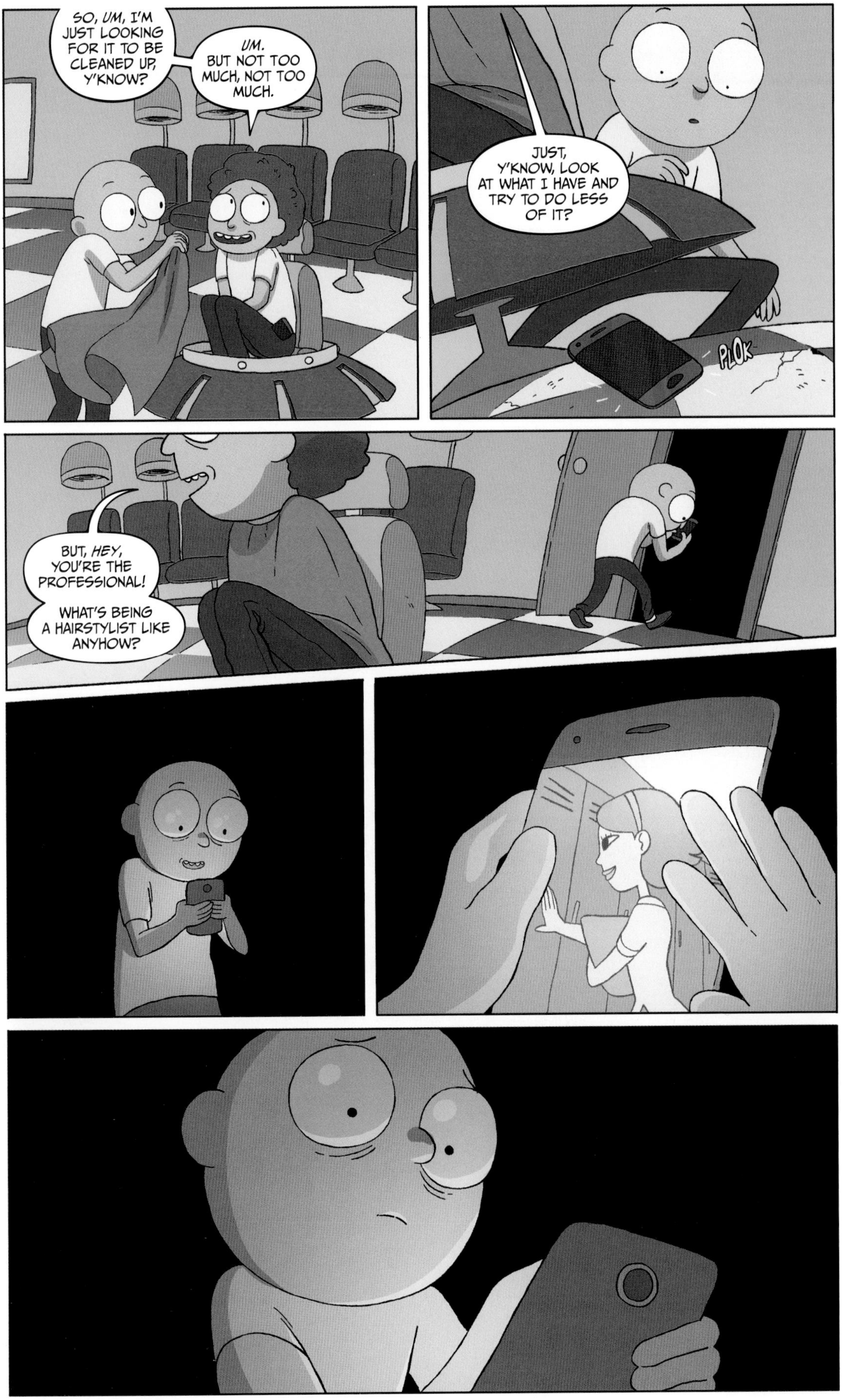
SO, UM, I'M JUST LOOKING FOR IT TO BE CLEANED UP, Y'KNOW?
UM. BUT NOT TOO MUCH, NOT TOO MUCH.
JUST, Y'KNOW, LOOK AT WHAT I HAVE AND TRY TO DO LESS OF IT?
PLOK
BUT, HEY, YOU'RE THE PROFESSIONAL!
WHAT'S BEING A HAIRSTYLIST LIKE ANYHOW?

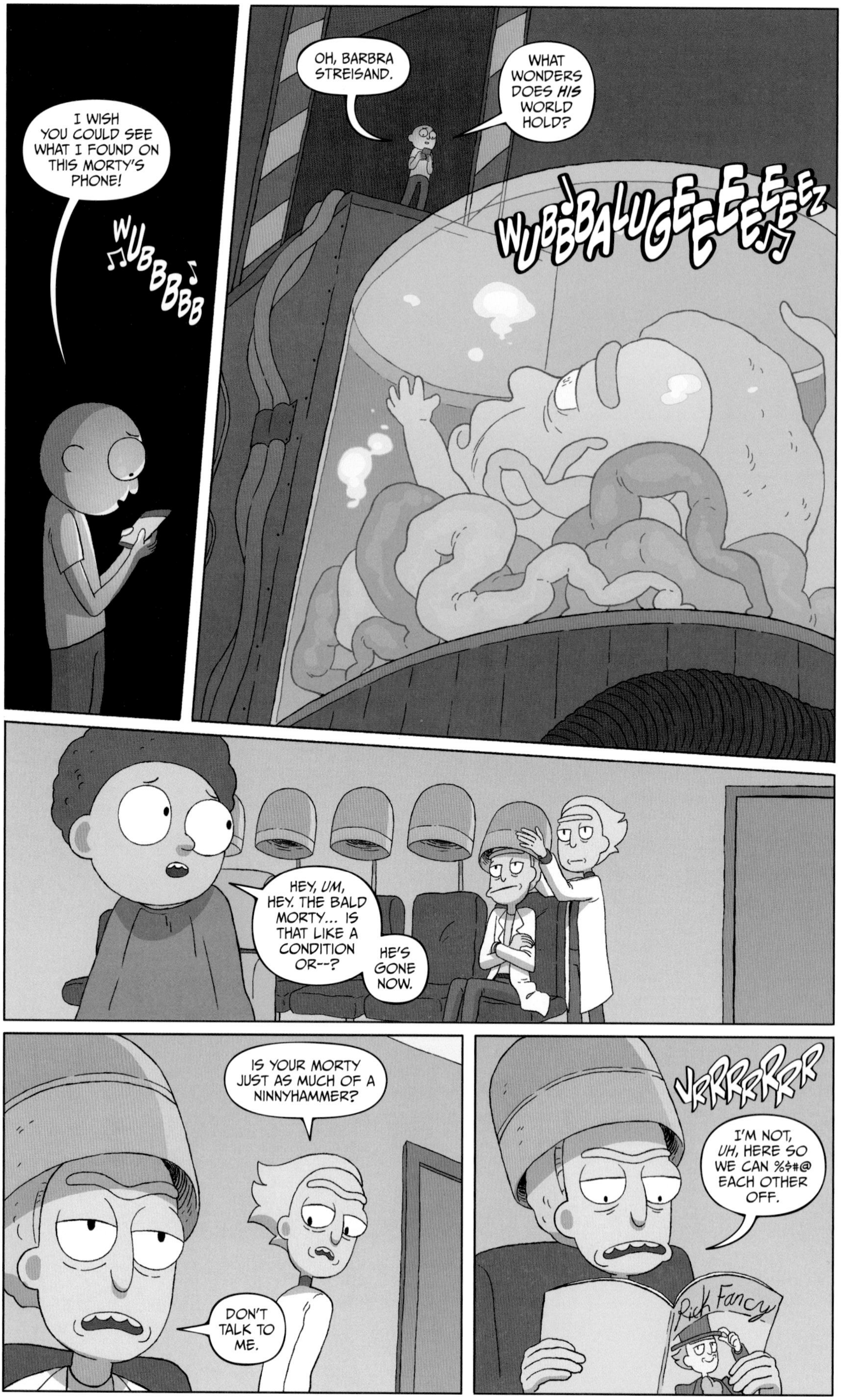
I WISH YOU COULD SEE WHAT I FOUND ON THIS MORTY'S PHONE!
WUBBBBB
OH, BARBRA STREISAND.
WHAT WONDERS DOES *HIS* WORLD HOLD?
WUBBBALUGEEEEEEEZ
HEY, *UM*, HEY. THE BALD MORTY... IS THAT LIKE A CONDITION OR--?
HE'S GONE NOW.
IS YOUR MORTY JUST AS MUCH OF A NINNYHAMMER?
DON'T TALK TO ME.
VRRRRRRR
I'M NOT, *UH*, HERE SO WE CAN %$#@ EACH OTHER OFF.
Rick Fancy

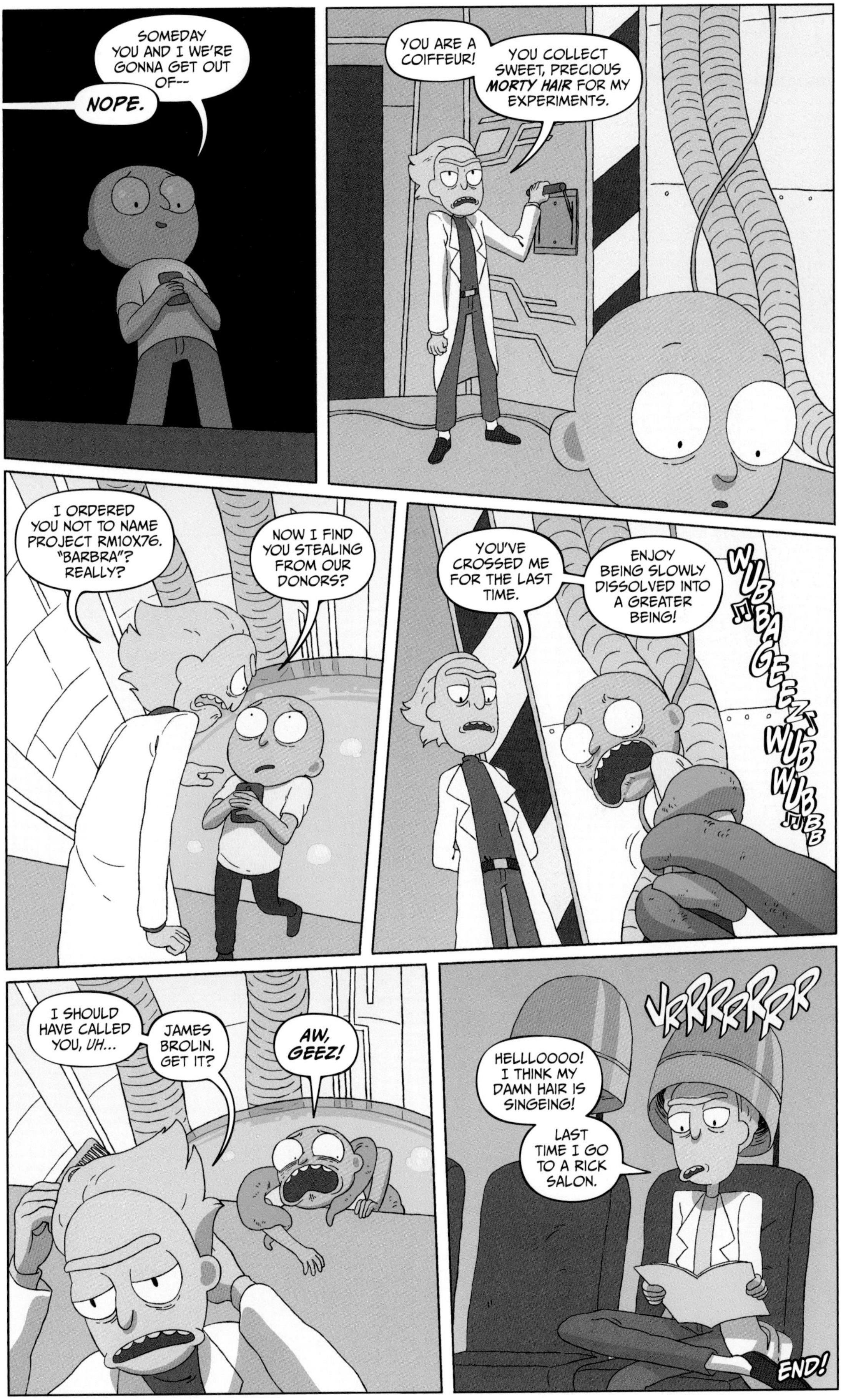
SOMEDAY YOU AND I WE'RE GONNA GET OUT OF--
NOPE.
YOU ARE A COIFFEUR!
YOU COLLECT SWEET, PRECIOUS **MORTY HAIR** FOR MY EXPERIMENTS.
I ORDERED YOU NOT TO NAME PROJECT RM10X76. "BARBRA"? REALLY?
NOW I FIND YOU STEALING FROM OUR DONORS?
YOU'VE CROSSED ME FOR THE LAST TIME.
ENJOY BEING SLOWLY DISSOLVED INTO A GREATER BEING!
WUBBA GEEZ WUB WUBB
I SHOULD HAVE CALLED YOU, *UH...*
JAMES BROLIN. GET IT?
AW, GEEZ!
VRRRRRRR
HELLLOOOO! I THINK MY DAMN HAIR IS SINGEING!
LAST TIME I GO TO A RICK SALON.
END!

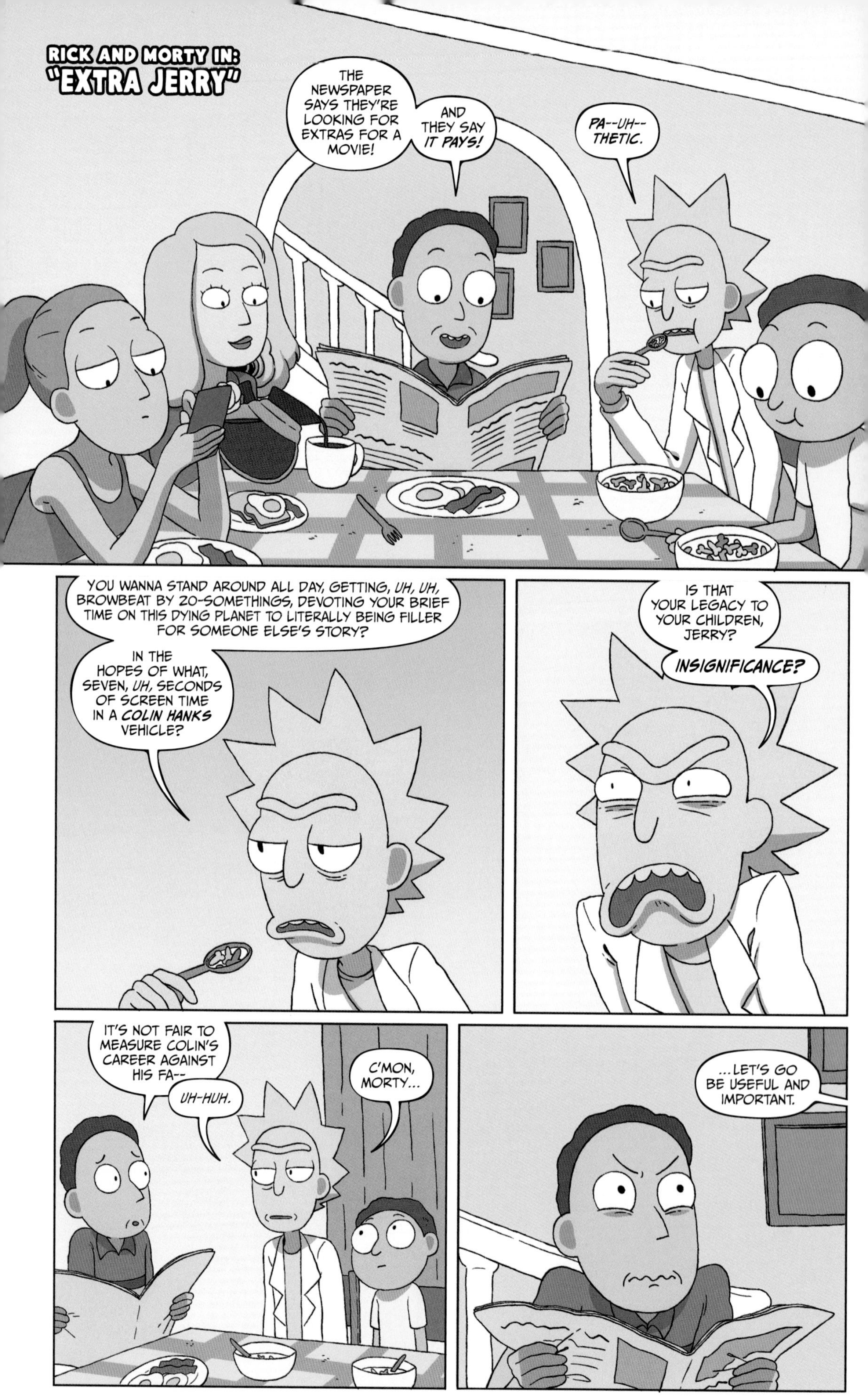
RICK AND MORTY IN:
"EXTRA JERRY"
THE NEWSPAPER SAYS THEY'RE LOOKING FOR EXTRAS FOR A MOVIE!
AND THEY SAY IT PAYS!
PA--UH--THETIC.
YOU WANNA STAND AROUND ALL DAY, GETTING, UH, UH, BROWBEAT BY 20-SOMETHINGS, DEVOTING YOUR BRIEF TIME ON THIS DYING PLANET TO LITERALLY BEING FILLER FOR SOMEONE ELSE'S STORY?
IN THE HOPES OF WHAT, SEVEN, UH, SECONDS OF SCREEN TIME IN A COLIN HANKS VEHICLE?
IS THAT YOUR LEGACY TO YOUR CHILDREN, JERRY?
INSIGNIFICANCE?
IT'S NOT FAIR TO MEASURE COLIN'S CAREER AGAINST HIS FA--
UH-HUH.
C'MON, MORTY...
...LET'S GO BE USEFUL AND IMPORTANT.

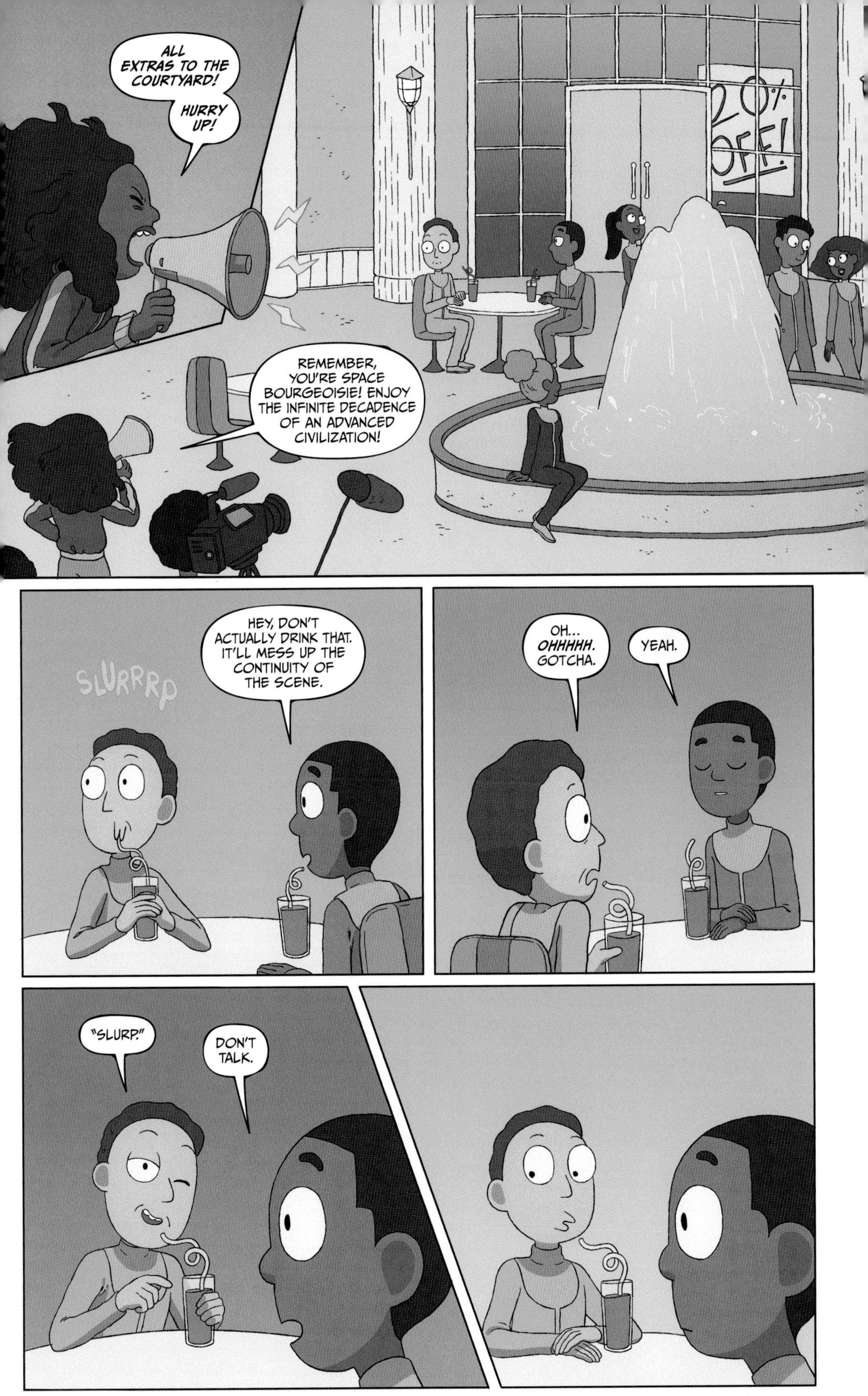
ALL EXTRAS TO THE COURTYARD!
HURRY UP!
20% OFF!
REMEMBER, YOU'RE SPACE BOURGEOISIE! ENJOY THE INFINITE DECADENCE OF AN ADVANCED CIVILIZATION!
SLURRRP
HEY, DON'T ACTUALLY DRINK THAT. IT'LL MESS UP THE CONTINUITY OF THE SCENE.
OH... *OHHHHH.* GOTCHA.
YEAH.
"SLURP."
DON'T TALK.

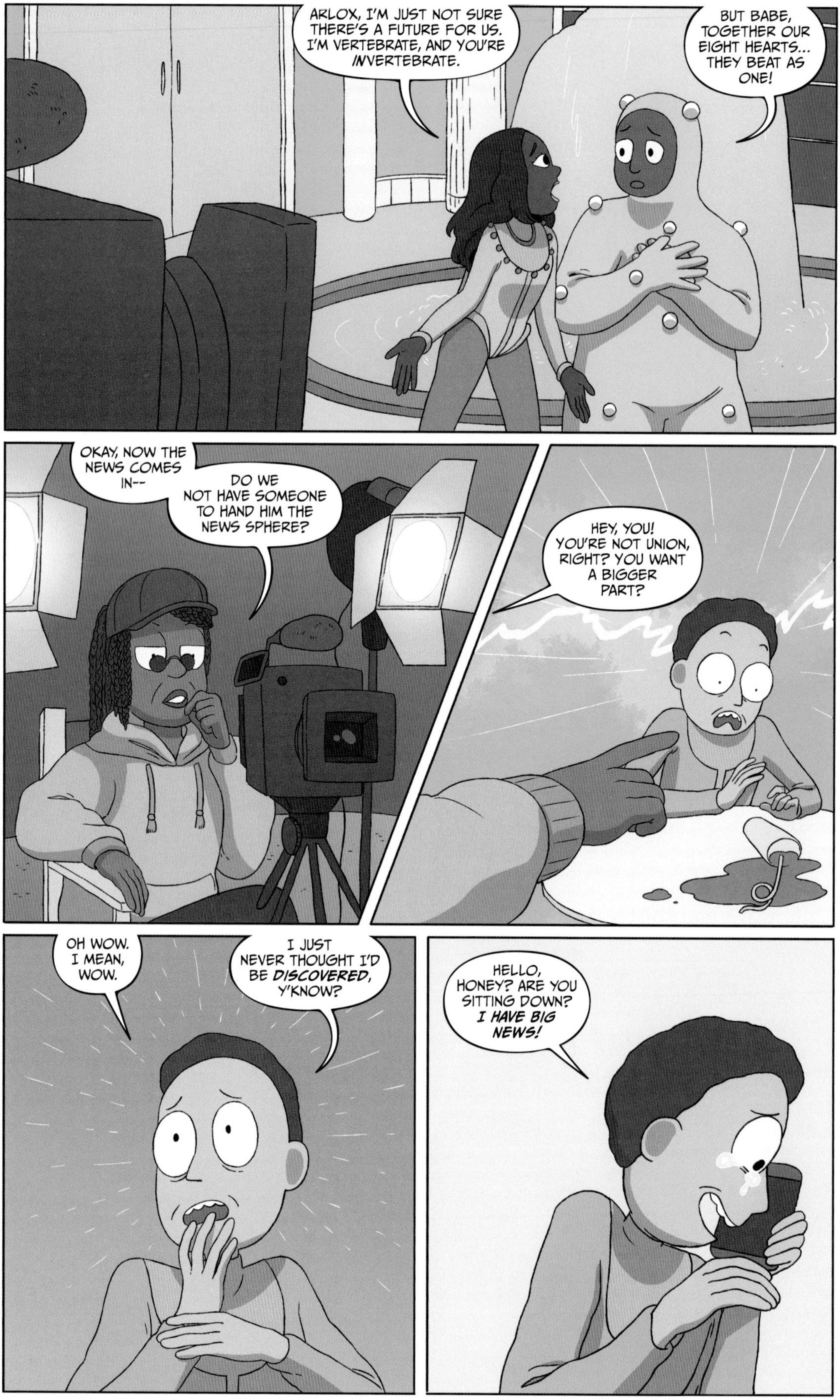
ARLOX, I'M JUST NOT SURE THERE'S A FUTURE FOR US. I'M VERTEBRATE, AND YOU'RE *IN*VERTEBRATE.
BUT BABE, TOGETHER OUR EIGHT HEARTS... THEY BEAT AS ONE!
OKAY, NOW THE NEWS COMES IN--
DO WE NOT HAVE SOMEONE TO HAND HIM THE NEWS SPHERE?
HEY, YOU! YOU'RE NOT UNION, RIGHT? YOU WANT A BIGGER PART?
OH WOW. I MEAN, WOW.
I JUST NEVER THOUGHT I'D BE ***DISCOVERED***, Y'KNOW?
HELLO, HONEY? ARE YOU SITTING DOWN? ***I HAVE BIG NEWS!***

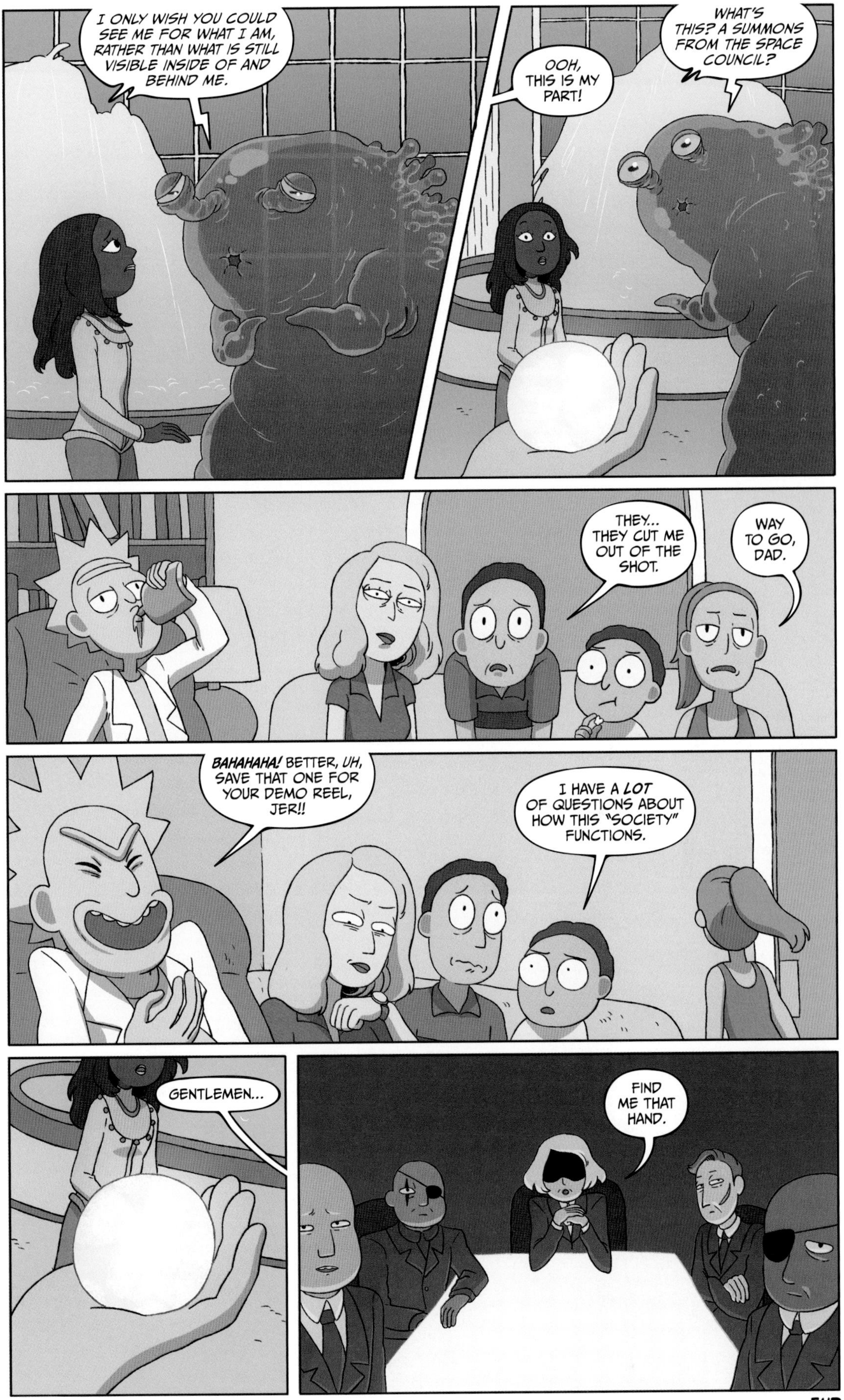
I ONLY WISH YOU COULD SEE ME FOR WHAT I AM, RATHER THAN WHAT IS STILL VISIBLE INSIDE OF AND BEHIND ME.
OOH, THIS IS MY PART!
WHAT'S THIS? A SUMMONS FROM THE SPACE COUNCIL?
THEY... THEY CUT ME OUT OF THE SHOT.
WAY TO GO, DAD.
BAHAHAHA! BETTER, UH, SAVE THAT ONE FOR YOUR DEMO REEL, JER!!
I HAVE A LOT OF QUESTIONS ABOUT HOW THIS "SOCIETY" FUNCTIONS.
GENTLEMEN...
FIND ME THAT HAND.
END

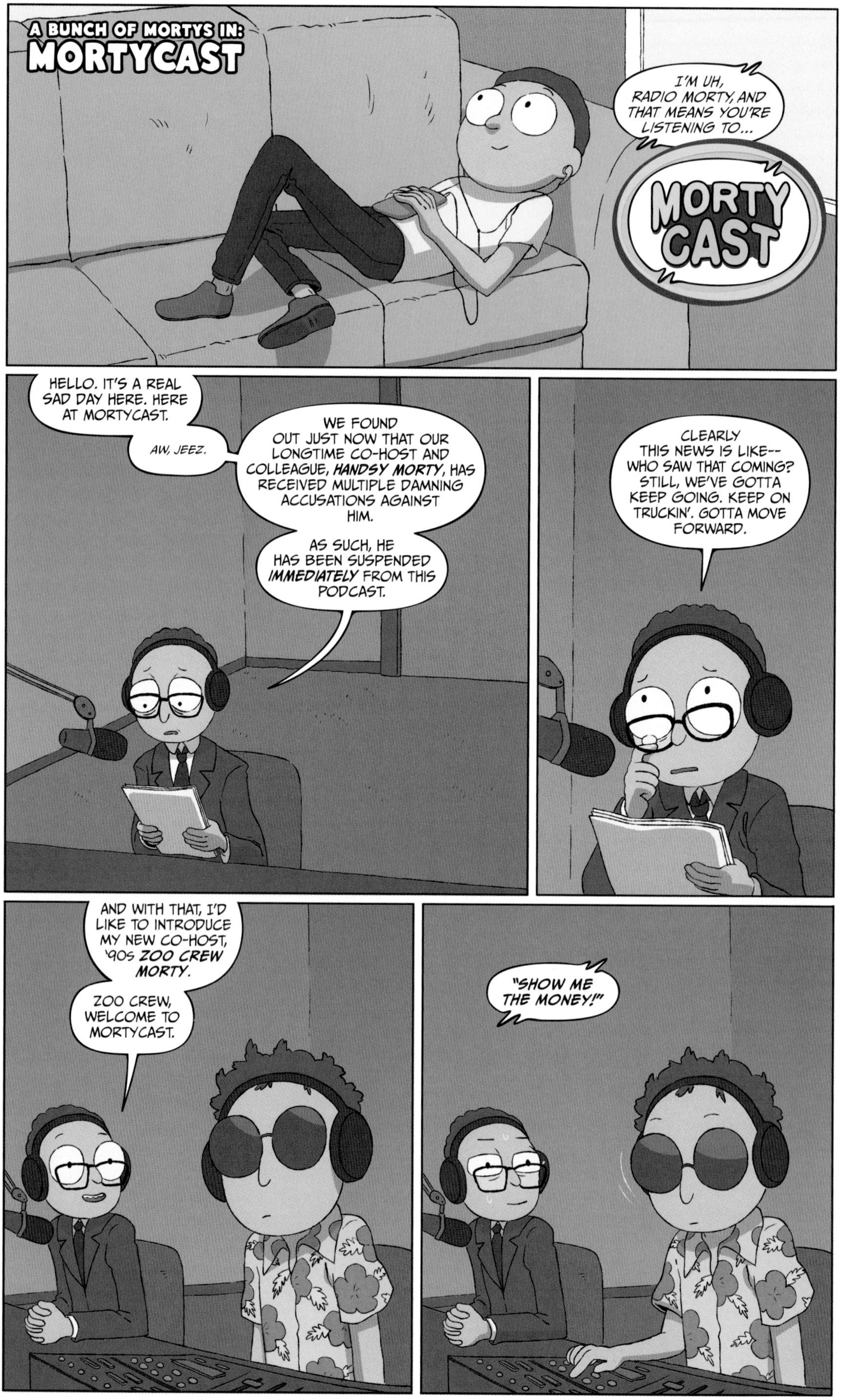
A BUNCH OF MORTYS IN:
MORTYCAST
I'M UH, RADIO MORTY, AND THAT MEANS YOU'RE LISTENING TO...
MORTY CAST
HELLO. IT'S A REAL SAD DAY HERE. HERE AT MORTYCAST.
AW, JEEZ.
WE FOUND OUT JUST NOW THAT OUR LONGTIME CO-HOST AND COLLEAGUE, HANDSY MORTY, HAS RECEIVED MULTIPLE DAMNING ACCUSATIONS AGAINST HIM.
AS SUCH, HE HAS BEEN SUSPENDED IMMEDIATELY FROM THIS PODCAST.
CLEARLY THIS NEWS IS LIKE-- WHO SAW THAT COMING? STILL, WE'VE GOTTA KEEP GOING. KEEP ON TRUCKIN'. GOTTA MOVE FORWARD.
AND WITH THAT, I'D LIKE TO INTRODUCE MY NEW CO-HOST, '90S ZOO CREW MORTY.
ZOO CREW, WELCOME TO MORTYCAST.
"SHOW ME THE MONEY!"

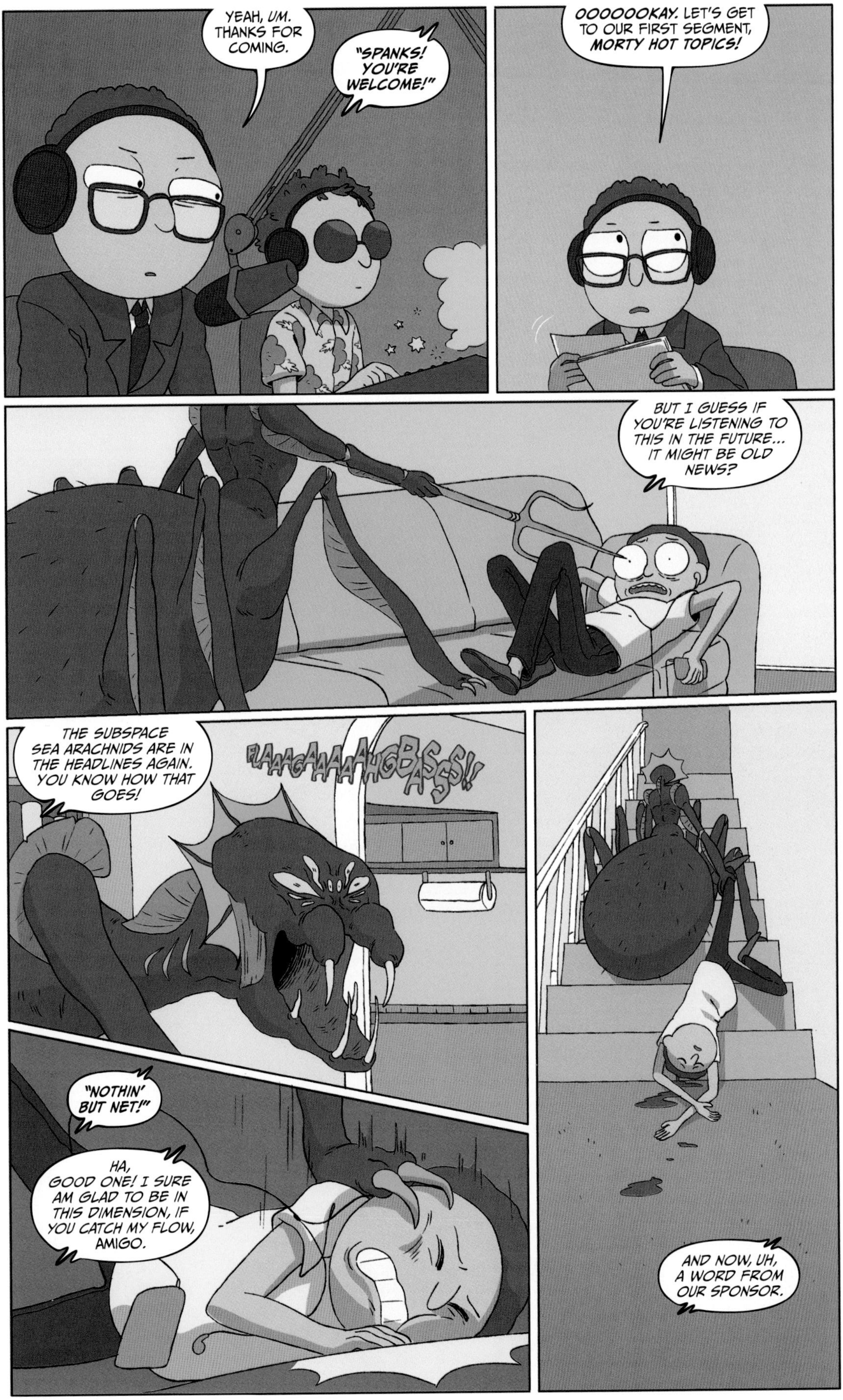
YEAH, UM. THANKS FOR COMING.
"SPANKS! YOU'RE WELCOME!"
OOOOOOKAY. LET'S GET TO OUR FIRST SEGMENT, MORTY HOT TOPICS!
BUT I GUESS IF YOU'RE LISTENING TO THIS IN THE FUTURE... IT MIGHT BE OLD NEWS?
THE SUBSPACE SEA ARACHNIDS ARE IN THE HEADLINES AGAIN. YOU KNOW HOW THAT GOES!
FLAAAGAAAAAHGBASSS!!
"NOTHIN' BUT NET!"
HA, GOOD ONE! I SURE AM GLAD TO BE IN THIS DIMENSION, IF YOU CATCH MY FLOW, AMIGO.
AND NOW, UH, A WORD FROM OUR SPONSOR.

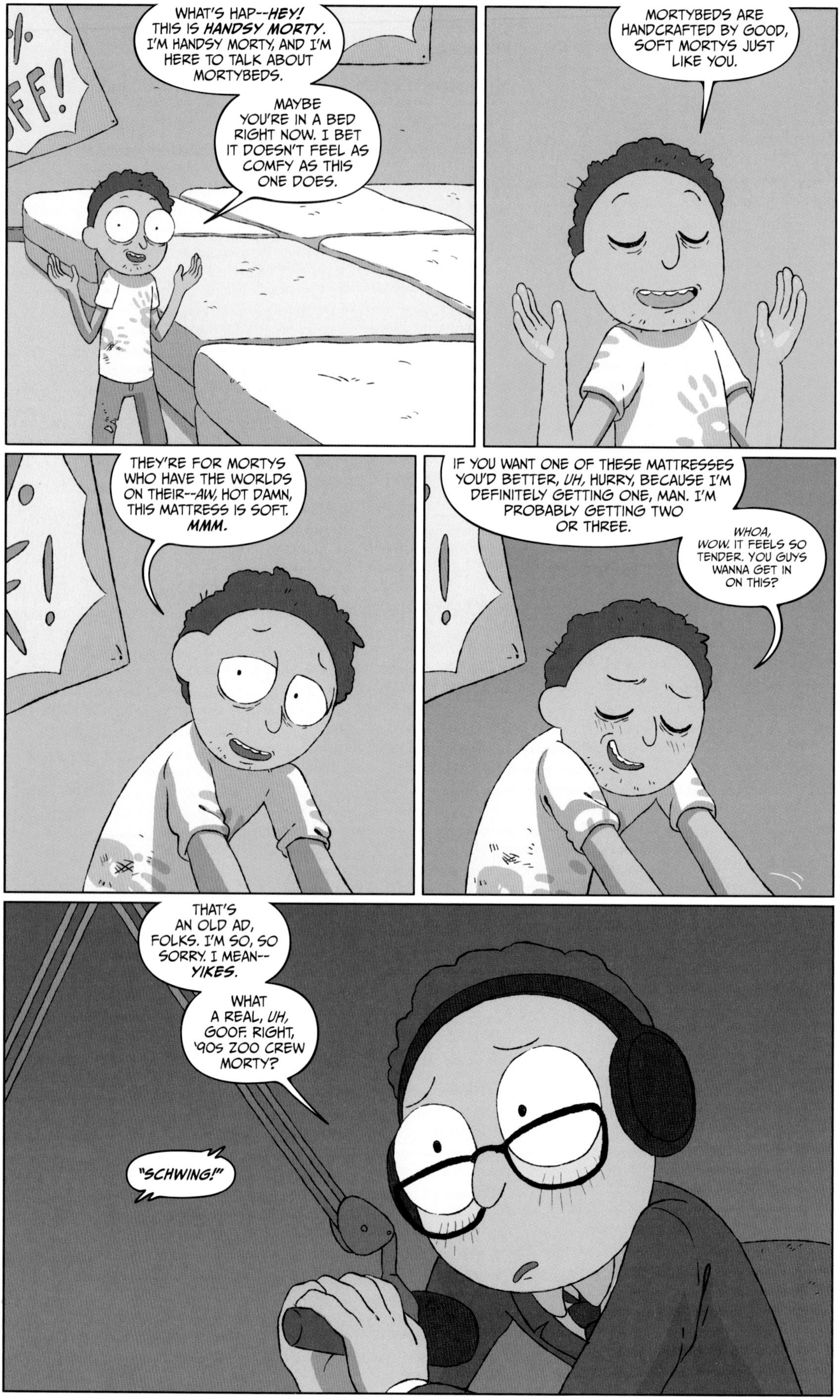
WHAT'S HAP--HEY! THIS IS HANDSY MORTY. I'M HANDSY MORTY, AND I'M HERE TO TALK ABOUT MORTYBEDS.
MAYBE YOU'RE IN A BED RIGHT NOW. I BET IT DOESN'T FEEL AS COMFY AS THIS ONE DOES.
MORTYBEDS ARE HANDCRAFTED BY GOOD, SOFT MORTYS JUST LIKE YOU.
THEY'RE FOR MORTYS WHO HAVE THE WORLDS ON THEIR--AW, HOT DAMN, THIS MATTRESS IS SOFT. MMM.
IF YOU WANT ONE OF THESE MATTRESSES YOU'D BETTER, UH, HURRY, BECAUSE I'M DEFINITELY GETTING ONE, MAN. I'M PROBABLY GETTING TWO OR THREE.
WHOA, WOW. IT FEELS SO TENDER. YOU GUYS WANNA GET IN ON THIS?
THAT'S AN OLD AD, FOLKS. I'M SO, SO SORRY. I MEAN-- YIKES.
WHAT A REAL, UH, GOOF. RIGHT, '90s ZOO CREW MORTY?
"SCHWING!"

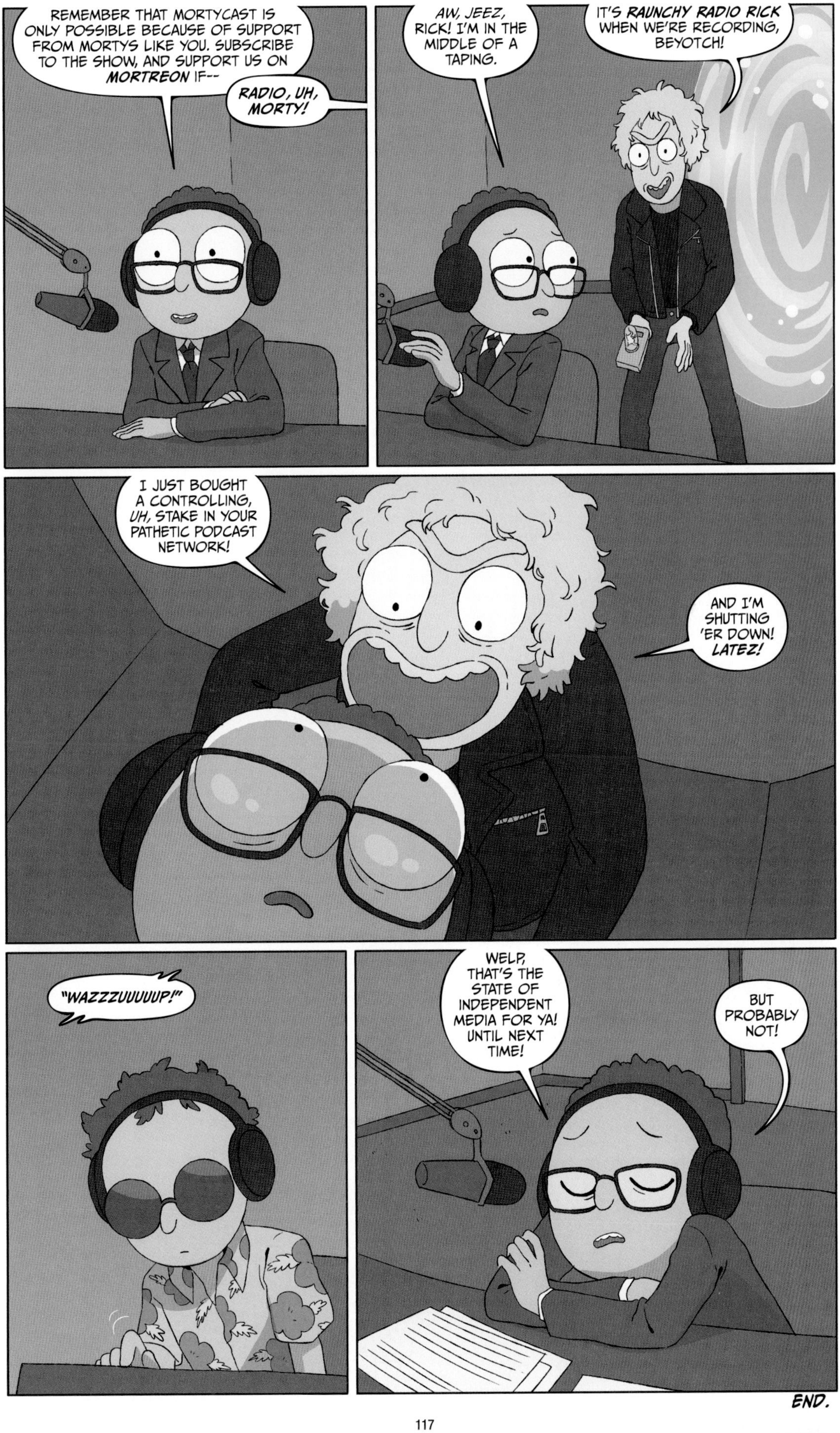
REMEMBER THAT MORTYCAST IS ONLY POSSIBLE BECAUSE OF SUPPORT FROM MORTYS LIKE YOU. SUBSCRIBE TO THE SHOW, AND SUPPORT US ON MORTREON IF--
RADIO, UH, MORTY!
AW, JEEZ, RICK! I'M IN THE MIDDLE OF A TAPING.
IT'S RAUNCHY RADIO RICK WHEN WE'RE RECORDING, BEYOTCH!
I JUST BOUGHT A CONTROLLING, UH, STAKE IN YOUR PATHETIC PODCAST NETWORK!
AND I'M SHUTTING 'ER DOWN! LATEZ!
"WAZZZUUUUUP!"
WELP, THAT'S THE STATE OF INDEPENDENT MEDIA FOR YA! UNTIL NEXT TIME!
BUT PROBABLY NOT!
END.

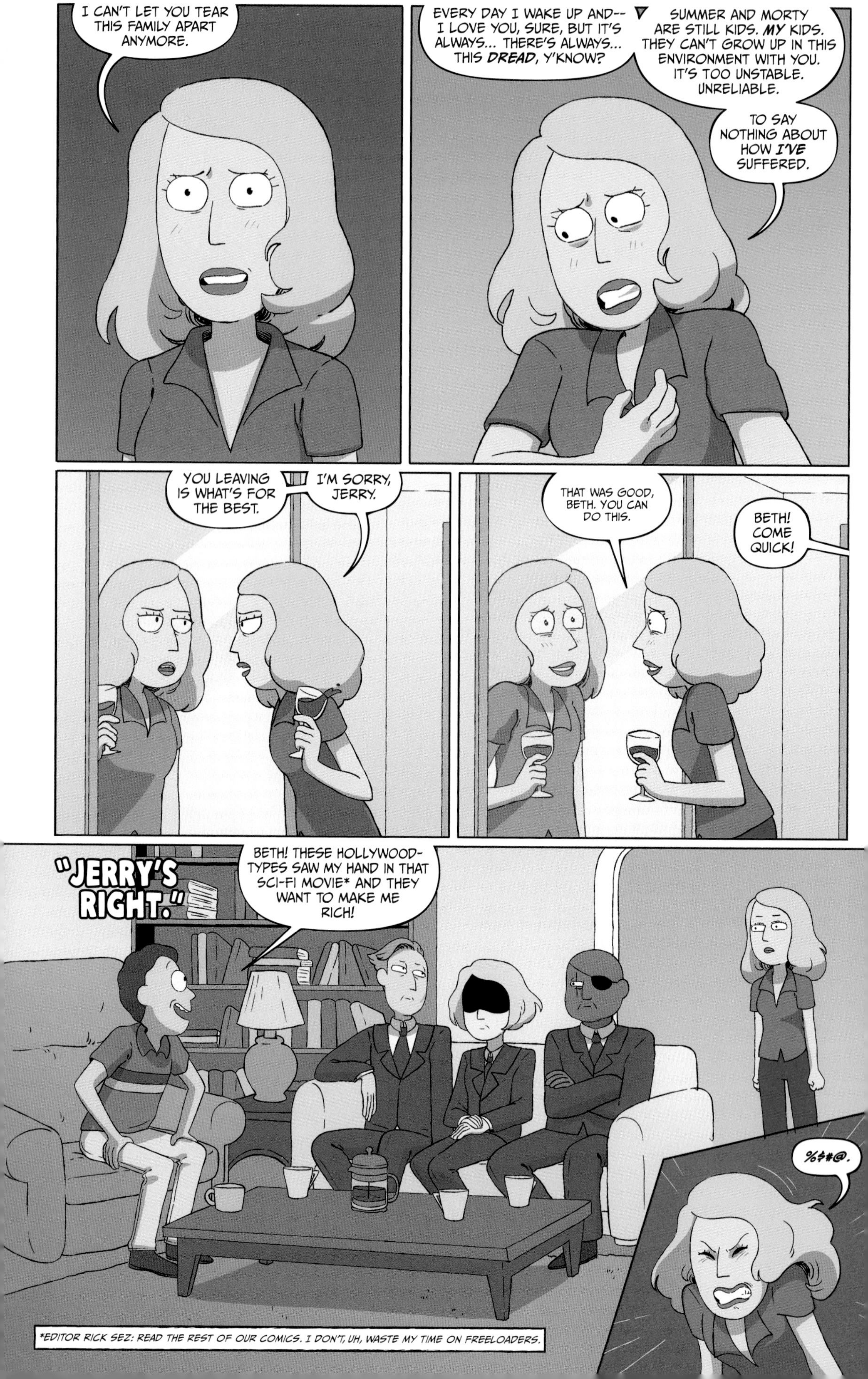
I CAN'T LET YOU TEAR THIS FAMILY APART ANYMORE.
EVERY DAY I WAKE UP AND-- I LOVE YOU, SURE, BUT IT'S ALWAYS... THERE'S ALWAYS... THIS DREAD, Y'KNOW?
SUMMER AND MORTY ARE STILL KIDS. MY KIDS. THEY CAN'T GROW UP IN THIS ENVIRONMENT WITH YOU. IT'S TOO UNSTABLE. UNRELIABLE.
TO SAY NOTHING ABOUT HOW I'VE SUFFERED.
YOU LEAVING IS WHAT'S FOR THE BEST.
I'M SORRY, JERRY.
THAT WAS GOOD, BETH. YOU CAN DO THIS.
BETH! COME QUICK!
"JERRY'S RIGHT."
BETH! THESE HOLLYWOOD-TYPES SAW MY HAND IN THAT SCI-FI MOVIE* AND THEY WANT TO MAKE ME RICH!
%$#@.
*EDITOR RICK SEZ: READ THE REST OF OUR COMICS. I DON'T, UH, WASTE MY TIME ON FREELOADERS.

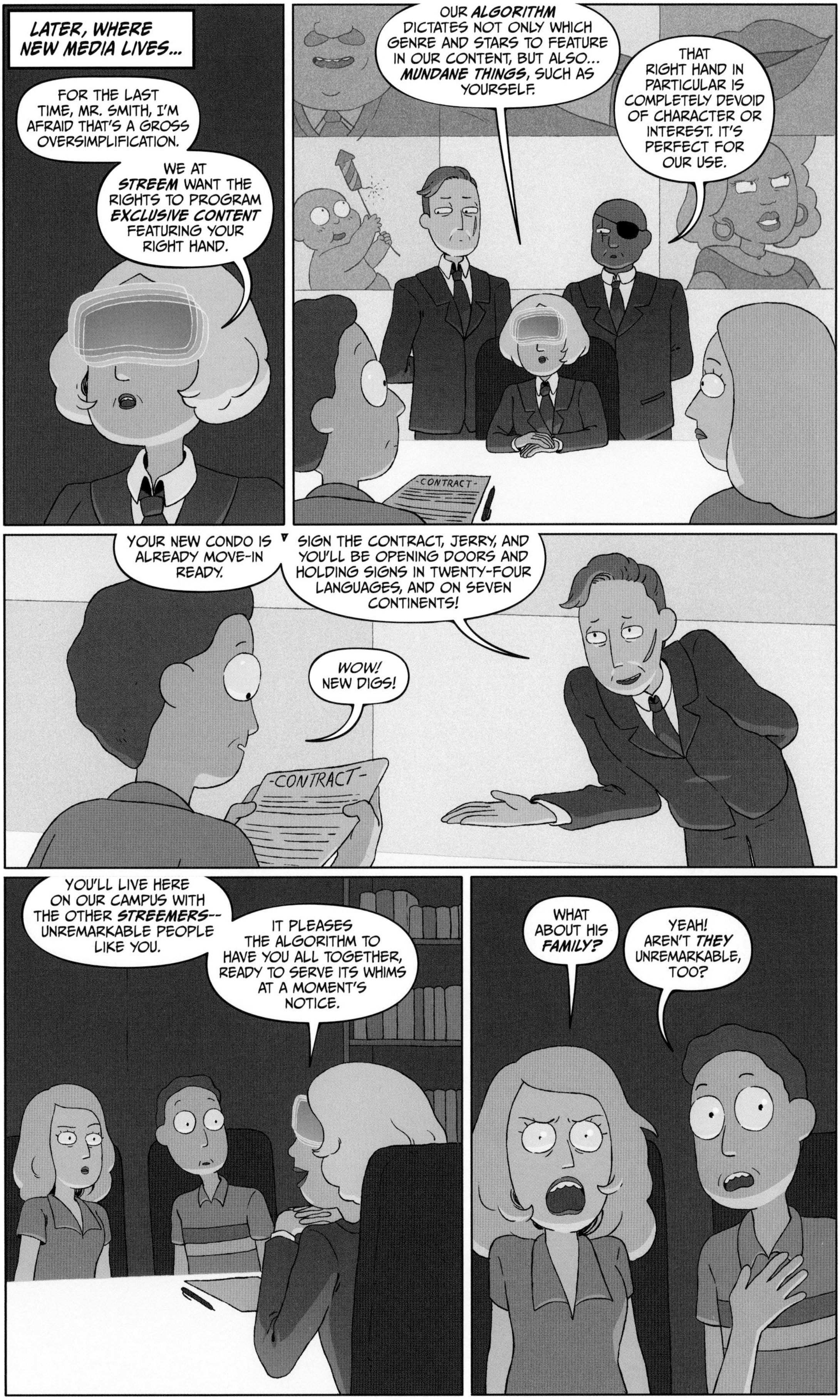
LATER, WHERE NEW MEDIA LIVES...
FOR THE LAST TIME, MR. SMITH, I'M AFRAID THAT'S A GROSS OVERSIMPLIFICATION.
WE AT STREEM WANT THE RIGHTS TO PROGRAM EXCLUSIVE CONTENT FEATURING YOUR RIGHT HAND.
OUR ALGORITHM DICTATES NOT ONLY WHICH GENRE AND STARS TO FEATURE IN OUR CONTENT, BUT ALSO... MUNDANE THINGS, SUCH AS YOURSELF.
THAT RIGHT HAND IN PARTICULAR IS COMPLETELY DEVOID OF CHARACTER OR INTEREST. IT'S PERFECT FOR OUR USE.
-CONTRACT-
YOUR NEW CONDO IS ALREADY MOVE-IN READY.
SIGN THE CONTRACT, JERRY, AND YOU'LL BE OPENING DOORS AND HOLDING SIGNS IN TWENTY-FOUR LANGUAGES, AND ON SEVEN CONTINENTS!
WOW! NEW DIGS!
-CONTRACT-
YOU'LL LIVE HERE ON OUR CAMPUS WITH THE OTHER STREEMERS-- UNREMARKABLE PEOPLE LIKE YOU.
IT PLEASES THE ALGORITHM TO HAVE YOU ALL TOGETHER, READY TO SERVE ITS WHIMS AT A MOMENT'S NOTICE.
WHAT ABOUT HIS FAMILY?
YEAH! AREN'T THEY UNREMARKABLE, TOO?

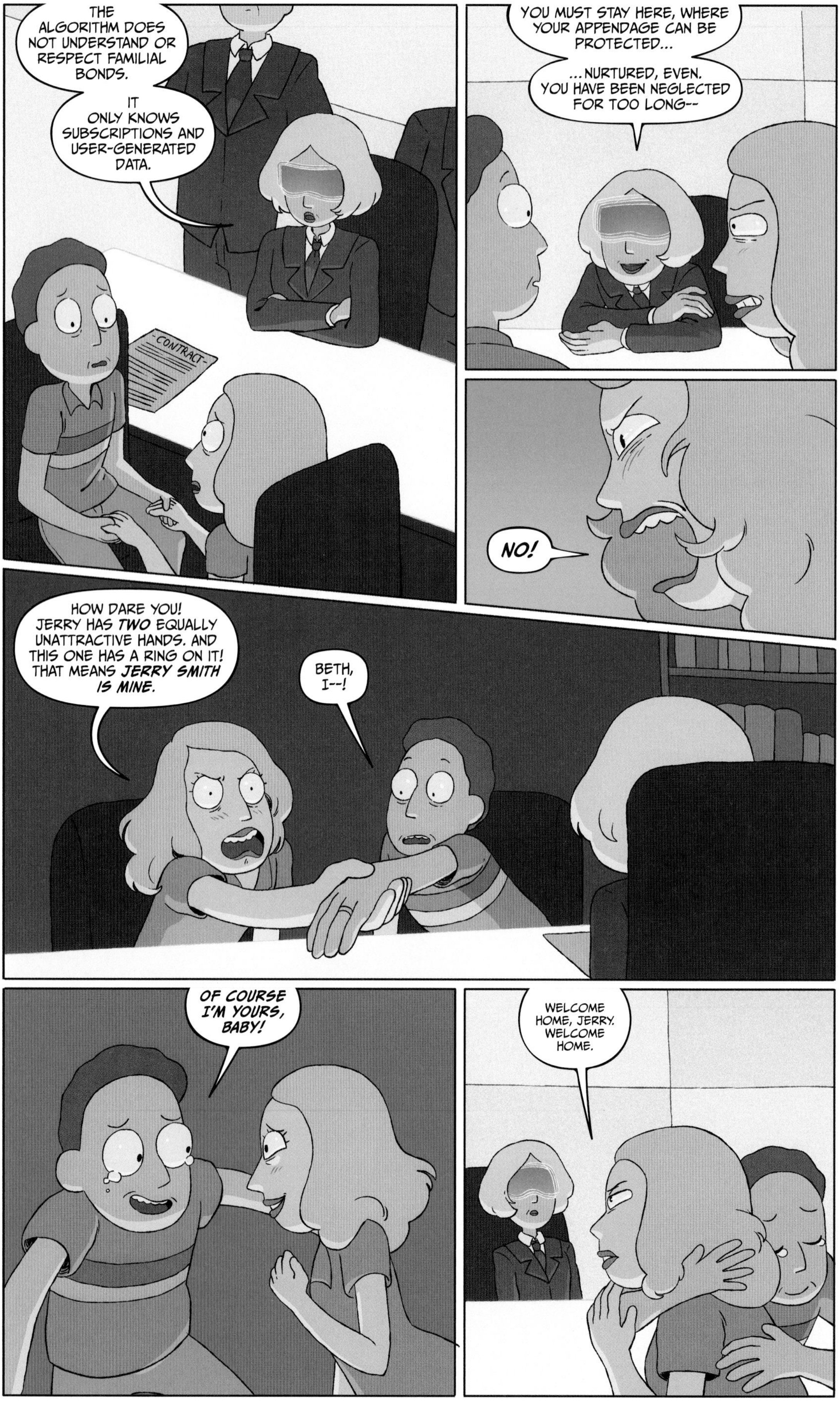
THE ALGORITHM DOES NOT UNDERSTAND OR RESPECT FAMILIAL BONDS.
IT ONLY KNOWS SUBSCRIPTIONS AND USER-GENERATED DATA.
-CONTRACT-
YOU MUST STAY HERE, WHERE YOUR APPENDAGE CAN BE PROTECTED...
...NURTURED, EVEN. YOU HAVE BEEN NEGLECTED FOR TOO LONG--
NO!
HOW DARE YOU! JERRY HAS TWO EQUALLY UNATTRACTIVE HANDS. AND THIS ONE HAS A RING ON IT! THAT MEANS JERRY SMITH IS MINE.
BETH, I--!
OF COURSE I'M YOURS, BABY!
WELCOME HOME, JERRY. WELCOME HOME.

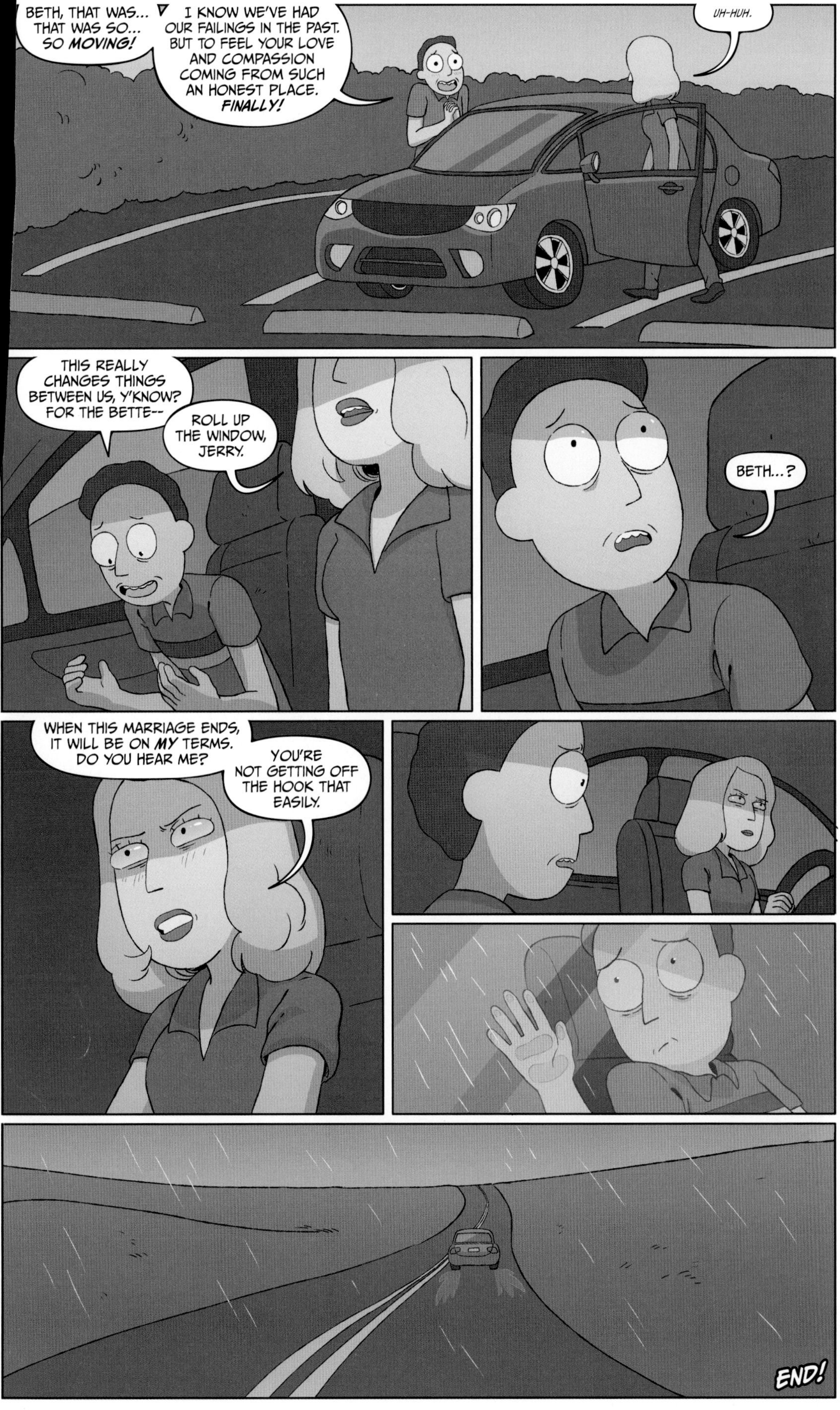
BETH, THAT WAS... THAT WAS SO... SO *MOVING!*
I KNOW WE'VE HAD OUR FAILINGS IN THE PAST. BUT TO FEEL YOUR LOVE AND COMPASSION COMING FROM SUCH AN HONEST PLACE. ***FINALLY!***
UH-HUH.
THIS REALLY CHANGES THINGS BETWEEN US, Y'KNOW? FOR THE BETTE--
ROLL UP THE WINDOW, JERRY.
BETH...?
WHEN THIS MARRIAGE ENDS, IT WILL BE ON *MY* TERMS. DO YOU HEAR ME?
YOU'RE NOT GETTING OFF THE HOOK THAT EASILY.
END!

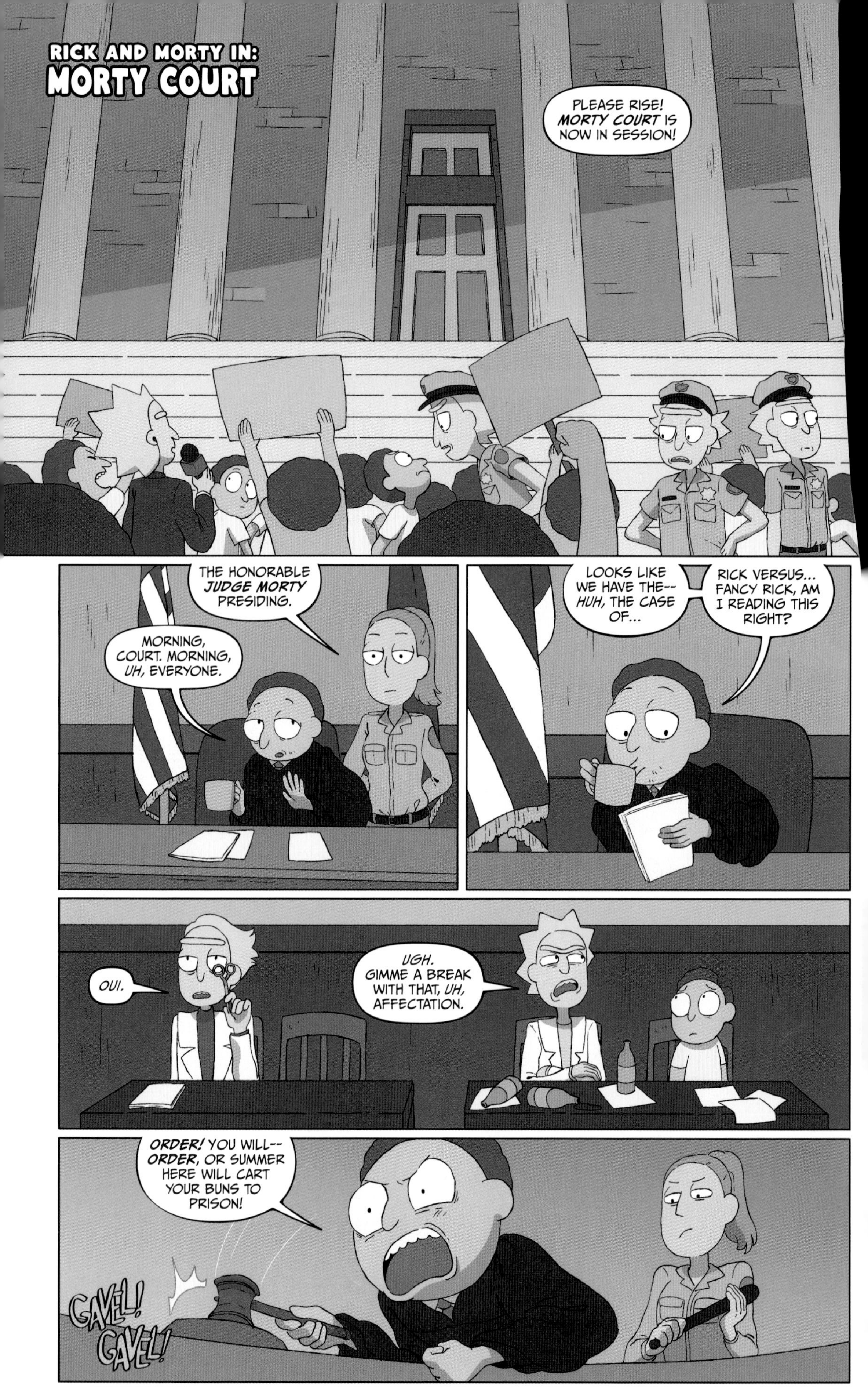
RICK AND MORTY IN:
MORTY COURT
PLEASE RISE! MORTY COURT IS NOW IN SESSION!
THE HONORABLE JUDGE MORTY PRESIDING.
MORNING, COURT. MORNING, UH, EVERYONE.
LOOKS LIKE WE HAVE THE-- HUH, THE CASE OF...
RICK VERSUS... FANCY RICK, AM I READING THIS RIGHT?
OUI.
UGH. GIMME A BREAK WITH THAT, UH, AFFECTATION.
ORDER! YOU WILL-- ORDER, OR SUMMER HERE WILL CART YOUR BUNS TO PRISON!
GAVEL! GAVEL!

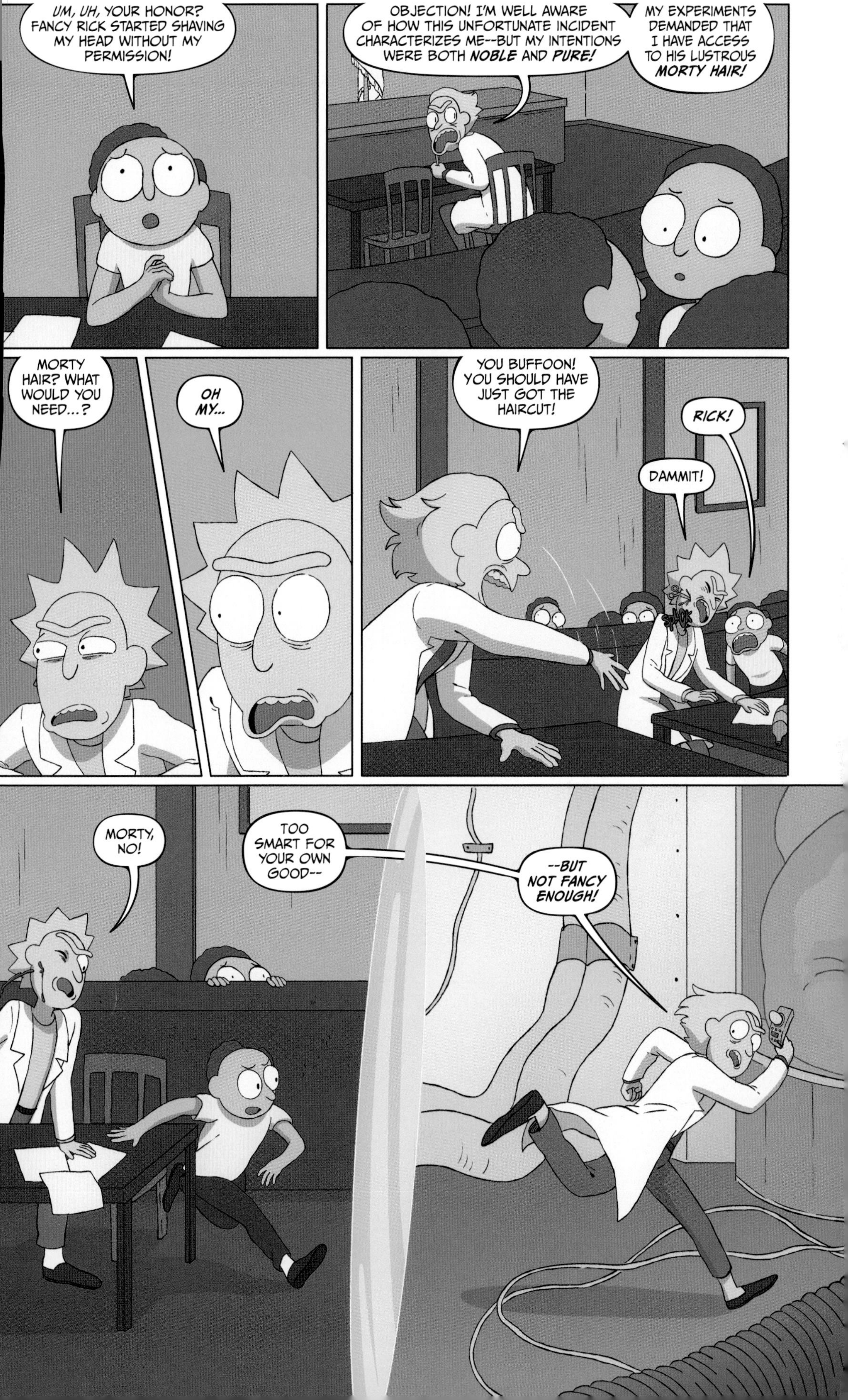
UM, UH, YOUR HONOR? FANCY RICK STARTED SHAVING MY HEAD WITHOUT MY PERMISSION!
OBJECTION! I'M WELL AWARE OF HOW THIS UNFORTUNATE INCIDENT CHARACTERIZES ME--BUT MY INTENTIONS WERE BOTH NOBLE AND PURE!
MY EXPERIMENTS DEMANDED THAT I HAVE ACCESS TO HIS LUSTROUS MORTY HAIR!
MORTY HAIR? WHAT WOULD YOU NEED...?
OH MY...
YOU BUFFOON! YOU SHOULD HAVE JUST GOT THE HAIRCUT!
RICK!
DAMMIT!
MORTY, NO!
TOO SMART FOR YOUR OWN GOOD--
--BUT NOT FANCY ENOUGH!

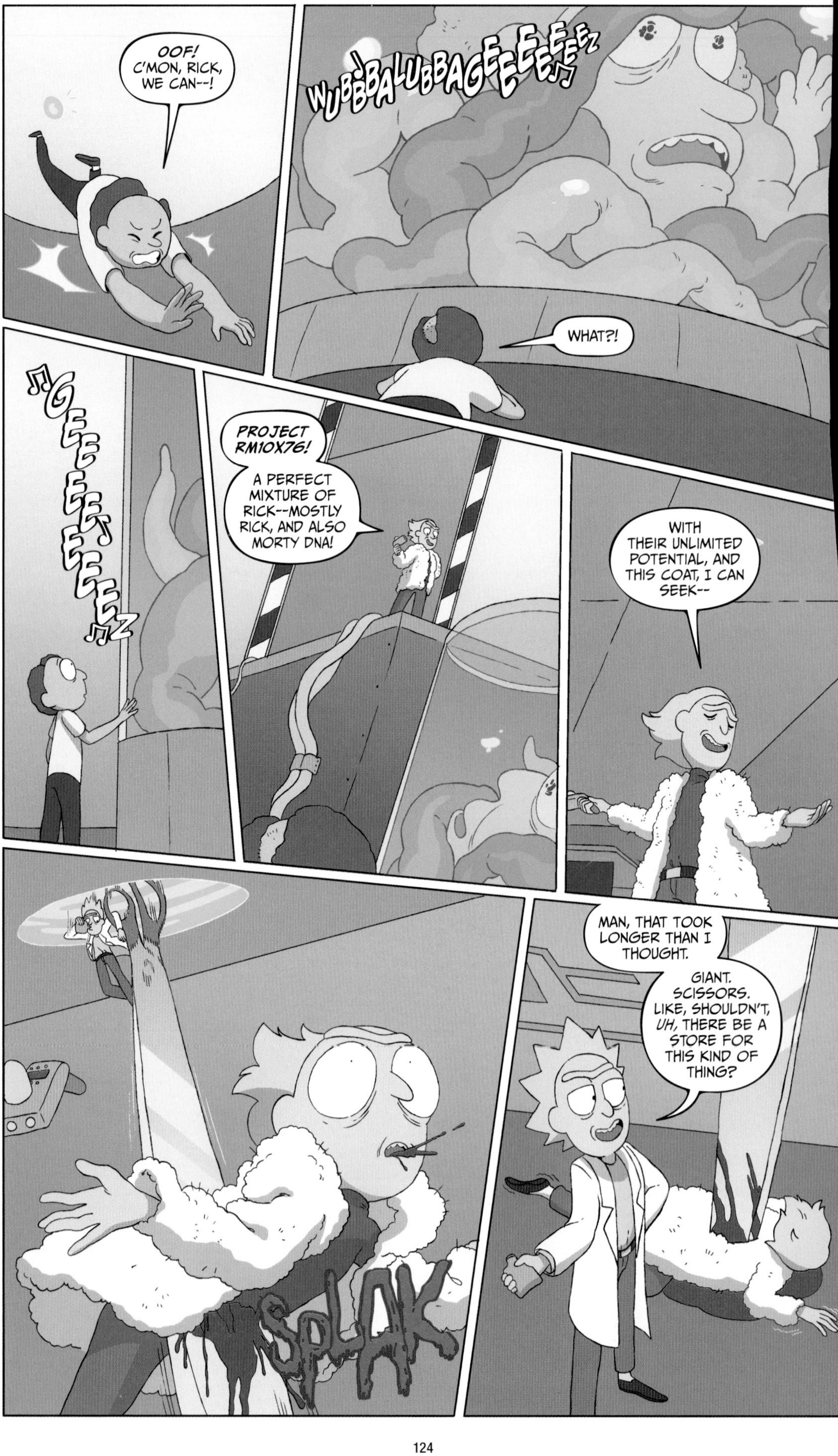
OOF! C'MON, RICK, WE CAN--!
WUBBALUBBAGEEEEEEZ
WHAT?!
GEEEEEEEEEZ
PROJECT RM10X76!
A PERFECT MIXTURE OF RICK--MOSTLY RICK, AND ALSO MORTY DNA!
WITH THEIR UNLIMITED POTENTIAL, AND THIS COAT, I CAN SEEK--
SPLAK
MAN, THAT TOOK LONGER THAN I THOUGHT.
GIANT. SCISSORS. LIKE, SHOULDN'T, *UH,* THERE BE A STORE FOR THIS KIND OF THING?

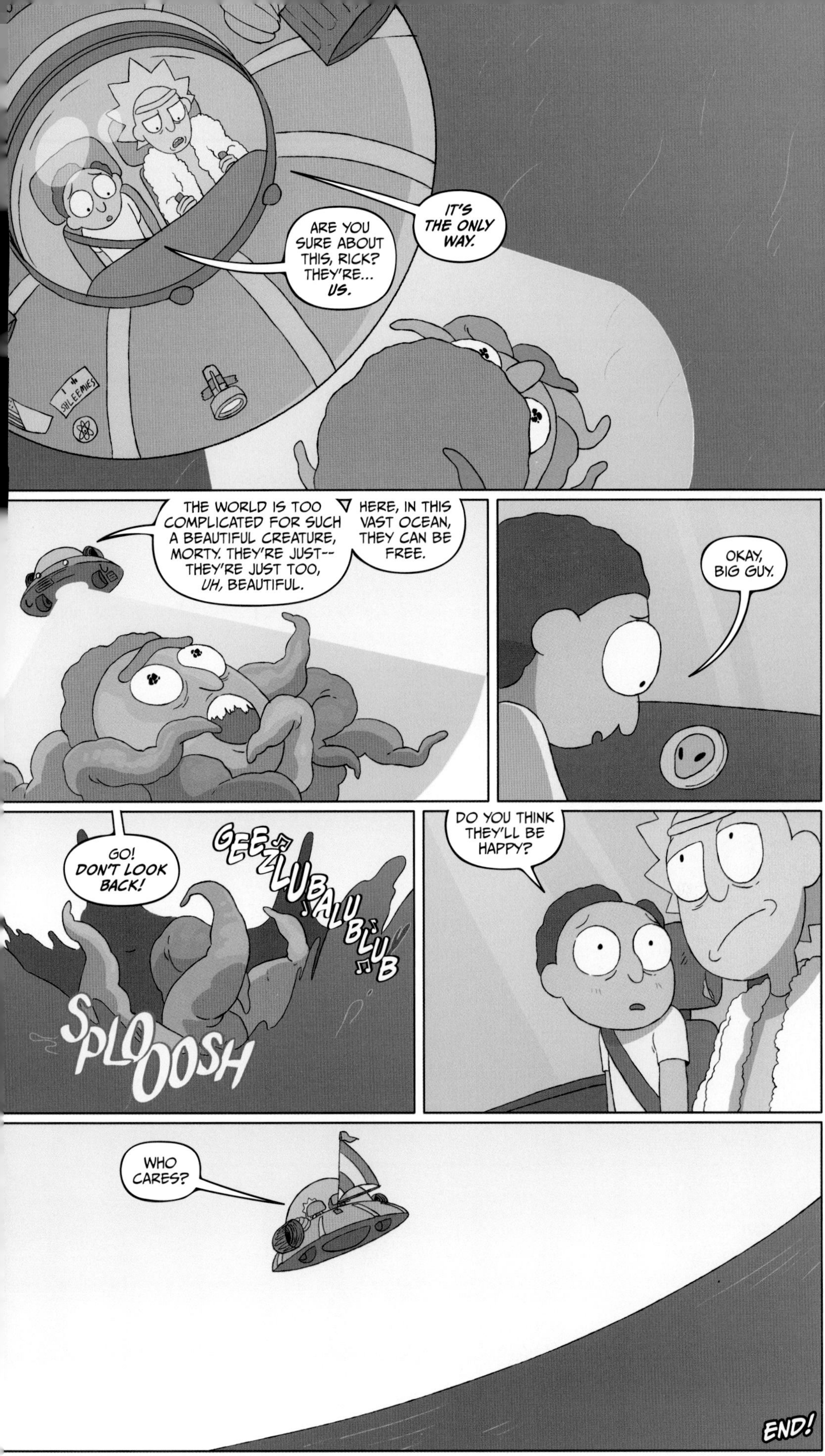
SHLEEMIES
ARE YOU SURE ABOUT THIS, RICK? THEY'RE... US.
IT'S THE ONLY WAY.
THE WORLD IS TOO COMPLICATED FOR SUCH A BEAUTIFUL CREATURE, MORTY. THEY'RE JUST-- THEY'RE JUST TOO, UH, BEAUTIFUL.
HERE, IN THIS VAST OCEAN, THEY CAN BE FREE.
OKAY, BIG GUY.
GO! DON'T LOOK BACK!
GEEZLUBALUBLUB
SPLOOOSH
DO YOU THINK THEY'LL BE HAPPY?
WHO CARES?
END!

DAN HARMON is the Emmy® winning creator/executive producer of the comedy series *Community* as well as the co-creator/executive producer of Adult Swim's *Rick and Morty*™.

Harmon's pursuit of minimal work for maximum reward took him from stand-up to improv to sketch comedy, then finally to Los Angeles, where he began writing feature screenplays with fellow Milwaukeean Rob Schrab. As part of his deal with Robert Zemeckis at Imagemovers, Harmon co-wrote the feature film *Monster House*. Following this, Harmon co-wrote the Ben Stiller-directed pilot *Heat Vision and Jack*, starring Jack Black and Owen Wilson.

Disillusioned by the legitimate industry, Harmon began attending classes at nearby Glendale Community College. At the same time, Harmon and Schrab founded Channel 101, an untelevised non-profit audience-controlled network for undiscovered filmmakers, many of whom used it to launch mainstream careers, including the boys behind SNL's Digital Shorts. Harmon, along with Schrab, partnered with Sarah Silverman to create her Comedy Central series, *The Sarah Silverman Program*, where he served as head writer for the first season.

Harmon went on to create, write, and perform in the short-lived VH1 sketch series *Acceptable TV* before eventually creating the critically acclaimed and fan-favorite comedy *Community*. The show originally aired on NBC for five seasons before being acquired by Yahoo, which premiered season six of the show in March 2015. In 2009, he won an Emmy for Outstanding Music and Lyrics for the opening number of the 81st Annual Academy Awards.

Along with Justin Roiland, Harmon created the breakout Adult Swim animated series *Rick and Morty*™. The show premiered in December 2013 and quickly became a ratings hit. Harmon and Roiland have wrapped up season three, which premiered in 2017.

In 2014, Harmon was the star of the documentary *Harmontown*, which premiered at the SXSW Film Festival and chronicled his 20-city stand-up/podcast tour of the same name. The documentary was released theatrically in October 2014.

JUSTIN ROILAND grew up in Manteca, California, where he did the basic stuff children do. Later in life he traveled to Los Angeles. Once settled in, he created several popular online shorts for Channel 101. Justin is afraid of his mortality and hopes the things he creates will make lots of people happy. Then maybe when modern civilization collapses into chaos, people will remember him and they'll help him survive the bloodshed and violence. Global economic collapse is looming. It's going to be horrible, and honestly, a swift death might be preferable than living in the hell that awaits mankind.

Justin also really hates writing about himself in the third person. I hate this. That's right. It's me. I've been writing this whole thing. Hi. The cat's out of the bag. It's just you and me now. There never was a third person. If you want to know anything about me, just ask. Sorry this wasn't more informative.

KYLE STARKS is an Eisner-nominated comic creator from Southern Indiana, where he resides with his beautiful wife and two amazing daughters. Stealy values him at 32 and a half Grepples or 17-and-a-half Smeggles depending on market value at the current time. Check out his creator-owned work: *Kill Them All* and *Sexcastle*.

MARC ELLERBY is a comics illustrator living in Essex, UK. He has worked on such titles as *Doctor Who*, *Regular Show*, and *The Amazing World of Gumball*. His own comics (which you should totally check out!) are *Chloe Noonan: Monster Hunter* and *Ellerbisms*. You can read some comics if you like at marcellerby.com.

TINI HOWARD is a writer and swamp witch from the Carolina Wilds. Her work includes *Magdalena* from Image/Top Cow Comics, *Rick and Morty*™: *Pocket Like You Stole It* from Oni Press, and *Assassinistas* from IDW/Black Crown! Her previous work includes *Power Rangers: Pink* (BOOM! Studios), *The Skeptics* (Black Mask Studios), and a contribution to the hit *Secret Loves of Geek Girls*, from Dark Horse Comics. She lives with her husband, Blake, and her son, Orlando, who is a cat.

JOSH TRUJILLO is a writer, editor, and comic book creator based in San Rafael, California. He has worked with clients including Boom! Studios, Dark Horse Comics, Shanken Creative Group, Oni Press, Telltale Games, and DC Comics, among others. His work spans different genre and audiences, specializing in children's fiction, fantasy, humor, history, romance, gaming, and LGBTQ issues.

Trujillo speaks for inclusiveness and diversity in popular media, and works alongside groups including the USC ONE Archive and Prism Comics. Josh loves his dog, his country, and is of good moral fiber. You can remain updated on his work by following Josh on Twitter @LostHisKeysMan.

RII ABREGO is a southern USA-based illustrator who has contributed to titles such as *Steven Universe*, *Adventure Time*, and *Rick and Morty*™. They can be found at twitter.com/riibrego—just follow the rat emoji.

KATY FARINA is a comic artist and illustrator based in Los Angeles, CA. She's currently a background painter at Dreamworks TV. In the past, she's done work with Boom! Studios, Oni Press, and Z2 Publishing. In the rare instance she isn't working on comics, she moonlights as the Baba Yaga; enticing local youth into ethical dilemmas and scooting around in her chicken-legged hut.

SARAH STERN is a comic artist and colorist from New York. Find her at sarahstern.com or follow her on Twitter at @worstwizard.

RIAN SYGH is a freelance comic artist and living enigma working out of Los Angeles, CA with his partner and two cats. He's done both illustration and sequential work with Boom! Studios, Diamond, HarperCollins, Oni Press, Valiant, and Z2 Publishing. He is the artist and co-creator of the Prism Award-winning comic *The Backstagers*. Which is pretty good, honestly.

CHRIS CRANK letters a bunch of books put out by Image, Dark Horse and Oni Press. He also has a podcast with Mike Norton (crankcast.net) and makes music (sonomorti.bandcamp.com). Catch him on Twitter: @ccrank.

MORE BOOKS FROM ONI PRES

RICK AND MORTY˜, VOL. 1
By Zac Gorman, CJ Cannon,
Marc Ellerby, and more
128 pages, softcover, color
ISBN 978-1-62010-281-7

RICK AND MORTY˜, VOL. 2
By Zac Gorman, CJ Cannon,
Marc Ellerby, and more
128 pages, softcover, color
ISBN 978-1-62010-319-7

RICK AND MORTY˜, VOL. 3
By Tom Fowler, CJ Cannon,
Marc Ellerby, and more
128 pages, softcover, color
ISBN 978-1-62010-343-2

RICK AND MORTY˜, VOL. 4
By Kyle Starks, CJ Cannon,
Marc Ellerby, and more
128 pages, softcover, color
ISBN 978-1-62010-377-7

RICK AND MORTY˜: VOL
By Kyle Starks, CJ Canne
Marc Ellerby, and more
128 pages, softcover, co
ISBN 978-1-62010-41

RICK AND MORTY˜, VOL. 6
By Zac Gorman, CJ Cannon,
Marc Ellerby, and more
128 pages, softcover, color
ISBN 978-1-62010-452-1

RICK AND MORTY˜, VOL. 7
By Zac Gorman, CJ Cannon,
Marc Ellerby, and more
128 pages, softcover, color
ISBN 978-1-62010-509-2

**RICK AND MORTY˜:
LIL' POOPY SUPERSTAR**
By Sarah Graley, Marc Ellerby,
and Mildred Louis
128 pages, softcover, color
ISBN 978-1-62010-374-6

**RICK AND MORTY˜:
POCKET LIKE YOU STOLE IT**
By Tini Howard, Marc Ellerby,
and Katy Farina
128 pages, softcover, color
ISBN 978-1-62010-474-3

**RICK AND MORTY˜
DELUXE EDITION, BOOK O**
By Zac Gorman, CJ Canno
Marc Ellerby, and more
296 pages, hardcover, col
ISBN 978-1-62010-360-

**RICK AND MORTY˜
DELUXE EDITION, BOOK TWO**
By Tom Fowler, Kyle Starks,
CJ Cannon, Marc Ellerby, and more
288 pages, hardcover, color
ISBN 978-1-62010-439-2

**RICK AND MORTY˜:
HARDCOVER, BOOK THREE**
By Kyle Starks, CJ Cannon, Marc
Ellerby, Sarah Graley, and more
288 pages, hardcover, color
ISBN 978-1-62010-535-1

For more information on these and other fine Oni Press comic books
and graphic novels visit **www.onipress.com**. To find a comic specialty
store in your area visit **www.comicshops.us**.